THE COMPLETE
LOW-FAT
COOKBOOK

THE COMPLETE
LOW-FAT
COOKBOOK

MURDOCH
BOOKS

Veal Cutlets in Chilli Tomato Sauce, page 53

Lamb Casserole with Beans, page 111

Potato Gnocchi with Tomato Sauce, page 218

Contents

Vegetable and Pasta Soup, page 19

You will find the following cookery ratings on the recipes in this book:

A single pot symbol indicates a recipe that is simple and generally straightforward to make—perfect for beginners.

Two symbols indicate the need for just a little more care and a little more time.

Three symbols indicate special recipes that need more investment in time, care and patience—but the results are worth it.

Pork Rolls with Roasted Capsicum, page 77

Mushroom, Ricotta and Olive Pizza, page 195

Pork, Bok Choy and Black Bean Stir-fry, page 78

Fruit Tarts, page 229

The Low-down on Low-fat

Eating low-fat isn't the same as being on a diet, but rather a change in eating habits that can stay with you for life, altering your tastes for good. Can't imagine a world without mayonnaise and cream? We'll show you how to 'adjust' some of your favourite recipes.

This isn't a diet book, but a cookbook of wholesome family meals with reduced fat—delicious alternatives to buying pre-packed supermarket low-fat dinners, many of which tend to be bland, insubstantial and quite expensive. What we've done is taken a selection of popular recipes and looked at reducing their fat content. We certainly haven't wanted to compromise on taste, so if your personal favourite isn't included, it may be because it tastes so great the way it is that a low-fat version would be a poor substitute. Luckily, our spaghetti bolognese, lasagne, potato wedges and even fudgy chocolate brownies all passed the taste test.

Fat is often portrayed as a villain and we must remember that it is not—everyone needs a certain amount of fat in their body, to help with growth and development and to carry fat-soluble vitamins throughout the body. It is the quantity and type of fat we eat that can cause problems. Foods contain a mix of different fats, but one type usually predominates in each food.

Saturated fats, those that have been implicated in some health problems and can raise cholesterol levels, are found mainly in animal products, including butter, cream, fat on meat and other fats which are solid at room temperature, like dripping or lard.

Mono-unsaturated fats, which are generally regarded as being better for

us, are found in olives, olive oil, many vegetable oils, most nuts, avocados and, in small amounts, in fish, chicken, lean meat and also eggs.

Polyunsaturated fats, found in nuts, grains, seeds and oily fish, usually remain soft at room temperature and also do not have the poor health implications of saturated fats.

However, although some fats are undoubtedly better for us than others, most tend to be high in calories. So if you are wanting to reduce the fat in your diet, don't eat too many nuts or avocados. If you are aiming to lose weight, cutting back on your fat intake is a good place to start and this book will certainly help you monitor that, but you do also need to consult your doctor and take advice about an exercise programme.

If you want to limit your fat intake, it is recommended you have no more than about 30–40 g of fat per day (30 g for women and small men, 40 g for men and taller women). With this in mind, we have developed recipes with the following amounts of fat per serve:

■ Soups and starters with up to 8 g fat
■ Main courses with up to 15 g fat
■ Desserts with up to 8 g fat.

You will find a variety of recipes, from hearty family dinners to dishes suitable for entertaining. Eating low-fat doesn't mean missing out on anything.

HELPFUL INGREDIENTS

As well as using the recipes in this book, once you get used to cooking and eating the low-fat way, you will find you don't need to completely give up many of your favourite dishes but you can adapt them yourself by using lower-fat ingredients. There are simple ways to change your cooking habits and other ways will become obvious when you use the recipes. Try low-fat natural yoghurt instead of sour cream, or whipped ricotta with orange (page 49) instead of whipped cream. Use fish canned in brine or spring water instead of oil. Buy chicken breast fillets that are sold without the skin, or remove the skin when you unpack them.

These days we are lucky with the choice and variety of low-fat foods available—dairy products such as cheese and spreads for bread, and meat which is sold well trimmed and labelled according to its fat content. The lean pre-trimmed cuts of meat (pork and lamb as well as beef) are excellent for making your own mince. Some shop-bought mince has quite a high proportion of fat, so make your own in a food processor. Avoid sausages, pies, pasties and burgers as these are made from poorer quality meat with higher proportions of fat. Eat more seafood, chicken and turkey (with the skin removed).

BETTER TIPS FOR BETTER EATING

- Trim all visible fat from meat or chicken, before and after cooking.
- Remove any chicken skin before cooking, to avoid the temptation to eat it when it's crispy and cooked.
- Use less meat in stews and casseroles. Instead, add lots of fresh vegetables or pulses such as chickpeas or kidney beans instead.
- Increase the amount of fish and legumes in your diet.
- Serve meals with plain pasta, boiled or dry-roasted potatoes or boiled/steamed rice to help you fill up with no extra added fats. Remember it's not the potato that contains the fat, but what goes on top.
- Skim stews or soups to remove excess fat or, better still, refrigerate overnight and lift off solidified fat. The flavour of most soups and stews is better after a day's refrigeration.
- Use low-fat plain or skim milk yoghurt in sauces and stews instead of cream.
- Thicken sauces by reducing the liquid and adding puréed vegetables, instead of making buttery sauces.
- Try alternatives to oil for basting and moistening (lemon or orange juice, vegetable juices, mustards, soy sauce, wine or fortified wines such as sherry). For tomato-based sauces such as bolognese, try frying onions in a little of the juice from tinned tomatoes.
- Use stock in soups instead of cream.
- Use light evaporated skim milk as a substitute for regular cream and light coconut milk instead of regular.
- Never go shopping when you're hungry and your resistance is low.

DON'T GO HUNGRY

Snack on low-fat, high fibre and no-fat foods between meals:

- Fresh fruit and vegetables (but not too much avocado).
- Fruit and vegetable juices.
- Skim milk and low-fat milk drinks; low-fat yoghurt.
- Pasta with tomato-based sauces.
- Steamed rice.
- Baked jacket potato with low-fat yoghurt and chives.
- Home-made muffins (pages 250–1).
- Wholegrain bread and bread rolls; bagels; English muffins; crumpets with low-fat spread such as honey, jam or Marmite.
- Some crispbreads (read the labels).
- Rice cakes.
- Plain popcorn and baked pretzels.
- Dried fruit.

For those who love cheese, there are many fat-reduced Cheddars on the market but it is also worth knowing that other cheeses, such as feta and ricotta, have low-fat versions.

Read all the labels on food packaging. These will tell you how much fat is contained in a recommended serving size or in a 100 g portion. If there isn't a nutritional table on the packaging, the manufacturers must list the ingredients in order of the quantities used. If the fat is near the top of the list, try another brand.

Be aware that just because a product is labelled 'light', this doesn't necessarily mean light in fat: it can mean low in salt, flavour, colour and weight or low in alcohol. As well, don't be confused by foods claiming to be low-cholesterol or no-cholesterol— this doesn't necessarily mean low in fat—just low in animal fats. These foods, which may include nuts, nut products, margarines or oils, can still contain a high percentage of other fats. Processed foods tend to be higher in fat. The more natural and less prepared the food, the better it is for you.

LOW-FAT COOKING HINTS

Using a light spray of oil from an aerosol and a non-stick pan to cook will save many tablespoons of cooking oil over time. The aerosol cans simply contain oil under pressure; no chemicals have been added. Avoid deep frying foods. In this book you will find occasional recipes for shallow-frying which don't break the 'fat-bank', but drain the food thoroughly on paper towels and enjoy these recipes in moderation.

Boiling, poaching and braising are all excellent ways to cook without adding fat. Steaming is a very good alternative to roasting, as it locks in the natural flavours. Add herbs, spices or lemon juice to meat, chicken or fish, or drizzle with sauce, then wrap in foil or baking paper and seal securely to keep in all the flavours. Steam in a bamboo or metal steamer, open the parcels at the table and enjoy the aroma and flavour. If you do roast joints of meat or poultry, place on a rack over a roasting tin so that the fat can collect below and be poured away. Once the meat is cooked, cut off any visible fat.

Stir-frying is a quick, healthy and relatively low-fat way to cook. This method uses a minimal amount of oil to seal meat and cooking is done quickly and at high temperatures so there is less opportunity for fat to be absorbed. The meat is then usually removed from the wok (it can be draining on paper towels) and set aside. When stir-frying vegetables, add a tablespoon of water to prevent them from sticking—this also produces steam which speeds up the cooking process even more. Return the meat to the pan, add any sauces and flavourings and toss well.

Grilling and barbecuing are not only low-fat but produce wonderful flavours. Lightly grease the grill or barbecue with oil spray or brush lightly with oil. If you grill on a rack, rather than a hotplate, fat can run off the meat. Try marinating or basting meat with orange juice, vinegar or yoghurt rather than oil. Chargrill pans, lightly brushed or sprayed with oil, are a good low-fat method of cooking.

Soups & Starters

THAI-STYLE CHICKEN AND CORN SOUP

Preparation time: 10 minutes
Total cooking time: 5 minutes
Serves 4
Fat per serve: 5 g

500 g (1 lb) can corn kernels, undrained
2 chicken stock cubes, crumbled
8 spring onions, sliced
1 tablespoon finely chopped fresh ginger
500 g (1 lb) chicken breast, finely sliced
1 tablespoon sweet chilli sauce
1 tablespoon fish sauce
125 g (4 oz) vermicelli rice noodles
1 cup (30 g/1 oz) chopped fresh coriander leaves
2 teaspoons grated lime rind
2 tablespoons lime juice

1 Bring 1 litre water to the boil in a large saucepan over high heat. Add the corn kernels and their juice, stock cubes, spring onion and ginger, then reduce the heat and allow to simmer for 1 minute.

2 Add the chicken, sweet chilli sauce and fish sauce and simmer for 3 minutes, or until the chicken is cooked through.

3 Meanwhile, place the noodles in a small heatproof bowl and pour in enough boiling water to cover. Leave for 4 minutes, or until softened. Drain the noodles and cut them into short lengths.

4 Add the noodles, coriander, lime rind and lime juice to the soup and serve immediately.

NUTRITION PER SERVE
Protein 33 g; Fat 5 g; Carbohydrate 35 g; Dietary Fibre 5.8 g; Cholesterol 63 mg; 1327 kJ (317 cal)

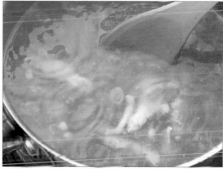

Add the corn kernels, stock cubes, spring onion and ginger to the saucepan.

Place the noodles in a heatproof bowl and cover with boiling water.

SEAFOOD RAVIOLI IN GINGERY SOUP

Preparation time: 30 minutes
Total cooking time: 20 minutes
Serves 4
Fat per serve: 7 g

8 raw prawns
1 carrot, chopped
1 onion, chopped
1 celery stick, chopped
3 spring onions, thinly sliced
6 cm (2¹/₂ inch) piece fresh ginger,
    thinly shredded
1 tablespoon mirin
1 teaspoon kecap manis
1 tablespoon soy sauce
4 large scallops
100 g (3¹/₂ oz) boneless white fish fillet
1 egg white
200 g (6¹/₂ oz) round gow gee
    wrappers
¹/₃ cup (10 g/¹/₄ oz) fresh coriander
    leaves

1 To make the soup, peel the prawns, reserve 4 for the ravioli filling and chop the rest into small pieces and reserve. Put the prawn heads and shells in a large pan, cook over high heat until starting to brown, then cover with 1 litre water. Add the carrot, onion and celery, bring to the boil, reduce the heat and simmer for 10 minutes. Strain and discard the prawn heads, shells and vegetables. Return the stock to a clean pan and add the spring onion, ginger, mirin, kecap manis and soy sauce. Set aside.
2 To make the ravioli, chop the whole reserved prawns with the scallops and fish in a food processor until smooth. Add enough egg white to bind. Lay half the gow gee wrappers on a work surface and place a rounded teaspoon of filling in the centre of each. Brush the edges with water. Top each with another wrapper and press the edges to seal, eliminating air bubbles as you go. Trim with a fluted cutter. Cover with plastic wrap.
3 Bring a large pan of water to the boil. Meanwhile, heat the stock and leave simmering. Just prior to serving, drop a few ravioli at a time into the boiling water. Cook for 2 minutes, remove with a slotted spoon and divide among heated bowls. Cook the chopped reserved prawns in the same water for 2 minutes; drain. Pour the hot stock over the ravioli and serve, sprinkled with the chopped cooked prawns and coriander leaves.

NUTRITION PER SERVE
Protein 17 g; Fat 7 g; Carbohydrate 65 g;
Dietary Fibre 4.5 g; Cholesterol 125 mg;
1765 kJ (420 cal)

Stir the prawn heads and shells in a pan over high heat until lightly browned.

Brush the edge of one wrapper with water, then cover with another.

Cook each batch of ravioli for 2 minutes, then remove with a slotted spoon.

POTATO, BROCCOLI AND CORIANDER SOUP

Preparation time: 15 minutes
Total cooking time: 30 minutes
Serves 6
Fat per serve: 0.5 g

500 g (1 lb) broccoli
cooking oil spray
2 onions, finely chopped
2 cloves garlic, finely chopped
2 teaspoons ground cumin
1 teaspoon ground coriander
750 g (1½ lb) potatoes, cubed
2 small chicken stock cubes

1½ cups (375 ml/12 fl oz) skim milk
3 tablespoons finely chopped fresh coriander

1 Cut the broccoli into small pieces. Lightly spray the base of a large saucepan with cooking oil, then place over medium heat and add the onion and garlic. Add 1 tablespoon water to prevent sticking. Cover and cook, stirring occasionally, over low heat for 5 minutes, or until the onion has softened and is lightly golden. Add the ground cumin and coriander and cook for 2 minutes.

2 Add the potato and broccoli to the pan, stir well and add the stock cubes

and 1 litre of water. Slowly bring to the boil, reduce the heat, cover and simmer over low heat for 20 minutes, or until the vegetables are tender. Allow to cool slightly.

3 Blend the soup in batches in a food processor or blender until smooth. Return to the pan and stir in the milk. Slowly reheat, without boiling. Stir the chopped coriander through and season well before serving.

NUTRITION PER SERVE
Protein 10 g; Fat 0.5 g; Carbohydrate 20 g;
Dietary Fibre 6 g; Cholesterol 2 mg;
580 kJ (140 cal)

Chop all the broccoli into small, even-sized florets for quick cooking.

Stir the ground cumin and coriander into the onion and cook for about 2 minutes.

Purée the mixture in batches, in a food processor or blender, until it is smooth.

LEEK AND POTATO SOUP

Preparation time: 20 minutes
Total cooking time: 45 minutes
Serves 4
Fat per serve: 1 g

cooking oil spray
2 leeks, white part only, sliced
3 cloves garlic, crushed
1 teaspoon ground cumin

1 kg (2 lb) potatoes, chopped
5 cups (1.25 litres) vegetable stock
1/2 cup (125 ml/4 fl oz) skim milk

1 Lightly spray a non-stick frying pan with oil. Add the leek, garlic and 1 tablespoon water to prevent sticking, then cook over low heat, stirring frequently, for 25 minutes, or until the leek turns golden. Add the cumin and cook for 2 minutes.
2 Put the potato in a large pan with the leek mixture and stock, bring to the boil, reduce the heat and simmer for 10–15 minutes, or until tender. Purée in a processor or blender until smooth. Return to the pan.
3 Stir in the milk, season and heat through before serving.

NUTRITION PER SERVE
Protein 8 g; Fat 1 g; Carbohydrate 35 g;
Dietary Fibre 5.5 g; Cholesterol 1 mg;
795 kJ (190 cal)

Stir the leek and garlic over low heat for about 25 minutes, until golden.

Add the cooked leek mixture to the chopped potato and stock.

Purée the soup in a food processor or blender, in batches if necessary.

WON TON NOODLE SOUP

Preparation time: 25 minutes
Total cooking time: 25 minutes
Serves 4
Fat per serve: 5 g

70 g (2¹/₄ oz) raw prawns
70 g (2¹/₄ oz) veal mince
3 tablespoons soy sauce
1 tablespoon finely chopped spring onion
1 tablespoon finely chopped water chestnuts
1 teaspoon finely chopped fresh ginger
2 cloves garlic, finely chopped
24 gow gee wrappers
5 cups (1.25 litres) chicken stock
2 tablespoons mirin
500 g (1 lb) baby bok choy, finely shredded
8 spring onions, sliced

1 Peel, devein and finely chop the prawns. Mix with the veal mince, 2 teaspoons soy sauce, spring onion, water chestnuts, ginger and garlic. Lay the round wrappers out on a work surface and place a teaspoon of mixture in the middle of each.
2 Moisten the edges of the wrappers and bring up the sides to form a pouch. Pinch together to seal. Cook in batches in a large pan of rapidly boiling water for 4–5 minutes. Drain and divide among soup bowls.
3 Bring the stock, remaining soy sauce and mirin to the boil in a large saucepan. Add the bok choy, cover and simmer for 2 minutes, or until the bok choy has just wilted. Add the sliced spring onion and season. Ladle the stock, bok choy and spring onion over the won tons.

NUTRITION PER SERVE
Protein 10 g; Fat 5 g; Carbohydrate 30 g; Dietary Fibre 5 g; Cholesterol 25 mg; 760 kJ (180 cal)

Peel the prawns and devein them before chopping them finely.

Bring the sides of the wrappers up around the filling and pinch to seal.

Add the finely shredded bok choy to the pan and simmer until just wilted.

TOM YAM GOONG

Preparation time: 25 minutes
Total cooking time: 45 minutes
Serves 6
Fat per serve: 5 g

500 g (1 lb) raw prawns
1 tablespoon oil
2 tablespoons tom yam curry paste
2 tablespoons tamarind purée
2 teaspoons ground turmeric
1 teaspoon chopped small red
    chillies
4 kaffir lime leaves, shredded
2 tablespoons fish sauce
2 tablespoons lime juice

2 teaspoons grated palm sugar
    or soft brown sugar
kaffir lime leaves, shredded, extra,
    to garnish

1 Peel the prawns, leaving the tails intact. Devein the prawns, starting at the head end. Reserve the shells and heads. Cover and refrigerate the prawn meat. Heat the oil in a wok or large saucepan and cook the shells and heads over medium heat, stirring frequently, for 10 minutes, or until the shells turn orange.
2 Add 1 cup (250 ml/8 fl oz) water and the tom yam paste to the pan. Bring to the boil and cook for 5 minutes, or until reduced slightly.

Add another 2 litres water, bring to the boil, reduce the heat and simmer for 20 minutes. Strain, discarding the shells and heads, and return the stock to the pan.
3 Add the tamarind, turmeric, chilli and lime leaves to the pan, bring to the boil and cook for 2 minutes. Add the prawns and cook for 5 minutes, or until pink. Stir in the fish sauce, lime juice and sugar. Garnish with shredded kaffir lime leaves.

NUTRITION PER SERVE
Protein 15 g; Fat 5 g; Carbohydrate 11 g;
Dietary Fibre 1.3 g; Cholesterol 158 mg;
608 kJ (145 cal)

Kaffir lime leaves can be tough and need to be very finely shredded before use.

Cook the prawn shells and tom yam paste until the liquid has reduced and thickened slightly.

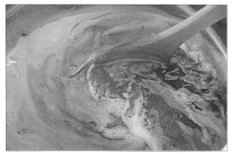

Stir in the tamarind, turmeric, chilli and lime leaves and cook for 2 minutes.

ROASTED RED CAPSICUM SOUP

Preparation time: 50 minutes
Total cooking time: 1 hour
Serves 6
Fat per serve: 7 g

4 large red capsicums
4 ripe tomatoes
2 tablespoons oil
1 red onion, chopped
1 clove garlic, crushed
4 cups (1 litre) vegetable stock
1 teaspoon sweet chilli sauce
Parmesan and pesto, to garnish

1 Cut the capsicums into large flat pieces, removing the seeds and membrane. Place skin-side-up under a hot grill until blackened. Leave covered with a tea towel until cool, then peel away the skin and chop the flesh.
2 Score a small cross in the base of each tomato, put them in a large heatproof bowl and cover with boiling water. Leave for 1 minute, then plunge into cold water and peel the skin from the cross. Cut in half, scoop out the seeds and roughly chop the flesh.
3 Heat the oil in a large heavy-based pan and add the onion. Cook over medium heat for 10 minutes, stirring

frequently, until very soft. Add the garlic and cook for a further minute. Add the capsicum, tomato and stock; bring to the boil, reduce the heat and simmer for about 20 minutes.
4 Purée the soup in a food processor or blender until smooth (in batches if necessary). Return to the pan to reheat gently and stir in the chilli sauce. Serve topped with shavings of Parmesan and a little pesto.

NUTRITION PER SERVE
Protein 3 g; Fat 7 g; Carbohydrate 5 g;
Dietary Fibre 2 g; Cholesterol 0 mg;
380 kJ (90 cal)

Once the skin of the capsicum has been blackened it should peel away easily.

Scoring a cross in the base of the tomato makes it easier to remove the skin.

Use a spoon to scoop out the seeds from the tomatoes once they have been peeled.

PUMPKIN SOUP WITH CORIANDER PASTE

Preparation time: 20 minutes
Total cooking time: 40 minutes
Serves 6
Fat per serve: 8 g

2 teaspoons vegetable oil
2 teaspoons ground coriander
2 teaspoons ground cumin
1/2 teaspoon ground turmeric
1 onion, chopped
1 celery stick, chopped
1.5 kg (3 lb) pumpkin, chopped
2 1/2 cups (600 ml/20 fl oz) chicken
    stock
1 cup (250 ml/8 fl oz) light coconut
    milk (see NOTE)

CORIANDER PASTE
1 cup (30 g/1 oz) coriander leaves
1/2 cup (10 g/1/4 oz) mint leaves
1 tablespoon grated fresh ginger
1 teaspoon caster sugar

1 Heat the oil in a large pan, add the spices and cook over low heat for 2 minutes, without allowing them to brown. Add the onion, celery and pumpkin and stir for 2 minutes to coat the vegetables in the spice mixture. Add the stock and bring to the boil. Cover and simmer for 30 minutes, or until the pumpkin is tender. Leave to cool slightly.
2 Purée the mixture in batches in a food processor until smooth. Return to the pan, stir in the coconut milk, season with salt and pepper and

reheat gently. If the soup is too thick, stir in a little extra stock.
3 To make the coriander paste, finely chop the coriander and mint leaves by hand or in a food processor. Combine in a bowl with the ginger and sugar. Spoon a little on top of the soup and stir through to serve.

NUTRITION PER SERVE
Protein 6 g; Fat 8 g; Carbohydrate 18 g;
Dietary Fibre 3.5 g; Cholesterol 0 mg;
1600 kJ (382 cal)

NOTE: Light coconut milk is simply fat-reduced coconut milk and is available in cans from most supermarkets. Ordinary coconut milk contains a very high amount of fat, so shouldn't be used as a substitute.

Stir the vegetables thoroughly until they are coated in the spices.

Let the mixture cool a little before puréeing, in case of hot splashes.

Mix the chopped coriander and mint with the ginger and sugar to make the paste.

CHICKEN SOUP

Preparation time: 10 minutes
Total cooking time: 30 minutes
Serves 4
Fat per serve: 5 g

2 teaspoons oil
1 small leek, white part only, finely
    sliced
2 potatoes, cubed

2 chicken breast fillets, thinly sliced
420 g (13 oz) can creamed corn
3 cups (750 ml/24 fl oz) chicken stock
1 tablespoon chopped chives

1 Heat the oil in a large pan, add the leek, cover and cook over low heat for 5 minutes, stirring occasionally, until the leek is very soft.
2 Add the potato, chicken, corn and stock to the pan. Stir to combine, bring to the boil, then reduce the heat and

leave to simmer for 20 minutes, or until the potato is very soft. Just before serving, season the soup with salt and pepper and garnish with the chopped chives.

NUTRITION PER SERVE
Protein 30 g; Fat 5 g; Carbohydrate 25 g;
Dietary Fibre 5 g; Cholesterol 50 mg;
1110 kJ (265 cal)

Discard any excess fat from the chicken fillets and cut into small, thin strips.

Cook the sliced leek slowly over low heat until it is very soft.

Add the potato, chicken, corn and stock to the pan and bring to the boil.

OXTAIL SOUP

Preparation time: 20 minutes + chilling
Total cooking time: 3 hours 20 minutes
Serves 4
Fat per serve: 7.5 g

1 tablespoon plain flour
1 kg oxtail, chopped into short pieces
  (ask your butcher to do this)
1 tablespoon oil
8 cups (2 litres) beef stock
1 onion, chopped
1 celery stick, chopped
2 carrots, chopped
1 swede or turnip, peeled and
  chopped
12 peppercorns
3 whole cloves
2 bay leaves
1 tablespoon plain flour, extra
2 tablespoons port
1 tablespoon tomato paste
3 tablespoons finely chopped fresh
  parsley

1 Put the flour and oxtail in a bag and shake to coat. Heat the oil in a large pan and brown the oxtail in batches for 5 minutes each batch. Return all the oxtail to the pan.
2 Add 1 1/2 cups (375 ml/12 fl oz) water and the stock, vegetables, peppercorns, cloves, bay leaves and 1/2 teaspoon salt to the pan. Bring slowly to the boil then reduce the heat and simmer, covered, for 3 hours.
3 Strain the vegetables and meat, reserving the liquid. Discard the vegetables and leave the meat to cool. Pull the meat from the bone, shred

and refrigerate. Meanwhile, refrigerate the stock until the fat has solidified on the surface and can be removed with a spoon. Add the meat to the liquid.
4 Put the soup in a clean pan. Mix together the extra flour, port and tomato paste, and add to the pan. Bring to the boil, stirring, until the soup thickens slightly. Simmer for 10 minutes, then stir in the parsley.

NUTRITION PER SERVE
Protein 25 g; Fat 7.5 g; Carbohydrate 9.5 g;
Dietary Fibre 2.5 g; Cholesterol 65 mg;
1700 kJ (405 cal)

Put the seasoned flour and oxtail pieces in a plastic bag and shake to coat.

Heat the oil and cook the oxtail pieces in batches until browned.

VEGETABLE AND PASTA SOUP

Preparation time: 20 minutes
Total cooking time: 40 minutes
Serves 6
Fat per serve: 2 g

2 teaspoons olive oil
1 onion, chopped
1 carrot, chopped
2 celery sticks, chopped

350 g (11 oz) sweet potato, chopped
400 g (13 oz) can corn kernels, drained
1 litre vegetable stock
1 cup (90 g/3 oz) pasta spirals

1 Heat the oil in a large pan and add the onion, carrot and celery. Cook the vegetables over low heat, stirring regularly, for 10 minutes, or until they are soft.
2 Add the sweet potato, corn kernels and stock. Bring to the boil and then reduce the heat and simmer for 20 minutes, or until the vegetables are tender.
3 Add the pasta to the pan and return to the boil. Reduce the heat and simmer for 10 minutes, or until the pasta is tender. Season the soup and serve immediately.

NUTRITION PER SERVE
Protein 4 g; Fat 2 g; Carbohydrate 25 g; Dietary Fibre 5 g; Cholesterol 0 mg; 555 kJ (135 cal)

Stir the onion, carrot and celery over low heat until they are soft.

Add the sweet potato, drained corn kernels and stock to the pan.

When the vegetables are tender add the pasta to the pan.

19

PEA AND HAM SOUP

Preparation time: 20 minutes + soaking
Total cooking time: 1 hour 40 minutes
Serves 10
Fat per serve: 1 g

500 g (1 lb) green split peas
1 kg (2 lb) ham hock or bacon bones,
    chopped into short pieces
    (ask your butcher to do this)
1 large onion, chopped
1 large carrot, chopped
1 celery stick, chopped
1 turnip, peeled and chopped
1 parsnip, peeled and chopped
3 tablespoons chopped fresh parsley

1 Leave the peas for at least 4 hours in a large bowl of water. Drain, discarding the soaking water.
2 Put the hock or bones in a large heavy-based pan and add 2 litres water, the peas, onion, carrot, celery, turnip and parsnip. Bring slowly to the boil and then reduce the heat, cover partially and simmer for 1½ hours, or until the peas are reduced to a mush. Stir occasionally and skim the surface regularly to remove any froth, using either a spoon or a folded piece of paper towel. Remove the pan from the heat and allow to cool a little.
3 Lift out the hock or bones with a pair of tongs or a slotted spoon. Leave them to cool a little before removing the meat. Discard the bones, dice the meat and set aside.
4 When the soup has cooled, purée it in small batches in a food processor or blender. Return the soup to the pan and add the diced meat. Stir in the parsley and reheat gently to serve.

NUTRITION PER SERVE
Protein 12 g; Fat 1 g; Carbohydrate 26 g;
Dietary Fibre 6.5 g; Cholesterol 0 mg;
685 kJ (164 cal)

STORAGE TIME: Refrigerate for up to 4 days or freeze for up to 1 month.

HINT: Ham hock has more meat than bacon bones, however bacon bones have a more intense flavour.

Peel and chop the parsnip. Ask your butcher to chop the ham hock for you.

Simmer the soup until the split peas are reduced to a mush.

Lift out the ham hock or bacon bones with a pair of tongs.

Return the chopped meat to the soup once it has been puréed.

HOT BEEF BORSCHT

Preparation time: 30 minutes
Total cooking time: 2 hours
Serves 6
Fat per serve: 2.5 g

500 g (1 lb) shin of beef, cut into large
   pieces
500 g (1 lb) fresh beetroot
1 onion, finely chopped
1 carrot, cut into short strips
1 parsnip, cut into short strips
1 cup (75 g/2$^1/_2$ oz) finely shredded
   cabbage

1 Put the meat in a large heavy-based
pan with 1 litre water and bring slowly
to the boil. Reduce the heat, cover and
simmer for 1 hour. Skim the surface
frequently to get rid of any froth.
2 Discard the stems from the beetroot
and place in a large heavy-based pan
with 1 litre water. Bring slowly to the
boil, reduce the heat and simmer for
40 minutes, or until the beetroot are
tender when pierced with a skewer.
Drain, reserving the liquid. Cool the
beetroot, then peel and grate.
3 Use tongs to remove the meat from
the stock, leave to cool then dice. Skim
any fat from the stock. Return the meat
to the stock and add the onion, carrot,
parsnip and grated beetroot. Add
1 cup (250 ml/8 fl oz) of the beetroot
liquid. Bring to the boil, reduce the
heat, cover and simmer for 45 minutes.
Add more beetroot liquid if you prefer
a thinner soup.
4 Add the cabbage, stir and simmer
for a further 15 minutes. Season to
taste and serve hot.

NUTRITION PER SERVE
Protein 22 g; Fat 2.5 g; Carbohydrate 11 g;
Dietary Fibre 4 g; Cholesterol 55 mg;
645 kJ (154 cal)

STORAGE TIME: May be kept covered
in the fridge for up to 4 days. Suitable
to freeze for up to 1 month.

NOTE: Borscht is a very hearty soup.
You can serve it as a main meal with
rye or black bread.

Cut the parsnip into short thin strips, keeping the
sizes as even as possible.

Use a sharp knife to cut away the stems from the
beetroot bulbs.

You will need to let the beetroot cool before it can
be peeled and grated.

Use a pair of tongs to lift the pieces of meat from
the stock.

SCOTCH BROTH

Preparation time: 20 minutes
Total cooking time: 2¹/₂ hours
Serves 10
Fat per serve: 2 g

750 g (1¹/₂ lb) neck lamb chops or
    lamb shanks
250 g (8 oz) pearl barley or soup mix
    (see NOTE)
1 carrot, peeled and diced
1 turnip, peeled and diced
1 parsnip, peeled and diced
1 onion, finely chopped
1 small leek, thinly sliced
1 cup (75 g/2¹/₂ oz) shredded
    cabbage
¹/₂ cup (15 g/¹/₂ oz) chopped parsley

1 Cut away any excess fat from the
meat. Put the meat in a large heavy-
based pan with 10 cups (2¹/₂ litres)
water. Bring to the boil, reduce the
heat and simmer, covered, for 1 hour.
Skim any froth from the surface
frequently. Meanwhile, soak the pearl
barley or soup mix in a large bowl of
water for about 1 hour.
2 Add the carrot, turnip, parsnip,
onion and leek to the pan. Drain the
barley or soup mix and add to the pan.
Stir well to combine, cover and
simmer for a further 1¹/₂ hours. Stir in
the cabbage 10 minutes before the end
of cooking time. (Add more water at
this stage if you like a thinner soup.)
3 Remove the meat from the pan
using tongs. Leave to cool before
removing the meat from the bones.

Chop the meat finely and return it to
the soup. Add parsley and season with
salt and pepper.

NUTRITION PER SERVE
Protein 21 g; Fat 2 g; Carbohydrate 20 g;
Dietary Fibre 4 g; Cholesterol 50 mg;
750 kJ (180 cal)

STORAGE TIME: May be kept covered
and refrigerated for up to 3 days.
Suitable to freeze up to 1 month.

NOTE: Soup mix is a combination of
pearl barley, split peas and lentils.
Both pearl barley and soup mix are
readily available from supermarkets.

Instead of a spoon, use paper towels to skim any
froth from the surface.

Drain the barley or soup mix and add to the pan
of simmering meat and vegetables.

Use tongs to lift the bones out of the soup and
then cut the meat from the bones.

CHICKEN CURRY LAKSA

Preparation time: 30 minutes
Total cooking time: 25 minutes
Serves 4
Fat per serve: 8 g

LAKSA PASTE
1 large onion, roughly chopped
5 cm (2 inch) piece fresh ginger, chopped
8 cm (3 inch) piece galangal, peeled and chopped
1 stem lemon grass, white part only, roughly chopped
2 cloves garlic
1 fresh red chilli, seeded and diced
2 teaspoons vegetable oil
2 tablespoons mild curry paste

500 g (1 lb) chicken breast fillets, cut into cubes
2 cups (500 ml/16 fl oz) chicken stock
60 g (2 oz) rice vermicelli
50 g (1¾ oz) dried egg noodles
400 ml (13 fl oz) light coconut milk
10 snow peas, halved
3 spring onions, finely chopped
1 cup (90 g/3 oz) bean sprouts
½ cup (15 g/½ oz) fresh coriander leaves

1 To make the laksa paste, process the onion, ginger, galangal, lemon grass, garlic and chilli in a food processor until finely chopped. Add the oil and process until the mixture has a paste like consistency. Spoon into a large wok, add the curry paste and stir over low heat for 1–2 minutes, until aromatic. Take care not to burn.
2 Increase the heat to medium, add the chicken and stir for 2 minutes, or until the chicken is well coated. Stir in the chicken stock and mix well. Bring slowly to the boil, then simmer for 10 minutes, or until the chicken is cooked through.
3 Meanwhile, cut the vermicelli into shorter lengths. Cook the vermicelli and egg noodles separately in large pans of boiling water for 5 minutes

each. Drain and rinse in cold water.
4 Just prior to serving, add the light coconut milk and snow peas to the chicken and heat through. To serve, divide the vermicelli and noodles among four warmed serving bowls. Pour the hot laksa over the top and garnish with the spring onion, bean sprouts and coriander leaves.

NUTRITION PER SERVE
Protein 30 g; Fat 8 g; Carbohydrate 4.5 g; Dietary Fibre 3 g; Cholesterol 65 mg; 945 kJ (225 cal)

HINT: If you prefer a more fiery laksa, use a medium or hot brand of curry paste or increase the amount of chillies in your laksa paste.

Over low heat, stir the curry paste into the onion mixture until aromatic.

Just before serving, stir the light coconut milk into the chicken until heated.

MINESTRONE

Preparation time: 30 minutes +
  overnight soaking
Total cooking time: 2³/₄ hours
Serves 8
Fat per serve: 7 g

250 g (8 oz) dried borlotti beans
2 tablespoons oil
2 onions, chopped
2 cloves garlic, crushed
90 g (3 oz) chopped bacon pieces
4 plum tomatoes, peeled and
  chopped
3 tablespoons chopped fresh parsley
8 cups (2 litres) beef or vegetable
  stock

3 tablespoons red wine
1 carrot, chopped
1 swede, peeled and diced
2 potatoes, diced
3 tablespoons tomato paste
2 zucchini, sliced
90 g (3 oz) peas
¹/₂ cup (90 g/3 oz) small macaroni
Parmesan, to serve

1 Soak the borlotti beans in water
overnight then drain. Add to a pan of
boiling water, simmer for 15 minutes
and then drain. Heat the oil in a large
heavy-based pan and cook the onion,
garlic and bacon pieces until the onion
is soft and the bacon golden.
2 Add the tomato, parsley, borlotti
beans, stock and red wine. Simmer,

covered, over low heat for 2 hours.
Add the carrot, swede, potato and
tomato paste, cover and simmer for a
further 15–20 minutes.
3 Add the zucchini, peas and pasta.
Cover and simmer for 10–15 minutes,
or until the vegetables and macaroni
are tender. Season and serve with a
little grated Parmesan.

NUTRITION PER SERVE
Protein 15 g; Fat 7 g; Carbohydrate 25 g;
Dietary Fibre 10 g; Cholesterol 12 mg;
955 kJ (228 cal)

HINT: The macaroni can be cooked
separately in boiling water and added
to the soup just before serving.

Soak the borlotti beans in a bowl of water
overnight and then drain.

Use a sharp knife to peel and dice the swede
and other vegetables.

Stir the onion and bacon over the heat until they
are soft and golden.

CURRIED SWEET POTATO SOUP

Preparation time: 20 minutes
Total cooking time: 40 minutes
Serves 6
Fat per serve: 8 g

1 tablespoon oil
1 large onion, chopped
2 cloves garlic, crushed
3 teaspoons curry powder
1.25 kg (2 lb 8 oz) orange sweet potato, peeled and cubed
4 cups (1 litre) chicken stock
1 large apple, peeled, cored and grated
1/2 cup (125 ml/4 fl oz) light coconut milk

1 Heat the oil in a large pan over medium heat and cook the onion for 10 minutes, stirring occasionally, until very soft. Add the garlic and curry powder and cook for a minute further.
2 Add the sweet potato, stock and apple. Bring to the boil, reduce the heat and simmer, partially covered, for 30 minutes, until very soft.
3 Cool the soup a little before processing in batches until smooth.

Return to the pan, stir in the coconut milk and reheat gently without boiling. Serve with warm pitta bread.

NUTRITION PER SERVE
Protein 5 g; Fat 8 g; Carbohydrate 35 g; Dietary Fibre 5.5 g; Cholesterol 0 mg; 975 kJ (233 cal)

STORAGE TIME: Can be kept in the fridge for 1 day without the coconut milk: add this when you reheat.

HINT: The soup will become quite thick on standing. Thin with stock or water if necessary.

Add the garlic and curry powder to the softened onion and cook for another minute.

Stir in the stock with the cubed sweet potato and grated apple.

Once the soup has been processed stir in the coconut milk.

JUNGLE SOUP

Preparation time: 10 minutes
Total cooking time: 35 minutes
Serves 4
Fat per serve: 4 g

2 teaspoons oil
1 onion, finely sliced
225 g (7 oz) butternut pumpkin,
    peeled and diced
225 g (7 oz) fresh pineapple or
    mango, chopped

1 clove garlic, crushed
1 dried red chilli, finely chopped
2 teaspoons grated fresh ginger
4 cups (1 litre) chicken stock
2 tablespoons lime juice
350 g (11 oz) chicken breast, skinned,
    cut diagonally into thin strips

1 Heat the oil in a large heavy-based
pan and cook the onion for 5 minutes,
or until golden brown. Add the
pumpkin and cook for 5 minutes, or
until just browned. Add the pineapple
or mango, garlic, chilli and ginger and

toss the contents of the pan together.
2 Add the stock and lime juice, bring
to the boil and then reduce the heat to
simmer for 20 minutes, or until the
pumpkin is nearly tender.
3 Add the chicken and simmer for
5 minutes, or until the chicken is
cooked. Serve immediately.

NUTRITION PER SERVE
Protein 22 g; Fat 4 g; Carbohydrate 10 g;
Dietary Fibre 2.5 g; Cholesterol 45 mg;
700 kJ (170 cal)

Peel and chop the pineapple or mango into bite-
sized pieces.

Add the pumpkin to the onion in the pan and
cook until browned.

Use two wooden spoons to toss together the
contents of the pan.

HOMESTYLE VEGETABLE SOUP

Preparation time: 25 minutes +
  overnight soaking
Total cooking time: 55 minutes
Serves 6
Fat per serve: 7 g

1 cup (220 g/7 oz) soup mix or pearl
  barley (see NOTE)
2 tablespoons oil
1 large onion, finely chopped
1 green capsicum, chopped
2 zucchini, sliced
2 celery sticks, sliced
125 g (4 oz) button mushrooms, sliced
2 carrots, sliced
1 large potato, chopped
500 g (1 lb) pumpkin, peeled and
  chopped
8 cups (2 litres) vegetable stock

1 Soak the soup mix in water for
8 hours, then drain. Heat the oil in a
large heavy-based pan and cook the
onion for 5 minutes, until soft. Add the
capsicum, zucchini, celery and
mushrooms and cook for 5 minutes.
2 Add the carrot, potato and
pumpkin. Pour in the stock and add
the soup mix; bring to the boil, then
reduce the heat.

3 Partially cover the pan and simmer
for 45 minutes, until the vegetables
and soup mix are very soft. For a
thinner soup add a little water.

NUTRITION PER SERVE
Protein 5 g; Fat 7 g; Carbohydrate 15 g;
Dietary Fibre 5 g; Cholesterol 0.5 mg;
595 kJ (140 cal)

STORAGE TIME: Keep for 2 days in
the refrigerator or freeze for 1 month.

NOTE: Soup mix is a combination of
pearl barley, split peas and lentils.
Both pearl barley and soup mix are
readily available from supermarkets.

Cover the soup mix with water and leave to soak
and rehydrate.

Add the stock and the soup mix to the pan of
chopped vegetables.

Partially cover the pan and simmer until the
vegetables are very soft.

CHUNKY CHICKEN AND VEGETABLE SOUP

Preparation time: 15 minutes
Total cooking time: 20 minutes
Serves 4
Fat per serve: 7 g

1 tablespoon oil
1 carrot, sliced
1 leek, chopped
2 chicken thigh fillets, cut into 2 cm
    (1 inch) pieces
1/4 cup (35 g/1 oz) ditalini pasta
4 cups (1 litre) vegetable stock
2 ripe tomatoes, diced

1 Heat the oil in a saucepan and cook the carrot and leek over medium heat for 4 minutes, or until soft. Add the chicken and cook for a further 2 minutes, or until the chicken has changed colour.

2 Add the pasta and the vegetable stock, cover and bring to the boil. Reduce the heat and simmer for 10 minutes, or until the pasta is cooked. Add the tomato halfway through the cooking. Season to taste with salt and pepper. Serve with fresh crusty bread.

NUTRITION PER SERVE
Protein 20 g; Fat 7 g; Carbohydrate 9 g;
Dietary Fibre 2 g; Cholesterol 40 mg;
725 kJ (173 cal)

NOTE: Ditalini pasta can be replaced with any small soup pasta.

Cook the carrot and leek until it is soft, then add the chicken to the pan.

Simmer the soup for 10 minutes, or until the pasta is cooked and tender.

CHICKEN NOODLE AND MUSHROOM SOUP

Preparation time: 10 minutes
Total cooking time: 10 minutes
Serves 6
Fat per serve: 6.5 g

cooking oil spray
2 teaspoons grated fresh ginger
4 spring onions, finely chopped
1 chicken breast fillet, cut into thin
    strips
120 g (4 oz) button mushrooms, sliced
410 g (13 oz) can chicken consommé
60 g (2 oz) instant noodles
3 teaspoons kecap manis

1 Heat a little oil in a saucepan, add
the ginger, spring onion and chicken
and stir-fry over high heat for
4–5 minutes, or until the chicken
changes colour. Add the mushrooms
and cook for a further 1 minute.
2 Add the consommé and 2 cups
(500 ml/16 fl oz) water and bring to
the boil. Stir in the noodles, then
reduce the heat and simmer for
3 minutes, or until the noodles are
soft. Stir in the kecap manis and serve.

NUTRITION PER SERVE
Protein 9 g; Fat 6.5 g; Carbohydrate 4 g;
Dietary Fibre 1 g; Cholesterol 20 mg;
520 kJ (110 cal)

NOTE: Kecap manis is a thick, sweet
sauce. If it is unavailable, use soy
sauce sweetened with a little soft
brown sugar.

Stir-fry the ginger, spring onion and chicken over
high heat for 5 minutes.

Add the consommé and water, then add the
noodles and cook until soft.

AUTUMN GARDEN SOUP

Preparation time: 35 minutes
Total cooking time: 1 hour
Serves 6
Fat per serve: 5 g

30 g (1 oz) butter
1 large leek, sliced
1 clove garlic, crushed
1 teaspoon grated fresh ginger
2 parsnips, peeled and chopped
1 medium celeriac, peeled and
    chopped
2 large carrots, chopped

3 potatoes, chopped
2 turnips, peeled and chopped
5 cups (1.25 litres) vegetable stock
2 tablespoons chopped chives

1 Melt the butter in a large heavy-based pan and add the leek. Cook over low heat for about 15 minutes until very soft and lightly golden.
2 Add the garlic and ginger and cook, stirring, for 1 minute further. Add the vegetables and stock to the pan and bring to the boil.
3 Reduce the heat to simmer, partially covered, for about 40 minutes until very soft. Stir in the chives and serve.

NUTRITION PER SERVE
Protein 4 g; Fat 5 g; Carbohydrate 18 g;
Dietary Fibre 6 g; Cholesterol 13 mg;
535 kJ (128 cal)

STORAGE TIME: The soup will keep for up to 2 days in the refrigerator.

HINT: The soup becomes very thick on standing. Thin it down with extra stock or water.

VARIATION: Allow the soup to cool and then process in batches until smooth. Return to the pan and thin with a little stock if necessary.

Peel away the outer rough surface of the celeriac with a potato peeler.

Cook the leek until soft and golden and then add the garlic and ginger.

Simmer for about 40 minutes, until the vegetables are very soft.

MEDITERRANEAN FISH SOUP

Preparation time: 30 minutes
Total cooking time: 45 minutes
Serves 4
Fat per serve: 7.5 g

1/2 teaspoon saffron threads
3 teaspoons oil
2 large onions, thinly sliced
1 leek, white part only, chopped
4 cloves garlic, finely chopped
1 bay leaf, torn
1/2 teaspoon dried marjoram
1 teaspoon grated orange rind

2 tablespoons dry white wine
1 red capsicum, cut into chunks
500 g (1 lb) tomatoes, chopped
125 ml (4 fl oz) crushed tomatoes
2 cups (500 ml/16 fl oz) fish stock
2 tablespoons tomato paste
2 teaspoons soft brown sugar
500 g (1 lb) firm white fish, cut into
    bite-sized pieces
3 tablespoons chopped fresh parsley

1 Soak the saffron in 2 tablespoons boiling water; set aside. Heat the oil in a large heavy-based pan over low heat. Add the onion, leek, garlic, bay leaf and marjoram. Cover and cook for 10 minutes, shaking the pan occasionally, until the onion is soft. Add the rind, wine, capsicum and tomato, cover and cook for 10 minutes.
2 Stir in the crushed tomatoes, stock, tomato paste, sugar and saffron (with liquid). Bring to the boil and then simmer, uncovered, for 15 minutes.
3 Add the fish to the soup, cover and cook for 8 minutes, or until tender. Season and add the parsley.

NUTRITION PER SERVE
Protein 30 g; Fat 7.5 g; Carbohydrate 15 g;
Dietary Fibre 5 g; Cholesterol 90 mg;
1020 kJ (245 cal)

Soak the saffron threads in 2 tablespoons boiling water to release the flavour.

Add the orange rind, wine, capsicum and tomato, cover and cook for 10 minutes.

Add the fish pieces to the soup, cover and cook until tender.

ASIAN CHICKEN NOODLE SOUP

Preparation time: 10 minutes
Total cooking time: 10 minutes
Serves 4
Fat per serve: 3 g

90 g (3 oz) fresh egg noodles
5 cups (1.25 litres) chicken stock
1 tablespoon mirin (see NOTE)
2 tablespoons soy sauce
3 cm (1 inch) piece fresh ginger,
    julienned
2 chicken breast fillets, finely sliced
2 bunches baby bok choy, stalks
    trimmed, leaves separated
fresh coriander leaves, to garnish

1 Soak the noodles in boiling water for 1 minute, drain and set aside. In a large saucepan, heat the stock to simmering, add the mirin, soy sauce, ginger, chicken and noodles. Cook for 5 minutes, or until the chicken is tender and the noodles are warmed through. Skim the surface of the soup.
2 Add the bok choy and cook for a further 2 minutes, or until the bok choy has wilted. Serve in deep Chinese bowls and garnish with fresh coriander leaves. Serve with sweet chilli sauce.

NUTRITION PER SERVE
Protein 30 g; Fat 3 g; Carbohydrate 15 g;
Dietary Fibre 1 g; Cholesterol 65 mg;
915 kJ (220 cal)

NOTE: Mirin is a Chinese sweet rice wine used for cooking. Sweet sherry, with a little sugar added, can be used if mirin is unavailable.

Cook for 5 minutes, or until the chicken is tender and the noodles warmed through.

Add the bok choy to the soup and cook for a couple of minutes to wilt it.

CHARGRILLED BABY OCTOPUS

Preparation time: 15 minutes
  + overnight marinating
Total cooking time: 10 minutes
Serves 4
Fat per serve: 3.5 g

1 kg (2 lb) baby octopus
3/4 cup (185 ml/6 fl oz) red wine
2 tablespoons balsamic vinegar
2 tablespoons soy sauce
2 tablespoons hoisin sauce
1 clove garlic, crushed

1 Cut off the octopus heads below the eyes with a sharp knife. Discard the heads and guts. Push the beaks out with your index finger, remove and discard. Wash the octopus thoroughly under running water and drain on crumpled paper towels. If the octopus are large, cut the tentacles into quarters.

2 Put the octopus in a large bowl. Stir together the wine, vinegar, soy sauce, hoisin sauce and garlic in a jug and pour over the octopus. Toss to coat, then cover and refrigerate for several hours, or overnight.

3 Heat a chargrill pan or barbecue hotplate until very hot and then lightly oil. Drain the octopus, reserving the marinade. Cook in batches for 3–5 minutes, or until the octopus flesh turns white. Brush the marinade over the octopus during cooking. Be careful not to overcook or the octopus will be tough. Serve warm or cold. Delicious with a green salad and lime wedges.

NUTRITION PER SERVE
Protein 42.5 g; Fat 3.5 g; Carbohydrate 4 g;
Dietary Fibre 1 g; Cholesterol 497.5 mg;
1060 kJ (255 cal)

Remove and discard the head from each octopus with a sharp knife.

Push the beaks through the centre with your index finger.

Brush the octopus all over with the reserved marinade while cooking.

STEAMED PRAWN NORI ROLLS

Preparation time: 15 minutes
  + 1 hour refrigeration
Total cooking time: 5 minutes
Makes 25 rolls
Fat per roll: 0.5 g

500 g (1 lb) peeled raw prawns,
  deveined
1½ tablespoons fish sauce
1 tablespoon sake
2 tablespoons chopped fresh
  coriander
1 large fresh kaffir lime leaf,
  finely shredded
1 tablespoon lime juice

2 teaspoons sweet chilli sauce
1 egg white, lightly beaten
5 sheets nori

DIPPING SAUCE
¼ cup (60 ml/2 fl oz) sake
¼ cup (60 ml/2 fl oz) soy sauce
1 tablespoon mirin
1 tablespoon lime juice

1 Process the prawns in a food
processor or blender with the fish
sauce, sake, coriander, kaffir lime leaf,
lime juice and sweet chilli sauce, until
smooth. Add the egg white and pulse
for a few seconds to just combine.
2 Lay the nori sheets on a flat surface
and spread some prawn mixture over
each sheet, leaving a 2 cm (1 inch)

border at one end. Roll up tightly,
cover and refrigerate for 1 hour to
firm. Using a sharp knife, trim the ends
and cut into 2 cm (1 inch) lengths.
3 Place the rolls in a lined bamboo
steamer. Cover the steamer and place
it over a wok of simmering water,
making sure it doesn't touch the water.
Steam the rolls for 5 minutes, or until
heated thoroughly.
4 For the dipping sauce, thoroughly
mix all the ingredients together in a
small bowl. Serve with the nori rolls.

NUTRITION PER ROLL
Protein 4 g; Fat 0.5 g; Carbohydrate 0.5 g;
Dietary Fibre 0.5 g; Cholesterol 39.5 mg;
95 kJ (23 cal)

Spread prawn mixture over each nori sheet,
leaving a 2 cm (1 inch) border at one end.

Roll each sheet up tightly, then cover and
refrigerate to firm.

Cut the nori rolls into short lengths with a very
sharp knife.

PEPPER AND ALMOND BREAD

Preparation time: 10 minutes +
   3 hours standing
Total cooking time: 1 hour 10 minutes
Makes about 70 pieces
Fat per piece: 1.5 g

2 teaspoons black peppercorns
2 egg whites
1/3 cup (90 g/3 oz) caster sugar
3/4 cup (90 g/3 oz) plain flour
1/4 teaspoon ground ginger
1/4 teaspoon ground cinnamon
1 cup (155 g/5 oz) almonds

1 Preheat the oven to moderate 180°C
(350°F/Gas 4). Grease an 8 x 26 cm
(3 x 10½ inch) bar tin. Line the base
and sides with baking paper. Lightly
crush the peppercorns with the back
of a spoon or in a mortar and pestle.
2 Beat the egg whites and sugar with
electric beaters for 4 minutes, or until
the mixture turns white and thickens.
Sift the flour, ginger and cinnamon and
fold in with the almonds and the
crushed peppercorns.
3 Spread the mixture into the tin.
Bake for 35 minutes, or until lightly
browned. Cool in the tin for at least
3 hours, before turning out onto a
board. (You can wrap the bread
in foil and slice the next day at this
stage.) Using a serrated knife, cut
the bread into 3 mm (1/8 inch) slices.
Place the slices in a single layer
on baking trays. Bake in a slow
150°C (300°F/Gas 2) oven for about
25–35 minutes, or until the slices
are dry and crisp. Allow to cool
completely before serving. Serve with
soups as an alternative to plain bread.

NUTRITION PER PIECE
Protein 1 g; Fat 1.5 g; Carbohydrate 2.5 g;
Dietary Fibre 0 g; Cholesterol 0 mg;
95 kJ (25 cal)

NOTE: To make a traditional
sweet almond bread, simply omit
the peppercorns.

Use the back of a large metal spoon to lightly
crush the peppercorns.

Beat the egg whites and caster sugar until the
mixture turns white and thickens.

Fold the flour, spices, almonds and peppercorns
into the egg white mixture.

Cut the bread into thin slices and arrange them in
a single layer on baking trays.

THAI CHICKEN BALLS

Preparation time: 20 minutes
Total cooking time: 40 minutes
Serves 6
Fat per serve: 8 g

1 kg (2 lb) chicken mince
1 cup (90 g/3 oz) fresh breadcrumbs
4 spring onions, sliced
1 tablespoon ground coriander
1 cup (50 g/1¾ oz) chopped fresh
    coriander

3 tablespoons sweet chilli sauce
1–2 tablespoons lemon juice
2 tablespoons oil

1 Preheat the oven to moderately hot 200°C (400°F/Gas 6). Mix the mince and breadcrumbs in a large bowl.
2 Add the spring onion, ground and fresh coriander, chilli sauce and lemon juice and mix well. Using damp hands, form the mixture into evenly shaped balls that are either small enough to eat with your fingers or large enough to use as burgers.

3 Heat the oil in a large non-stick frying pan and cook the chicken balls over high heat until browned all over. Drain well on paper towels and then place them on a baking tray and bake until cooked through. (The small chicken balls will take 5 minutes to cook and the larger ones will take 10–15 minutes.)

NUTRITION PER SERVE
Protein 40 g; Fat 8 g; Carbohydrate 10 g;
Dietary Fibre 1 g; Cholesterol 85 mg;
1160 kJ (275 cal)

Mix the spring onion, coriander, chilli sauce and lemon juice into the mince mixture.

With damp hands, form the mixture into evenly shaped balls.

Cook the chicken balls in batches until they are browned and then bake in the oven.

MELON AND PINEAPPLE WITH CHILLI SYRUP

Preparation time: 15 minutes
Total cooking time: 20 minutes
Serves 4
Fat per serve: 0 g

JALAPENO SYRUP
1/2 cup (125 ml/4 fl oz) fresh lime juice
1/2 cup (125 g/4 oz) sugar
2 jalapeno chillies, stems removed, sliced into thin rounds (see NOTE)

1/2 small round watermelon, cut into small cubes
1 small ripe pineapple, peeled and cut into small triangles
fresh mint sprigs, to serve

1 To make the jalapeno syrup, stir the lime juice, sugar and 1/2 cup (125 ml/4 fl oz) water in a small pan over medium-low heat without boiling until the sugar has completely dissolved. Bring to the boil, then simmer for 10–15 minutes, without stirring, or until thick and syrupy.

2 Add the chilli, cook for 5 minutes and cool to room temperature.
3 Arrange the fruit on a plate; drizzle with the syrup. Garnish with the mint and extra chilli slices. Serve chilled.

NUTRITION PER SERVE
Protein 2 g; Fat 0 g; Carbohydrate 45 g;
Dietary Fibre 3 g; Cholesterol 0 mg;
745 kJ (180 cal)

NOTE: Jalapeno chillies, or peppers, are very hot. You could use a milder chilli if you prefer.

Peel and slice the pineapple and cut the slices into small triangles.

Simmer the syrup, without boiling, until all the sugar has dissolved.

Add the sliced jalapeno chilli to the syrup and cook for 5 minutes.

TOFU SALAD WITH GINGER MISO DRESSING

Preparation time: 20 minutes +
  overnight marinating
Total cooking time: 5 minutes
Serves 4
Fat per serve: 8 g

90 ml (3 fl oz) light soy sauce
2 teaspoons soy bean oil
2 cloves garlic, crushed
1 teaspoon grated fresh ginger
1 teaspoon chilli paste
500 g (1 lb) firm tofu, cut into small
  cubes
400 g (13 oz) mesclun leaves
1 Lebanese cucumber, finely sliced
250 g (8 oz) cherry tomatoes, halved
2 teaspoons soy bean oil, extra

DRESSING
2 teaspoons white miso paste (see
  NOTE)
2 tablespoons mirin
1 teaspoon sesame oil
1 teaspoon grated fresh ginger
1 teaspoon finely chopped chives
1 tablespoon toasted sesame seeds

1 Mix together the tamari, soy bean oil, garlic, ginger, chilli paste and $1/2$ teaspoon salt in a bowl. Add the tofu and mix until well coated. Marinate for at least 10 minutes, or preferably overnight. Drain and reserve the marinade.
2 To make the dressing, combine the miso with $1/2$ cup (125 ml/4 fl oz) hot water and leave until the miso dissolves. Add the mirin, sesame oil, ginger, chives and sesame seeds and stir tuntil beginning to thicken.
3 Put the mesclun leaves, cucumber and tomato in a serving bowl.

4 Heat the extra soy bean oil on a chargrill or hotplate. Add the tofu and cook over medium heat for 4 minutes, or until golden brown. Pour on the reserved marinade and cook for a further 1 minute over high heat. Remove from the grill and cool for 5 minutes.
5 Add the tofu to the salad, drizzle with the dressing and toss well.

NUTRITION PER SERVE
Protein 12 g; Fat 8 g; Carbohydrate 4 g;
Dietary Fibre 4 g; Cholesterol 0 mg;
590 kJ (140 cal)

NOTE: Miso is Japanese bean paste and is commonly used in soups, dressings, on grilled foods and as a flavouring for pickles.

Gently stir the tofu cubes through the marinade until well coated.

Stir the dressing ingredients together until it begins to thicken.

Cook the tofu cubes over medium heat until each side is golden brown.

PRAWN SPRING ROLLS

Preparation time: 50 minutes
Total cooking time: 4 minutes
Makes about 18 spring rolls
Fat per spring roll: 1 g

50 g (1³/₄ oz) rice vermicelli
2 spring onions
1 Lebanese cucumber, peeled
1 carrot
24 cooked prawns, peeled and
    chopped
2 tablespoons chopped roasted
    unsalted peanuts
2 Chinese mushrooms, soaked,
    chopped finely
¹/₂ lettuce, finely shredded
¹/₂ cup (25 g/³/₄ oz) chopped
    fresh mint
50 g (1³/₄ oz) bean sprouts
375 g (12 oz) rice paper rounds,
    21 cm (8¹/₂ inch) diameter

DIPPING SAUCE
2 tablespoons caster sugar
2 tablespoons fish sauce
2 tablespoons lime juice
1 tablespoon rice vinegar or white
    vinegar
1 spring onion, finely chopped
1 small red chilli, seeded and finely
    chopped
1 clove garlic, crushed

1 Put the vermicelli in a bowl, cover with boiling water and leave for 1–2 minutes, or until soft. Rinse under cold water, drain, chop roughly with scissors and put in a bowl.
2 Very finely shred the spring onions, cucumber and carrot into thin 5 cm (2 inch) strips. Blanch the carrot in boiling water for 1 minute, drain and cool. Add the carrot, spring onion and cucumber to the cooled vermicelli with the prawns, peanuts, mushrooms, lettuce, mint and bean sprouts. Toss, using your hands.
3 For each spring roll, soften a rice paper in a bowl of warm water for 10–20 seconds. Lay it on a tea towel and place 3 tablespoons of filling in the centre. Fold in the sides and roll up into a parcel. Seal the edges by brushing with a little water. Place on a serving platter and cover with a damp cloth while you make the rest.
4 To make the dipping sauce, combine the sugar and 2 tablespoons warm water in a small bowl and stir until the sugar dissolves. Add the remaining ingredients and stir well. Serve with the spring rolls.

NUTRITION PER SPRING ROLL
Protein 6 g; Fat 1 g; Carbohydrate 5 g; Dietary Fibre 1 g; Cholesterol 35 mg; 246 kJ (60 cal)

The spring onion, cucumber and carrot should be cut into short, fine strips.

Soften one sheet of rice paper at a time in a bowl of warm water.

Put the filling in the centre of the rice paper, then roll and fold into a parcel.

CHICKEN WINGS MARINATED IN SOY

Preparation time: 10 minutes +
   20 minutes refrigeration
Total cooking time: 50 minutes
Serves 4
Fat per serve: 7 g

½ cup (125 ml/4 fl oz) soy sauce
3 tablespoons honey
2 cloves garlic, crushed
3 tablespoons sweet chilli sauce
4 tablespoons lemon juice
½ cup (15 g/½ oz) lightly packed
   fresh mint, roughly chopped
16 chicken wings

1 Preheat the oven to moderately hot 200°C (400°F/Gas 6). Mix together the soy, honey, garlic, sweet chilli sauce, lemon juice and mint. Put the chicken wings in a flat dish in a single layer, pour the marinade over the top, cover with plastic wrap and refrigerate for 20 minutes.

2 Place the wings and any excess marinade into a baking dish and bake for 50 minutes, or until the wings are cooked through and the soy marinade has caramelised. Turn the wings once or twice during cooking to ensure even caramelisation.

NUTRITION PER SERVE
Protein 25 g; Fat 7 g; Carbohydrate 18 g;
Dietary Fibre 0 g; Cholesterol 105 mg;
1004 kJ (240 cal)

NOTE: The wings can be eaten by themselves or, for a main course, serve with steamed rice and a green salad. They can marinate overnight and be cooked the next day.

Arrange the chicken wings in a single layer in a dish and pour the marinade over the top.

Bake for 50 minutes, or until the soy marinade has caramelised.

CHARGRILLED TUNA AND RUBY GRAPEFRUIT SALAD

Preparation time: 20 minutes
Total cooking time: 10 minutes
Serves 6
Fat per serve: 7 g

4 ruby grapefruit
cooking oil spray
3 tuna steaks
150 g (5 oz) rocket leaves
1 red onion, sliced

ALMOND AND RASPBERRY DRESSING
2 tablespoons almond oil
2 tablespoons raspberry vinegar
1/2 teaspoon sugar
1 tablespoon shredded fresh mint

1 Cut a slice off each end of the grapefruit and peel away the skin, removing all the pith. Separate the segments and set aside in a bowl.
2 Heat a chargrill plate and spray lightly with oil. Cook each tuna steak for 3–4 minutes on each side. This will leave the centre slightly pink. Cool,

then thinly slice or flake.
3 To make the dressing, put the almond oil, vinegar, sugar and mint in a small screw-top jar and shake until well combined.
4 Place the rocket on a serving plate and top with the grapefruit segments, then the tuna and onion. Drizzle with the dressing and serve.

NUTRITION PER SERVE
Protein 15 g; Fat 7 g; Carbohydrate 8 g;
Dietary Fibre 2 g; Cholesterol 50 mg;
1015 kJ (240 cal)

Cut a slice off the ends of the grapefruit and peel away the skin and pith.

Separate the grapefruit into segments and set aside in a bowl.

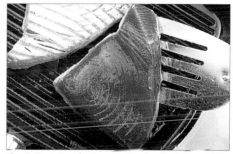

Cook the tuna steaks on a lightly oiled chargrill plate—they should still be pink in the centre.

TANDOORI LAMB SALAD

Preparation time: 20 minutes
 + overnight marinating
Total cooking time: 15 minutes
Serves 4 as a light lunch or starter
Fat per serve: 6.5 g

1 cup (250 g/8 oz) low-fat natural
  yoghurt
2 cloves garlic, crushed
2 teaspoons grated fresh ginger
2 teaspoons ground turmeric
2 teaspoons garam masala
1/4 teaspoon paprika

2 teaspoons ground coriander
red food colouring, optional
500 g (1 lb) lean lamb fillets
4 tablespoons lemon juice
1 1/2 teaspoons chopped fresh
  coriander
1 teaspoon chopped fresh mint
150 g (5 oz) mixed salad leaves
1 large mango, cut into strips
2 cucumbers, cut into matchsticks

1 Mix the yoghurt, garlic, ginger and
spices in a bowl, add a little colouring
and toss with the lamb to thoroughly
coat. Cover and refrigerate overnight.
2 Grill the lamb on a foil-lined baking

tray under high heat for 7 minutes
each side, or until the marinade starts
to brown. Set aside for 5 minutes
before serving.
3 Mix the lemon juice, coriander and
mint, then season. Toss with the salad
leaves, mango and cucumber, then
arrange on plates. Slice the lamb and
serve over the salad.

NUTRITION PER SERVE
Protein 30 g; Fat 6.5 g; Carbohydrate 8 g;
Dietary Fibre 2 g; Cholesterol 90 mg;
965 kJ (230 cal)

Coat the lamb with the marinade, cover and
refrigerate overnight.

Cut the mango flesh into long, thin strips, using a
sharp knife.

Turn the lamb after about 7 minutes and cook
until the marinade starts to brown.

CHARGRILLED VEGETABLE TERRINE

Preparation time: 30 minutes +
  overnight refrigeration
Total cooking time: Nil
Serves 8
Fat per serve: 5 g

350 g (11 oz) ricotta
2 cloves garlic, crushed
8 large slices chargrilled eggplant,
  drained (see NOTE)
10 slices chargrilled red capsicum,
  drained
8 slices chargrilled zucchini, drained
45 g (1 1/2 oz) rocket leaves
3 marinated artichokes, drained and
  sliced
85 g (3 oz) semi-dried tomatoes,
  drained and chopped
100 g (3 1/2 oz) marinated mushrooms,
  drained and halved

1 Line a 24 x 13 x 6 cm (9 x 5 x 2 1/2 inch) loaf tin with plastic wrap, leaving a generous amount hanging over the sides. Place the ricotta and garlic in a bowl and beat until smooth. Season with salt and pepper to taste and set aside.

2 Line the base of the tin with half the eggplant, cutting and fitting to cover the base. Top with a layer of half the capsicum, then all the zucchini slices. Spread evenly with the ricotta mixture and press down firmly. Place the rocket leaves on top of the ricotta. Arrange the artichoke, tomato and mushrooms in three rows lengthways on top of the ricotta.

3 Top with another layer of capsicum and finish with the eggplant. Fold the overhanging plastic wrap over the top of the terrine. Put a piece of cardboard on top and weigh it down with weights or small food cans. Refrigerate the terrine overnight.

4 To serve, peel back the plastic wrap and turn the terrine out onto a plate. Remove the plastic wrap and cut into thick slices.

NUTRITION PER SERVE
Protein 6 g; Fat 5 g; Carbohydrate 3 g;
Dietary Fibre 2 g; Cholesterol 20 mg;
350 kJ (85 cal)

NOTE: You can buy chargrilled eggplant, capsicum and zucchini and marinated mushrooms and artichokes at delicatessens.

STORAGE TIME: Cover any leftovers with plastic wrap and store in the refrigerator for up to 2 days.

Put the ricotta and crushed garlic in a bowl and beat until smooth.

Arrange the mushrooms, tomato and artichoke in three rows over the rocket.

Cover the terrine with cardboard and weigh down with small food cans.

PESTO BEEF SALAD

Preparation time: 30 minutes
Total cooking time: 25 minutes
Serves 8 as a starter
Fat per serve: 5 g

100 g (3½ oz) button mushrooms
1 large yellow capsicum
1 large red capsicum
cooking oil spray
100 g (3½ oz) lean fillet steak
1½ cups (135 g/4½ oz) penne

PESTO
1 cup (50 g/1¾ oz) tightly packed
    basil leaves
2 cloves garlic, chopped

2 tablespoons pepitas (pumpkin
    seeds)
1 tablespoon olive oil
2 tablespoons orange juice
1 tablespoon lemon juice

1 Cut the mushrooms into quarters.
Cut the capsicums into large flat
pieces, removing the seeds and
membrane. Place skin-side-up under a
hot grill until blackened. Leave
covered with a tea towel until cool,
then peel away the skin and chop
the flesh.
2 Spray a non-stick frying pan with oil
and cook the steak over high heat for
3–4 minutes each side until it is
medium-rare. Remove and leave for
5 minutes before cutting into thin

slices. Season with a little salt.
3 To make the pesto, finely chop the
basil leaves, garlic and pepitas in a
food processor. With the motor
running, add the oil, orange and
lemon juice. Season well.
4 Meanwhile, cook the penne in a
large pan of rapidly boiling salted
water until *al dente*. Drain, then toss
with the pesto in a large bowl.
5 Add the capsicum pieces, steak
slices and mushroom quarters to the
penne and toss to distribute evenly.
Serve immediately.

NUTRITION PER SERVE
Protein 8 g; Fat 5 g; Carbohydrate 15 g;
Dietary Fibre 2 g; Cholesterol 7 mg;
660 kJ (135 cal)

When the capsicum has cooled, peel away the
skin and dice the flesh.

Cook the steak in a non-stick frying pan until it is
medium-rare.

Add the oil with the orange and lemon juice, in a
thin stream.

THAI BEEF SALAD WITH MINT AND CORIANDER

Preparation time: 40 minutes
Total cooking time: 4 minutes
Serves 6 as a starter
Fat per serve: 6 g

2 tablespoons dried shrimp
125 g (4 oz) English spinach
1 tablespoon sesame oil
500 g (1 lb) rump steak
1 cup (90 g/3 oz) bean sprouts
1 small red onion, thinly sliced
1 small red capsicum, cut into thin
    strips
1 small Lebanese cucumber, cut into
    thin strips
200 g (6¹/₂ oz) daikon radish, peeled
    and cut into thin strips
1 small tomato, halved, seeded and
    thinly sliced
¹/₄ cup (5 g/¹/₄ oz) mint leaves
¹/₂ cup (15 g/¹/₂ oz) coriander leaves
2 cloves garlic, finely chopped
1–2 small red chillies, chopped
2 small green chillies, chopped

DRESSING
¹/₄ cup (60 ml/2 fl oz) lime juice
¹/₄ cup (60 ml/2 fl oz) fish sauce
1 tablespoon finely chopped lemon
    grass
1 teaspoon sugar

1 Soak the dried shrimp in hot water for 15 minutes; drain well and chop finely. Wash the English spinach and drain well. Trim the thick stalks and coarsely shred the leaves.
2 Heat the oil in a frying pan, add the steak and cook over high heat for 1¹/₂–2 minutes on each side until medium-rare. Allow to cool slightly and then slice the steak thinly.

3 To make the dressing, combine the lime juice, fish sauce, lemon grass and sugar in a small jug. Whisk until the ingredients are well combined.
4 To assemble the salad, combine the shrimp, sliced beef, bean sprouts, onion, capsicum, cucumber, radish, tomato, mint, coriander, garlic and chillies in a large bowl. Place the

spinach on a serving plate, top with the combined beef and vegetables, and drizzle with the dressing.

NUTRITION PER SERVE
Protein 25 g; Fat 6 g; Carbohydrate 6 g;
Dietary Fibre 4 g; Cholesterol 65 mg;
730 kJ (175 cal)

Slice the onion, and cut the capsicum, cucumber and daikon into thin strips.

Trim the thick stalks from the English spinach and coarsely shred the leaves.

Cook the steak over high heat for a couple of minutes until it is medium-rare.

Salads

On warm summer days salads can be satisfying as a light meal in themselves, but they can also be served as side dishes to many of the low-fat main courses in this book.

TOMATO AND BASIL

Quarter 6 ripe Roma tomatoes and mix with 1 sliced red onion, 1 crushed garlic clove, 2 tablespoons balsamic vinegar and 1 cup (60 g/2 oz) shredded basil leaves. Toss, season and set aside for 10 minutes, then transfer to a shallow dish. (If you find raw onion too strong, put it in a bowl and cover with boiling water for 5 minutes. Drain well.) Serves 4.

NUTRITION PER SERVE
Protein 2 g; Fat 0 g; Carbohydrate 5 g;
Dietary Fibre 2 g; Cholesterol 0 mg;
120 kJ (30 cal)

HOT BEANS WITH YOGHURT

Combine 100 g (3^1/$_2$ oz) each of dried chickpeas, pinto beans, red kidney beans and black-eyed beans in a large bowl. Cover with water and soak overnight. Drain, place in a large pan and cover with water. Bring to the boil, reduce the heat and simmer for 45 minutes, or until tender. Don't overcook or they will be mushy. Meanwhile, in a large, deep non-stick frying pan, cook 2 sliced onions over low heat for 25 minutes, or until golden. Add 2 teaspoons ground cumin and 1 teaspoon ground coriander with the beans; toss. Add a 420 g (13 oz) can drained corn kernels, 2 chopped tomatoes, ^{1}/$_3$ cup (80 ml/2^3/$_4$ fl oz) lemon juice and ^{1}/$_4$ cup (7 g/^{1}/$_4$ oz) chopped coriander leaves. Season and stir. Grate a Lebanese cucumber and, with your hands, squeeze out the moisture. Combine with 1 cup (250 g/8 oz) low-fat natural yoghurt. Season, then stir. Put the hot beans on a plate and top with the yoghurt mix. Serves 8.

NUTRITION PER SERVE
Protein 10 g; Fat 2 g; Carbohydrate 25 g;
Dietary Fibre 8.5 g; Cholesterol 1.5 mg;
745 kJ (180 cal)

ROAST PUMPKIN AND ONION WITH ROCKET

Preheat the oven to moderately hot 200°C (400°F/Gas 6). Cut 800 g (1 lb 10 oz) peeled jap pumpkin into 3 cm (1¼ inch) cubes and 2 small red onions into small wedges. Line a small baking dish with baking paper, add the vegetables and sprinkle with 2 finely chopped garlic cloves. Lightly spray with oil. Season and cook for 30–35 minutes, or until the pumpkin is just tender. Set aside. Tear the leaves from 150 g (5 oz) rocket into pieces. Arrange on a platter, then top with the pumpkin and onion. Drizzle all over with 1–2 tablespoons balsamic vinegar. Serve warm. Serves 4.

NUTRITION PER SERVE
Protein 5.5 g; Fat 1 g; Carbohydrate 15 g; Dietary Fibre 4 g; Cholesterol 0 mg; 400 kJ (95 cal)

GRILLED VEGETABLES

Mix 1.5 kg (3 lb) of thickly sliced vegetables (such as pumpkin, potato, parsnip, eggplant and zucchini) with 2 tablespoons olive oil and 4 finely chopped cloves garlic in a large baking dish. Heat a large flat grill or barbecue plate and spray lightly with cooking oil. Grill the vegetables separately (they will cook at different rates), turning until charred. Bake for 15 minutes on a lightly greased baking tray in a moderate 180°C (350°F/Gas 4) oven until cooked. Arrange 300 g (10 oz) baby spinach leaves on a platter, top with the vegetables and half a thinly sliced red capsicum. Drizzle with 2 tablespoons balsamic vinegar and chopped chives. Serves 4.

NUTRITION PER SERVE
Protein 9 g; Fat 10 g; Carbohydrate 25 g; Dietary Fibre 10 g; Cholesterol 0 mg; 1000 kJ (240 cal)

CITRUS FRUIT WITH HONEY DRESSING

Remove the rind from 1 grapefruit, 2 small red grapefruit and 4 oranges. Remove and discard all the pith from a few slices of the rind from each fruit and cut the rind into long thin strips. Remove any remaining pith from the fruit and slice between each section. Segment the fruit over a bowl to catch any juice; set the juice aside. Put the segments and rind in a salad bowl with 1 sliced red onion and ⅓ cup (10 g/¼ oz) fresh coriander leaves. Add 2 tablespoons honey and ⅓ cup (80 ml/2¾ fl oz) raspberry vinegar to the reserved fruit juice and whisk to combine. Pour over the salad and toss. Serve on a bed of rocket. Serves 6.

NUTRITION PER SERVE
Protein 3 g; Fat 0 g; Carbohydrate 25 g; Dietary Fibre 3.5 g; Cholesterol 0 mg; 505 kJ (120 cal)

Clockwise, from top left: Grilled vegetables; Hot beans with yoghurt; Citrus fruit with honey dressing; Roast pumpkin and onion with rocket; Tomato and basil.

Dressings

Most people think that low-fat eating means no more tangy dressings and creamy sauces. Not so. These dressings will give a lift to salads, meat, fish and even desserts and won't break the fat bank.

HERB, GARLIC AND YOGHURT

Whisk together 200 g (6½ oz) low-fat natural yoghurt, 4 tablespoons skim milk, 1 teaspoon Dijon mustard, 1 tablespoon finely chopped chives, 2 teaspoons finely chopped fresh parsley, 2 teaspoons chopped fresh oregano and 1 crushed clove garlic. Season with salt and pepper.
Makes 1 cup (250 ml/8 fl oz).

NUTRITION PER TABLESPOON
Protein 1 g; Fat 0 g; Carbohydrate 1 g;
Dietary Fibre 0 g; Cholesterol 0 mg;
50 kJ (10 cal)

BERRY DRESSING

Blend 100 g (3½ oz) fresh or thawed frozen strawberries, 1½ tablespoons oil, 3 tablespoons apple juice, 1 tablespoon lemon juice, 1 tablespoon cider vinegar and some cracked black pepper in a blender until smooth. Season with salt.
Makes ¾ cup (185 ml/6 fl oz).

NUTRITION PER TABLESPOON
Protein 0 g; Fat 3 g; Carbohydrate 1 g;
Dietary Fibre 0 g; Cholesterol 0 mg;
145 kJ (35 cal)

WALNUT VINAIGRETTE

Combine 2 tablespoons cider vinegar, 1 tablespoon balsamic vinegar, 1½ tablespoons walnut oil, 1 teaspoon Dijon mustard, 2 tablespoons water, ½ teaspoon caster sugar and 2 teaspoons finely chopped fresh parsley in a screw-top jar. Shake the jar, then season.
Makes ½ cup (125 ml/4 fl oz).

NUTRITION PER TABLESPOON
Protein 0 g; Fat 5 g; Carbohydrate 1 g;
Dietary Fibre 0 g; Cholesterol 0 mg;
210 kJ (50 cal)

ROASTED CAPSICUM SAUCE

Quarter 2 red capsicums, remove the seeds and membrane and grill until the skins blister and blacken. Cool under a damp tea towel before peeling. Cut one quarter into thin strips then set aside. Heat 1 teaspoon oil in a small pan, add 2 finely chopped spring onions and 1 tablepsoon water, then stir over heat until the spring onion is soft. Add the remaining capsicum, 3 tablespoons beef stock, 2 tablespoons white wine, 2 tablespoons tomato paste and $1/4$ teaspoon sugar. Simmer for 2 minutes, then blend until smooth. Season and stir in 1 tablespoon chopped chives. Garnish with red capsicum strips.
Makes 1 cup (250 ml/8 fl oz).

NUTRITION PER TABLESPOON
Protein 0.5 g; Fat 0.5 g; Carbohydrate 1.5 g;
Dietary Fibre 0.5 g; Cholesterol 0 mg;
55 kJ (15 cal)

TOMATO SAUCE

Heat 1 teaspoon oil in a pan, add a sliced small leek, 2 tablespoons water and 1 crushed clove garlic. Cover and stir until the leek is soft. Add a 440 g (14 oz) can chopped tomato, 1 tablespoon tomato paste, $1/4$ teaspoon sugar and 2 tablespoons red wine. Stir, then simmer for 5 minutes. Season.
Makes 2 cups (500 ml/16 fl oz).

NUTRITION PER TABLESPOON
Protein 0.5 g; Fat 0.5 g; Carbohydrate 1.5 g;
Dietary Fibre 0.5 g; Cholesterol 0 mg;
55 kJ (15 cal)

HUMMUS DRESSING

Drain a 425 g (14 oz) can chickpeas and put in a food processor with $3/4$ cup (185 ml/6 fl oz) vegetable stock, 1 tablespoon tahini paste and 2 chopped cloves garlic. Stir 1 teaspoon each of ground coriander and cumin in a dry frying pan over medium heat for 3 minutes, or until aromatic. Cool slightly, add to the processor and mix until nearly smooth. Mix in 2 tablespoons lemon juice. Season with cracked pepper and salt. If too thick, add a little water.
Makes 1 cup (250 ml/8 fl oz).

NUTRITION PER TABLESPOON
Protein 2 g; Fat 1.5 g; Carbohydrate 4 g;
Dietary Fibre 1.5 g; Cholesterol 0 mg;
160 kJ (40 cal)

SWEET RICOTTA CREAM

Beat together 200 g ($6^{1}/2$ oz) ricotta, 100 g ($3^{1}/2$ oz) low-fat natural yoghurt, $1/2$ teaspoon finely grated orange rind, 3 tablespoons orange juice and 1 tablepoon caster sugar until smooth.
Makes 1 cup (250 ml/8 fl oz).

NUTRITION PER TABLESPOON
Protein 2 g; Fat 1.5 g; Carbohydrate 2.5 g;
Dietary Fibre 0 g; Cholesterol 6.5 mg;
130 kJ (30 cal)

Clockwise, from top left: Berry dressing, Walnut vinaigrette; Hummus dressing; Tomato sauce; Sweet ricotta cream; Roasted capsicum sauce; Herb, garlic and yoghurt.

Meat

BEEF BOURGUIGNON

Preparation time: 10 minutes
Total cooking time: 2 hours
Serves 6
Fat per serve: 7 g

1 kg (2 lb) topside or round steak
plain flour, seasoned with salt and
    pepper
3 rashers bacon, rind removed
1 tablespoon oil
12 pickling onions
1 cup (250 ml/ 8 fl oz) red wine
2 cups (500 ml/16 fl oz) beef stock
1 teaspoon dried thyme
200 g (6½ oz) button mushrooms
2 bay leaves

1 Trim the steak of fat and sinew and cut into 2 cm (3/4 inch) cubes. Lightly toss in the seasoned flour to coat, shaking off the excess.
2 Cut the bacon into 2 cm (3/4 inch) squares. Heat the oil in a large pan and quickly cook the bacon over medium heat. Remove the bacon from the pan, then add the meat and brown well in batches. Remove and set aside. Add the onions to the pan and cook until golden.
3 Return the bacon and meat to the pan with the remaining ingredients. Bring to the boil, reduce the heat and simmer, covered, for 1½ hours, or until the meat is very tender, stirring now and then. Remove the bay leaves to serve.

NUTRITION PER SERVE
Protein 40 g; Fat 7 g; Carbohydrate 5 g;
Dietary Fibre 1 g; Cholesterol 90 mg;
1150 kJ (275 cal)

STORAGE TIME: Refrigerate in an airtight container for up to 3 days.

Trim the meat of any fat and sinew and cut it into cubes.

Return the bacon and meat to the pan and add the remaining ingredients.

BEEF AND VEGETABLE CASSEROLE

Preparation time: 40 minutes
Total cooking time: 1 hour 40 minutes
Serves 6
Fat per serve: 4 g

500 g (1 lb) lean round steak
cooking oil spray
1 onion, sliced
3 cloves garlic, crushed
2 teaspoons ground cumin
1 teaspoon dried thyme leaves
2 bay leaves
400 g (13 oz) can chopped tomatoes
500 g (1 lb) potatoes, chopped
2 large carrots, thickly sliced
4 zucchini, thickly sliced
250 g (8 oz) mushrooms, halved
250 g (8 oz) yellow squash, halved
2 tablespoons tomato paste
1/2 cup (125 ml/4 fl oz) red wine
1/3 cup (20 g/3/4 oz) chopped fresh
   parsley

1 Preheat the oven to moderate 180°C (350°F/Gas 4). Remove any excess fat and sinew from the meat and cut into 2 cm (3/4 inch) cubes. Spray a deep, non-stick frying pan with oil and fry the meat in batches until brown. Remove from the pan. Spray the pan again, add the onion and cook until lightly golden. Add the garlic, cumin, thyme and bay leaves and stir for 1 minute.
2 Return the meat and any juices to the pan, tossing to coat with spices. Add 1 1/2 cups (375 ml/12 fl oz) water and the tomato, scraping the pan. Simmer for 10 minutes, or until thickened. Mix in a large casserole dish with the vegetables, tomato paste and wine.

3 Bake, covered, for 1 hour. Stir well, then uncover and bake for 20 minutes. Season, remove the bay leaves and stir in the parsley.

NUTRITION PER SERVE
Protein 25 g; Fat 4 g; Carbohydrate 20 g; Dietary Fibre 6.5 g; Cholesterol 50 mg; 930 kJ (220 cal)

Discard any excess fat and sinew from the steak and cut the steak into cubes.

When the onion is golden, add the garlic, cumin, thyme and bay leaves.

Pour the wine into the casserole dish and stir through the vegetables.

VEAL CUTLETS IN CHILLI TOMATO SAUCE

Preparation time: 35 minutes
Total cooking time: 35 minutes
Serves 4
Fat per serve: 6 g

5 slices wholemeal bread
3 tablespoons fresh parsley
3 cloves garlic
4 thick veal cutlets, trimmed
3 tablespoons skim milk
2 teaspoons olive oil
1 onion, finely chopped
1 tablespoon capers, drained
1 teaspoon canned green
    peppercorns, chopped
1 teaspoon chopped red chilli
2 tablespoons balsamic vinegar
1 teaspoon soft brown sugar
2 tablespoons tomato paste
440 g (14 oz) can chopped tomatoes

1 Preheat the oven to moderate 180°C (350°F/Gas 4). Place a rack in a small baking dish. Chop the bread, parsley and garlic in a food processor to make fine breadcrumbs.

2 Season the cutlets on both sides with salt and black pepper. Pour the milk into a bowl and put the breadcrumbs on a plate. Dip the veal in the milk, then coat in the crumbs, pressing the crumbs on. Transfer to the rack and bake for 20 minutes.

3 Heat the oil in a small pan over medium heat. Add the onion, capers, peppercorns and chilli, cover and cook for 8 minutes. Stir in the vinegar, sugar and tomato paste and stir until boiling. Stir in the tomato, reduce the heat and simmer for 15 minutes.

4 Remove the cutlets from the rack and wipe the dish. Place about three-quarters of the tomato sauce in the base and put the cutlets on top. Spoon the remaining sauce over the cutlets and return to the oven. Reduce the oven to slow 150°C (300°F/Gas 2) and bake for 10 minutes to heat through.

NUTRITION PER SERVE
Protein 15 g; Fat 6 g; Carbohydrate 20 g; Dietary Fibre 5 g; Cholesterol 25 mg; 845 kJ (200 cal)

Trim the veal cutlets of any excess fat and gristle and then season with salt and pepper.

Dip the seasoned cutlets in the milk, then press into the breadcrumb mixture.

Put the cutlets on top of the tomato sauce, then top with the remaining sauce.

BEEF STROGANOFF

Preparation time: 20 minutes
Total cooking time: 25 minutes
Serves 4
Fat per serve: 4 g

500 g (1 lb) rump steak
cooking oil spray
1 onion, sliced
1/4 teaspoon paprika
250 g (8 oz) button mushrooms,
   halved

2 tablespoons tomato paste
1/2 cup (125 ml/4 fl oz) beef stock
1/2 cup (125 ml/4 fl oz) low-fat
   evaporated milk
3 teaspoons cornflour
3 tablespoons chopped fresh parsley

1 Remove any excess fat from the steak and slice into thin strips. Cook in batches in a large, lightly greased non-stick frying pan over high heat, until just cooked. Remove from the pan.
2 Lightly spray the pan and cook the onion, paprika and mushrooms over medium heat until the onion has softened. Add the meat, tomato paste, stock and 1/2 cup (125 ml/4 fl oz) water. Bring to the boil, then reduce the heat and simmer for 10 minutes.
3 In a small bowl, mix the evaporated milk with the cornflour. Add to the pan and stir until the sauce boils and thickens. Sprinkle with parsley.

NUTRITION PER SERVE
Protein 35 g; Fat 4 g; Carbohydrate 8 g;
Dietary Fibre 2.5 g; Cholesterol 85 mg;
900 kJ (215 cal)

Slice the rump steak into thin strips after removing any excess fat.

Stir the onion, paprika and mushrooms until the onion has softened.

Stir the evaporated milk into the cornflour until the mixture is smooth.

MEATLOAF

Preparation time: 15 minutes
Total cooking time: 1 hour 20 minutes
Serves 6
Fat per serve: 9 g

cooking oil spray
2 onions, finely chopped
2 cloves garlic, crushed
1½ cups (120 g/4 oz) fresh
  breadcrumbs
60 g (2 oz) pumpkin, coarsely grated
1 carrot, coarsely grated
2 tablespoons chopped fresh parsley
500 g (1 lb) lean beef mince
2 tablespoons Worcestershire sauce
1 teaspoon dried basil
1 tablespoon tomato paste
1 egg, lightly beaten
90 g (3 oz) button mushrooms, thinly
  sliced

TOMATO SAUCE
400 g (13 oz) can tomatoes
1 tablespoon dry white wine
2 teaspoons soft brown sugar

1 Preheat the oven to moderately hot
200°C (400°F/Gas 6). Lightly spray a
non-stick frying pan with oil and place
over medium heat. Add the onion
and cook, stirring, for 2 minutes. Add
1 tablespoon water to prevent sticking,
then add the crushed garlic and stir for
3 minutes, or until the onion is golden
brown. Allow to cool.
2 Use your hands to thoroughly mix
together the breadcrumbs, pumpkin,
carrot, parsley, mince, Worcestershire
sauce, basil, tomato paste and the
cooled onion mixture. Mix in the egg
and mushrooms. Season. Transfer to a
10 x 18 cm (4 x 7 inch) non-stick loaf
tin (or loaf tin lined with greaseproof

paper), pressing gently into the tin and
smoothing the top.
3 To make the tomato sauce, push the
undrained tomatoes through a sieve,
discarding the contents of the sieve.
Stir in the wine and sugar. Spoon
3 tablespoons over the meatloaf and
bake for 15 minutes. Spoon another
3 tablespoons of sauce over the
meatloaf, lower the oven temperature
to 190°C (375°F/Gas 5) and bake for

1 hour 10 minutes, basting
occasionally with sauce. Slice and
serve with any remaining sauce.

NUTRITION PER SERVE
Protein 7 g; Fat 9 g; Carbohydrate 25 g;
Dietary Fibre 4 g; Cholesterol 30 mg;
615 kJ (150 cal)

Lightly cover the base of the non-stick pan with
cooking oil spray.

Using your hands is the easiest way to combine
the ingredients.

Spoon 3 tablespoons of the tomato sauce over
the meatloaf.

SPAGHETTI BOLOGNESE

Preparation time: 30 minutes
Total cooking time: 1 hour 20 minutes
Serves 6
Fat per serve: 8 g

cooking oil spray
2 onions, finely chopped
2 cloves garlic, finely chopped
2 carrots, finely chopped
2 celery sticks, finely chopped
400 g (13 oz) lean beef mince
1 kg (2 1b) tomatoes, chopped

1/2 cup (125 ml/4 fl oz) red wine
350 g (11 oz) spaghetti
1/4 cup (15 g/1/2 oz) finely chopped
  fresh parsley

1 Lightly spray a large saucepan with oil. Place over medium heat and add the onion, garlic, carrot and celery. Stir for 5 minutes, or until the vegetables have softened. Add 1 tablespoon water, if necessary, to prevent sticking.
2 Increase the heat to high, add the mince and cook for 5 minutes, or until browned. Stir constantly to prevent the meat sticking. Add the tomato, wine

and 1 cup (250 ml/8 fl oz) water. Bring to the boil, reduce the heat and simmer, uncovered, for about 1 hour, until the sauce has thickened.
3 Cook the spaghetti in a large pan of rapidly boiling salted water for 10–12 minutes, or until *al dente*, then drain. Stir the parsley through the sauce, season with salt and pepper and serve over the pasta.

NUTRITION PER SERVE
Protein 9 g; Fat 8 g; Carbohydrate 50 g;
Dietary Fibre 7 g; Cholesterol 0 mg;
1695 kJ (405 cal)

Finely chop both the onions and then fry with the garlic, carrot and celery.

Stir the meat constantly and break up any lumps with the back of the spoon.

Simmer the bolognese sauce uncovered until the liquid has reduced and the sauce thickened.

BEEF AND LENTIL CURRY

Preparation time: 45 minutes +
  10 minutes soaking
Total cooking time: 1 hour 50 minutes
Serves 6
Fat per serve: 14 g

3–4 small dried red chillies
1 tablespoon oil
2 red onions, cut into thin wedges
4 cloves garlic, finely chopped
1 tablespoon grated fresh ginger
1 tablespoon garam masala
3 cardamom pods, lightly crushed
1 cinnamon stick
2 teaspoons ground turmeric
750 g (1¹/₂ lb) chuck or gravy beef,
  diced
400 g (13 oz) can chopped tomatoes
¹/₂ cup (90 g/3 oz) brown or green
  lentils
¹/₂ cup (125 g/4 oz) red lentils
200 g (6¹/₂ oz) pumpkin, diced
150 g (5 oz) baby eggplant, quartered
  lengthways, diced
125 g (4 oz) baby English spinach
  leaves
1 tablespoon tamarind purée
2 tablespoons grated palm sugar

1 Soak the chillies in boiling water for 10 minutes, drain and finely chop.
2 Heat the oil in a large saucepan. Add the onion and cook, stirring, over medium heat for 5 minutes, or until soft. Add the garlic and ginger, and cook for a further 2 minutes.
3 Add the chilli, garam masala, cardamom pods, cinnamon stick, turmeric and ¹/₂ teaspoon coarsely ground black pepper. Cook, stirring, for 2 minutes, or until fragrant. Add the beef and stir constantly for 3–4 minutes, or until the meat changes colour and is well coated in the spices.
4 Add the tomato, lentils, 1 teaspoon salt and 3 cups (750 ml) water. Simmer, covered, for 1 hour, or until the lentils are tender. Stir frequently to prevent any of the mixture sticking to the base of the pan. Add a little extra water, if necessary.
5 Add the pumpkin and eggplant to the pan, and cook, covered, for 20 minutes, or until the beef and vegetables are tender and the sauce thickens. Stir in the spinach, tamarind purée and palm sugar, and cook, covered, for a further 10 minutes. Remove the cinnamon stick and serve.

NUTRITION PER SERVE
Protein 34 g; Fat 14 g; Carbohydrate 22 g;
Dietary Fibre 6.5 g; Cholesterol 84 mg;
1452 kJ (347 cal)

NOTE: This dish is traditionally served with rice which is cooked pilaf-style with well-browned, slow-cooked onion slices.

Lightly crush the cardamom pods with the back of a heavy knife.

Add the beef to the pan and stir to coat with the fragrant spices.

Cook until the beef and vegetables are tender and the sauce thickens.

LASAGNE

Preparation time: 40 minutes
Total cooking time: 1 hour 35 minutes
Serves 8
Fat per serve: 12 g

2 teaspoons olive oil
1 large onion, chopped
2 carrots, finely chopped
2 celery sticks, finely chopped
2 zucchini, finely chopped
2 cloves garlic, crushed
500 g (1 lb) lean beef mince
2 x 400 g (13 oz) cans crushed
   tomatoes
1/2 cup (125 ml/4 fl oz) beef stock
2 tablespoons tomato paste
2 teaspoons dried oregano
375 g (12 oz) instant or fresh lasagne
   sheets

CHEESE SAUCE
1/3 cup (40 g/11/4 oz) cornflour
3 cups (750 ml/24 fl oz) skim milk
100 g (31/2 oz) reduced-fat cheese,
   grated

1 Heat the olive oil in a large non-stick frying pan. Add the onion and cook for 5 minutes, until soft. Add the carrot, celery and zucchini and cook, stirring constantly, for 5 minutes, or until the vegetables are soft. Add the crushed garlic and cook for another minute. Add the beef mince and cook over high heat, stirring, until well browned. Break up any lumps of meat with a wooden spoon.
2 Add the crushed tomato, beef stock, tomato paste and dried oregano to the pan and stir to thoroughly combine. Bring the mixture to the boil, then reduce the heat and simmer gently, partially covered, for 20 minutes,

stirring occasionally to prevent the mixture sticking to the pan.
3 Preheat the oven to moderate 180°C (350°F/Gas 4). Spread a little of the meat sauce into the base of a 23 x 30 cm (9 x 12 inch) ovenproof dish. Arrange a layer of lasagne sheets in the dish, breaking some of the sheets, if necessary, to fit in neatly.
4 Spread half the meat sauce over the top to cover evenly. Cover with another layer of lasagne sheets, a layer of meat sauce, then a final layer of lasagne sheets.
5 To make the cheese sauce, blend a little of the milk with the cornflour, to form a smooth paste, in a small pan. Gradually blend in the remaining milk and stir constantly over low heat until the mixture boils and thickens. Remove from the heat and stir in the grated cheese until melted. Spread evenly over the top of the lasagne and bake for 1 hour.
6 Check the lasagne after 25 minutes. If the top is browning too quickly, cover loosely with non-stick baking paper or foil. Take care when removing the baking paper or foil that the topping does not come away with the paper. Leave the lasagne to stand for 15 minutes before cutting into portions for serving.

NUTRITION PER SERVE
Protein 15 g; Fat 12 g; Carbohydrate 50 g; Dietary Fibre 5 g; Cholesterol 10 mg; 1885 kJ (450 cal)

STORAGE TIME: Can be frozen for up to 2–3 months. When required, thaw overnight in the refrigerator, then reheat, covered with foil, for about 30 minutes in a moderate oven.

Chop the garlic and crush using the flat side of a large knife.

Add the vegetables to the pan and stir constantly until soft.

When you add the meat, break up any lumps with a wooden spoon.

Spread a little of the meat sauce over the base and cover evenly with lasagne sheets.

Remove the pan from the heat and stir in the cheese until melted.

Spread the cheese sauce evenly over the top of the lasagne.

MEATBALLS IN TOMATO SAUCE

Preparation time: 40 minutes
Total cooking time: 1 hour 40 minutes
Serves 6
Fat per serve: 8 g

500 g (1 lb) lean veal mince
1 onion, very finely chopped
4 cloves garlic, finely chopped
1 egg white, lightly beaten
1 cup (80 g/2³/4 oz) fresh white
    breadcrumbs
¹/2 cup (30 g/1 oz) finely chopped
    fresh parsley
3 tablespoons finely chopped fresh
    oregano
cooking oil spray
1.5 kg (3 lb) ripe tomatoes
2 onions, finely sliced
¹/2 cup (125 g/4 oz) tomato paste
¹/2 teaspoon sugar
350 g (11 oz) penne

1 Combine the veal mince, onion, half the garlic, the egg white, breadcrumbs, two-thirds of the parsley and 1 tablespoon of the oregano in a large bowl. Season and mix well with your hands . Shape into 36 small balls. Spray a large non-stick frying pan with oil. Cook a third of the meatballs over high heat for 4–5 minutes, or until browned, turning constantly to prevent the meatballs sticking. Remove from the pan and repeat with the remaining meatballs.
2 Score a cross in the base of each tomato, place in a heatproof bowl and cover with boiling water. Leave for 1 minute, or until the skins start to come away. Drain, plunge into a bowl of iced water, then peel away the skin and roughly chop the flesh.

3 Lightly spray the base of a large, deep non-stick saucepan. Add the sliced onion and remaining garlic and cook over low heat for 2–3 minutes, stirring constantly. Add 2 tablespoons water, cover and cook gently for 5 minutes to soften the onion. Stir in the tomato and tomato paste. Cover and simmer for 10 minutes, uncover and simmer gently for 40 minutes. Add the meatballs, cover and simmer for another 15–20 minutes, or until the

meatballs are just cooked. Add the sugar, remaining parsley and oregano and season well.
4 Cook the penne in a large pan of boiling salted water until *al dente*, then drain. Serve with the meatballs.

NUTRITION PER SERVE
Protein 15 g; Fat 8 g; Carbohydrate 60 g;
Dietary Fibre 9 g; Cholesterol 60 mg;
1321 kJ (316 cal)

When the veal mixture is thoroughly combined, shape into balls.

Score a cross in the base of each tomato so that you can peel off the skin.

Remove the tomatoes from the hot water, plunge into iced water, then peel.

MADRAS BEEF CURRY

Preparation time: 20 minutes
Total cooking time: 1 hour 40 minutes
Serves 4
Fat per serve: 15 g

1 kg (2 lb) skirt or chuck steak
1 tablespoon oil
1 onion, chopped
3–4 tablespoons Madras curry paste

¹/₄ cup (60 g/2 oz) tomato paste
1 cup (250 ml/8 fl oz) beef stock

1 Trim the meat of any fat or sinew and cut it into bite-sized cubes. Heat the oil in a large frying pan, add the onion and cook over medium heat for 10 minutes, or until browned.
2 Add the curry paste and stir for 1 minute, or until fragrant. Then add the meat and cook, stirring, until coated with the curry paste. Stir in the tomato paste and stock. Reduce the heat and simmer, covered, for 1 hour 15 minutes. Uncover and simmer for 15 minutes, or until the meat is tender.

NUTRITION PER SERVE
Protein 53 g; Fat 15 g; Carbohydrate 4.5 g;
Dietary Fibre 1.5 g; Cholesterol 170 mg;
1514 kJ (362 cal)

STORAGE TIME: This dish can be refrigerated for 2–3 days

Trim the meat of any excess fat or sinew and cut into cubes.

Cook the chopped onion in a large frying pan until it is browned.

Add the meat to the pan and stir to coat in the curry paste.

STEAK WITH ROASTED RED ONION SAUCE

Preparation time: 20 minutes
Total cooking time: 1 hour 20 minutes
Serves 4
Fat per serve: 15 g

250 g (8 oz) red onions, thinly sliced
500 g (1 lb) pickling onions
2 cloves garlic
1 tablespoon olive oil
750 g (1 1/2 lb) Roma tomatoes
1/2 teaspoon salt
2 tablespoons chopped fresh oregano
220g (7 oz) can Italian peeled
    tomatoes
2 teaspoons muscatel liqueur or
    brandy
2 teaspoons soft brown sugar
4 scotch or rump fillet steaks, trimmed

1 Preheat the oven to moderately hot 200°C (400°F/Gas 6). Place the red onion, pickling onions and garlic cloves in a large roasting tin with half the olive oil. Roll the onions in the oil so that they are lightly coated.
2 Halve the tomatoes lengthways and add to the tin. Drizzle with the remaining olive oil, salt and oregano and roast for 1 hour.
3 Use a pair of kitchen scissors to roughly cut up the canned tomatoes, while they are still in the tin. Spoon the chopped tomatoes and their juice into the roasting tin, taking care not to break up the roasted tomatoes. Drizzle the muscatel or brandy over the top and sprinkle with the brown sugar. Return to the oven and roast for a further 20 minutes.
4 Chargrill the steaks on a lightly oiled chargrill pan until cooked to your liking. Serve with the hot sauce.

NUTRITION PER SERVE
Protein 60 g; Fat 15 g; Carbohydrate 13 g;
Dietary Fibre 5 g; Cholesterol 143 mg;
1900 kJ (450 cal)

SERVING SUGGESTION: This sauce is a great low-fat condiment for serving with grilled meats at barbecues.

Red onions will give a lovely colour to the sauce. Peel them and slice thinly.

Add the tomatoes to the roasting tin and sprinkle with oil, salt and oregano.

Use scissors to chop up tinned tomatoes without losing the juice.

Drizzle the muscatel or brandy over the pan and sprinkle with soft brown sugar.

VEAL, LEMON AND CAPER STEW

Preparation time: 30 minutes
Total cooking time: 2 hours
Serves 6
Fat per serve: 13 g

1 tablespoon olive oil
50 g (1³/₄ oz) butter
1 kg (2 lb) stewing veal,
  cut into 4 cm (1¹/₂ inch) chunks
300 g (10 oz) French shallots
3 leeks, cut into large chunks
2 cloves garlic, crushed
1 tablespoon plain flour
2 cups (500 ml/16 fl oz)
  chicken stock
1 teaspoon grated lemon rind
¹/₃ cup (80 ml/2³/₄ fl oz) lemon juice
2 bay leaves
2 tablespoons capers, drained and
  well rinsed

1 Preheat the oven to moderate 180°C (350°F/Gas 4). Heat the oil and half the butter in a large, heavy-based pan. Brown the veal in batches over medium high heat and transfer to a large casserole dish.

2 Blanch the shallots in boiling water for 30 seconds, then peel and add to the pan with the leeks. Gently cook for 5 minutes, or until soft and golden. Add the garlic, cook for 1 minute, then transfer to the casserole dish.

3 Melt the remaining butter in the pan, add the flour and cook for 30 seconds. Remove from the heat, add the stock and stir until well combined. Return to the heat and cook, stirring, until the sauce begins to bubble.

4 Pour the sauce into the casserole dish and stir in the lemon rind, lemon juice and bay leaves. Cover and bake for 1 1¹/₂ hours, or until the veal is tender. During the last 20 minutes of cooking, remove the lid to allow the sauces to reduce a little. Stir in the capers and season with salt and pepper before serving.

NUTRITION PER SERVE
Protein 40 g; Fat 13 g; Carbohydrate 5 g;
Dietary Fibre 2 g; Cholesterol 160 mg;
1300 kJ (300 cal)

Add the leeks and peeled shallots to the pan and gently fry until soft and golden.

Remove the pan from the heat and stir in the stock, scraping up the brown bits.

BOMBAY CURRY

Preparation time: 20 minutes
Total cooking time: 2 hours
Serves 6
Fat per serve: 15 g

1 kg (2 lb) chuck steak
1 tablespoon oil
2 onions, chopped
2 cloves garlic, crushed
2 green chillies, chopped
1 tablespoon grated fresh ginger
1½ teaspoons ground turmeric
1 teaspoon ground cumin

1 tablespoon ground coriander
½–1 teaspoon chilli powder
1 teaspoon salt
400 g (13 oz) can tomatoes
1 cup (250 ml/8 fl oz) light coconut
   milk

1 Cut the beef into cubes. Heat the oil in a large pan and cook the onion until just soft.

2 Add the garlic, chilli, ginger, turmeric, cumin, coriander and chilli powder. Stir until heated; add the beef and cook, stirring, over high heat until well coated with the spice mixture.

3 Add the salt and tomatoes. Simmer,

covered, for 1–1½ hours, or until the beef is tender. Stir in the coconut milk and simmer, uncovered, for a further 5–10 minutes, or until slightly thickened. Garnish with fresh ginger.

NUTRITION PER SERVE
Protein 35 g; Fat 15 g; Carbohydrate 5 g;
Dietary Fibre 2 g; Cholesterol 120 mg;
1325 kJ (315 cal)

NOTE: Bombay Curry is best made 1–2 days in advance to give the flavours time to develop. Store, covered, in the refrigerator.

Cut the beef into cubes, trimming any excess fat from the meat.

Add the garlic, chilli, ginger, turmeric, cumin, coriander and chilli powder.

Stir in the salt and tomatoes, then simmer, covered, until the meat is tender.

CHARGRILLED LEMON GRASS BEEF WRAPPED IN FLATBREAD

Preparation time: 30 minutes +
  5 hours freezing and refrigerating
Total cooking time: 8 minutes
Serves 6
Fat per serve: 15 g

1 kg (2 lb) piece rump steak
6 flatbreads (lavash breads)
200 g (6½ oz) bean sprouts
3 tomatoes, chopped
½ cup (25 g/¾ oz) chopped fresh
  mint

LEMON GRASS MARINADE
3 stems lemon grass, white part only,
  chopped
2 tablespoons sesame seeds, toasted
5 spring onions, chopped
2 cm (1 inch) piece fresh ginger,
  grated
2 red chillies, seeded
1 onion, chopped
1 teaspoon soft brown sugar
1 tablespoon fish sauce
2 teaspoons sesame oil
2 tablespoons peanut oil

1 Cut the beef into wide strips. Wrap each strip tightly in plastic wrap. Freeze for 2 hours to make the beef easier to slice.
2 To make the lemon grass marinade, combine the lemon grass, sesame seeds, spring onion, ginger, chilli, onion, sugar, fish sauce, sesame oil and peanut oil in a food processor. Process to a paste.
3 Remove the beef from the wrappers and cut into wafer-thin slices. Place in a dish with the lemon grass mixture. Cover; refrigerate for at least 3 hours.
4 Brush a heavy-based pan with oil and heat until very hot. Cook the beef briefly, in small batches, until just tender. Place onto the flatbreads; top with the bean sprouts, tomato and mint. Roll the flatbreads up to serve.

NUTRITION PER SERVE
Protein 55 g; Fat 15 g; Carbohydrate 55 g; Dietary Fibre 5 g; Cholesterol 110 mg; 2545 kJ (605 cal)

Lightly toast 2 tablespoons of sesame seeds in a dry frying pan.

Cover the strips of beef tightly in plastic wrap and place in the freezer to make them easy to slice.

Process the onions, spices, sugar, fish sauce and oils into a paste.

Take the beef out of the plastic wrappers and cut into wafer-thin slices.

OSSO BUCO WITH GREMOLATA

Preparation time: 30 minutes
Total cooking time: 2 hours 40 minutes
Serves 4
Fat per serve: 15 g

2 tablespoons olive oil
1 onion, finely chopped
1 clove garlic, crushed
1 kg (2 lb) veal shin slices (osso buco)
2 tablespoons plain flour
410 g (13 oz) can tomatoes, roughly
    chopped
1 cup (250 ml/8 fl oz) white wine
1 cup (250 ml/8 fl oz) chicken
    stock

GREMOLATA
2 tablespoons finely choppped fresh
    parsley
2 teaspoons grated lemon rind
1 teaspoon finely chopped garlic

1 Heat 1 tablespoon oil in a large shallow casserole. Add the onion and cook over low heat until soft and golden. Add the garlic. Cook for 1 minute, then remove from the dish.
2 Heat the remaining oil and brown the veal in batches, then remove. Return the onion to the casserole and stir in the flour. Cook for 30 seconds and remove from the heat. Slowly stir in the tomatoes, wine and stock, combining well with the flour. Return the veal to the casserole.

3 Return to the heat and bring to the boil, stirring. Cover and reduce the heat to low so that the casserole is just simmering. Cook for 2¹/₂ hours, or until the meat is very tender and almost falling off the bones.
4 To make the gremolata, combine the parsley, lemon rind and garlic in a bowl. Sprinkle over the osso buco and serve with risotto or plain rice.

NUTRITION PER SERVE
Protein 50 g; Fat 15 g; Carbohydrate 9.5 g;
Dietary Fibre 2.5 g; Cholesterol 165 mg;
1700 kJ (405 cal)

HINT: Try to make this a day in advance to give the flavours time to develop and blend.

Heat the oil in the casserole and cook the veal pieces in batches until browned.

Add the tomatoes, white wine and stock and mix until well combined.

Make the traditional gremolata topping by mixing together the parsley, lemon rind and garlic.

SILVERSIDE AND PARSLEY SAUCE

Preparation time: 20 minutes + soaking
Total cooking time: 2 hours
Serves 6
Fat per serve: 15 g

1.5 kg (3 lb) corned silverside
1 teaspoon black peppercorns
5 whole cloves
2 bay leaves, torn
2 tablespoons soft brown sugar

PARSLEY SAUCE
30 g (1 oz) butter
1 1/2 tablespoons plain flour
400 ml (13 fl oz) skim milk

1/2 cup (125 ml/4 fl oz) beef stock
2 tablespoons chopped fresh
   parsley

1 Soak the corned beef in cold water for 45 minutes, changing the water 3–4 times to reduce the saltiness.
2 Put the beef in a large heavy-based pan with the peppercorns, cloves, bay leaves, brown sugar and enough cold water to just cover. Bring to the boil, then reduce the heat to very low and simmer for 1 1/2–1 3/4 hours. Turn the meat every 30 minutes and add more water when needed. Do not let the water boil or the beef will be tough. Remove from the pan, wrap in foil and leave to stand for at least 15 minutes before carving. (Save the liquid and

use for cooking vegetables.)
3 To make the parsley sauce, melt the butter in a pan over medium heat, and stir in the flour. Cook, stirring with a wooden spoon, for 1 minute. Remove the pan from the heat and pour in the milk and stock, whisking until smooth. Return the pan to the heat and cook, whisking constantly, until the sauce boils and thickens. Reduce the heat and simmer for 2 minutes more. Stir in the parsley and season to taste.
4 Slice the meat across the grain and serve with the sauce.

NUTRITION PER SERVE
Protein 50 g; Fat 15 g; Carbohydrate 10 g;
Dietary Fibre 0 g; Cholesterol 100 mg;
1625 kJ (390 cal)

Soak the corned beef in cold water to help eliminate some of the saltiness.

Put the beef, peppercorns, cloves, bay leaves and sugar in a pan and cover with water.

Make sure you turn the meat every half hour or so and don't boil the water or the meat will toughen.

BEEF POT ROAST

Preparation time: 15 minutes
Total cooking time: 3 hours 15 minutes
Serves 6
Fat per serve: 10 g

300 g (10 oz) small pickling onions
2 carrots
3 parsnips, peeled
30 g (1 oz) butter
1–1.5 kg (2–3 lb) piece of silverside,
    trimmed of fat (see NOTE)
1/4 cup (60 ml/2 fl oz) dry red wine
1 large tomato, finely chopped
1 cup (250 ml/8 fl oz) beef stock

1 Put the onions in a heatproof bowl and cover with boiling water. Leave for 1 minute, then drain well. Allow to cool and then peel off the skins.

2 Cut the carrots and parsnips in half lengthways then into even-sized pieces. Heat half the butter in a large heavy-based pan that will tightly fit the meat (it will shrink during cooking), add the onions, carrot and parsnip and cook, stirring, over medium-high heat until browned. Remove from the pan.

3 Add the remaining butter to the pan and add the meat, browning well all over. Increase the heat to high and pour in the wine. Bring to the boil, then add the tomato and stock. Return to the boil, then reduce the heat to low, cover and simmer for 2 hours, turning once. Add the vegetables and simmer, covered, for 1 hour.

4 Remove the meat from the pan and put it on a board ready for carving. Cover with foil and leave it to stand while you finish the sauce.

5 Increase the heat to high and boil the pan juices with the vegetables for 10 minutes to reduce and thicken slightly. Skim off any fat and taste before seasoning. Serve the meat and vegetables with the pan juices. Serve with mustard.

NUTRITION PER SERVE
Protein 60 g; Fat 10 g; Carbohydrate 95 g;
Dietary Fibre 3.5 g; Cholesterol 185 mg;
1690 kJ (405 cal)

NOTE: Eye of silverside is a tender, long shaped cut of silverside which carves easily into serving-sized pieces. A regular piece of silverside or topside may be substituted.

Put the pickling onions in a bowl and cover with boiling water.

Add the piece of meat to the pan and brown well on all sides.

Put the vegetables in with the meat, then cover and simmer for 1 hour.

CHILLI CON CARNE

Preparation time: 25 minutes +
  overnight soaking
Total cooking time: 2 hours 15 minutes
Serves 6
Fat per serve: 10 g

185 g (6 oz) dried black eye beans
650 g (1 lb 5 oz) tomatoes
1½ tablespoons oil
900 g (1 lb 13 oz) trimmed chuck
  steak, cut into chunks
3 onions, thinly sliced
2 cloves garlic, chopped
2 teaspoons ground cumin
1 tablespoon paprika
½ teaspoon ground allspice
1–2 teaspoons chilli powder
1 tablespoon soft brown sugar
1 tablespoon red wine vinegar

1 Put the beans in a bowl, cover with plenty of water and leave overnight to soak. Drain well. Score a cross in the base of each tomato. Put the tomatoes in a bowl of boiling water for 30 seconds, then transfer to a bowl of cold water. Drain and peel the skin away from the cross. Halve the tomatoes and remove the seeds with a teaspoon. Chop the flesh finely.
2 Heat 1 tablespoon of the oil in a large heavy-based pan and add half the meat. Cook over medium-high heat for 2 minutes, or until well browned. Remove from the pan and repeat with the remaining meat, then remove from the pan.
3 Add the rest of the oil to the pan and add the onion. Cook over medium heat for 5 minutes, or until softened. Add the garlic and spices and cook, stirring, for 1 minute, or until aromatic. Add 2 cups (500 ml/16 fl oz) water and stir. Return the meat to the pan with the beans and tomatoes. Bring to the boil, then reduce the heat to low and simmer, partially covered, for 2 hours, or until the meat is tender and the chilli con carne is thick and dryish, stirring occasionally. Towards the end of the cooking time the mixture may start to catch, so add a little water if necessary. Stir through the sugar and vinegar, and season with salt to taste. Serve with flour tortillas, grated low-fat cheese and lime wedges.

NUTRITION PER SERVE
Protein 43 g; Fat 10 g; Carbohydrate 54 g;
Dietary Fibre 10 g; Cholesterol 100 mg;
2040 kJ (486 cal)

Soak the black eye beans in a bowl of water overnight before cooking them.

Drain the tomatoes then carefully peel the skin away from the cross.

Remove the tomato seeds with a teaspoon and then finely chop the flesh.

COUNTRY BEEF STEW

Preparation time: 40 minutes
Total cooking time: 2 hours 10 minutes
Serves 8
Fat per serve: 10 g

1 small eggplant, cubed
2–3 tablespoons olive oil
2 red onions, sliced
2 cloves garlic, crushed
1 kg (2 lb) chuck steak, cubed
1 teaspoon ground coriander
1/2 teaspoon allspice
3/4 teaspoon sweet paprika
6 ripe tomatoes, chopped
1 cup (250 ml/8 fl oz) red wine

3 cups (750 ml/24 fl oz) beef stock
2 tablespoons tomato paste
250 g (8 oz) baby new potatoes,
   halved
2 celery sticks, sliced
3 carrots, chopped
2 bay leaves
3 tablespoons chopped fresh parsley

1 Put the eggplant in a colander, sprinkle generously with salt and leave for 20 minutes. Rinse, pat dry with paper towels and set aside.
2 Heat the oil in a large heavy-based pan and cook the onion for 5 minutes until soft; add the garlic and cook for 1 minute. Remove and set aside. Add the eggplant and brown for 5 minutes.

Remove and set aside. Brown the meat in batches over medium heat, sprinkle with the spices, season and cook for 1–2 minutes. Add the tomato, onion, wine, stock and tomato paste and bring to the boil. Reduce the heat and simmer, covered, for 25 minutes.
3 Add the potato, celery, carrot and bay leaves, bring to the boil, reduce the heat, cover and simmer for 1 hour. Add the eggplant and simmer for 30 minutes, uncovered. Lift out the bay leaves and stir in the parsley.

NUTRITION PER SERVE
Protein 30 g; Fat 10 g; Carbohydrate 10 g;
Dietary Fibre 4 g; Cholesterol 85 mg;
1160 kJ (280 cal)

Put the eggplant in a colander and sprinkle with salt to draw out any bitterness.

Add the tomato, onion, wine, stock and tomato paste to the pan.

Add the potato, celery, carrot and bay leaves to the pan.

BEEF WITH MANGO, RAISIN AND FRESH TOMATO SALSA

Preparation time: 40 minutes
Total cooking time: 35 minutes
Serves 4
Fat per serve: 15 g

2 tomatoes
1 mango
60 g (2 oz) raisins
1 teaspoon canned green
    peppercorns, drained and crushed

1 teaspoon finely grated lemon rind
2 tablespoons red wine vinegar
1 tablespoon olive oil
1 spring onion, shredded
750 g piece eye fillet beef

1 Preheat the oven to 180°C (350°F/Gas 4). Score a cross in the base of each tomato. Place in a bowl of boiling water for 10 seconds, then plunge into cold water and peel the skin away from the cross. Scoop out the seeds and discard. Finely chop the tomato flesh and put in a bowl.
2 Peel and finely dice the mango and

mix with the tomato and raisins. Mix together the peppercorns, lemon rind, vinegar and oil and add to the salsa. Season and scatter with spring onion.
3 Place the beef in a lightly oiled roasting tin and roast in the oven for 30–35 minutes. Leave to stand for 10 minutes before slicing.

NUTRITION PER SERVE
Protein 56 g; Fat 15 g; Carbohydrate 21 g; Dietary Fibre 3 g; Cholesterol 148 mg; 2000 kJ (500 cal)

Score a cross in the base of each tomato to make it easier to peel off the skin.

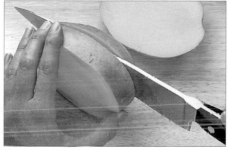

Cut the cheeks from the mango, remove the skin and dice the flesh.

Mix the peppercorns, rind, vinegar and oil with the rest of the salsa ingredients.

BEEF WITH OYSTER SAUCE

Preparation time: 15 minutes
Total cooking time: 5 minutes
Serves 4
Fat per serve: 12 g

1¹/₂ teaspoons cornflour
¹/₂ cup (125 ml/4 fl oz) beef stock
2 tablespoons oyster sauce
1 teaspoon finely crushed garlic
1 teaspoon caster sugar

1 tablespoon oil
350 g (11 oz) rump steak, finely sliced
250 g (8 oz) beans, topped and tailed,
    cut into 5 cm (2 inch) lengths
1 small red capsicum, sliced
¹/₂ cup (60 g/2 oz) bean sprouts

1 Dissolve the cornflour in a little of the stock. Mix with the remaining stock, oyster sauce, garlic and sugar and set aside.
2 Heat the wok until very hot, add the oil and swirl it around to coat the side. Add the beef in batches and stir-fry over high heat for 2 minutes, or until it browns.
3 Add the beans and capsicum and stir-fry another minute.
4 Add the cornflour mixture to the wok and cook until the sauce boils and thickens. Stir in the bean sprouts and serve immediately.

NUTRITION PER SERVE
Protein 23 g; Fat 12 g; Carbohydrate 10 g;
Dietary Fibre 2.5 g; Cholesterol 60 mg;
1016 kJ (243 cal)

Brown the steak in batches so the wok doesn't overcrowd and reduce the temperature.

Add the beans and capsicum to the browned meat and stir-fry for 1 minute.

Add the mixture of stock and cornflour and stir until the sauce boils and thickens.

RICE NOODLES WITH BEEF

Preparation time: 10 minutes +
  30 minutes marinating
Total cooking time: 15 minutes
Serves 6
Fat per serve: 13 g

2 cloves garlic, crushed
2 teaspoons chopped fresh ginger
3½ tablespoons oyster sauce
5 teaspoons soy sauce
500 g (1 lb) beef, thinly sliced

2 tablespoons oil
1 kg (2 lb) fresh rice noodles, sliced
  into 2 cm (1 inch) strips
100 g (3½ oz) garlic chives, chopped
1 teaspoon sugar

1 Mix the garlic, ginger, 1 tablespoon oyster sauce and 2 teaspoons soy sauce. Add the beef and toss to coat. Cover and refrigerate for 30 minutes.
2 Heat the wok until very hot, add half the oil and swirl it around to coat the side. Add half the beef and stir-fry for 5 minutes, or until cooked. Remove

and repeat with the remaining beef. Add the remaining oil, then add the noodles and stir fry for 3–5 minutes, or until softened.
3 Add the garlic chives and stir-fry until just wilted. Stir in the remaining oyster and soy sauces and sugar, return the beef to the wok and toss to heat through. Serve immediately.

NUTRITION PER SERVE
Protein 33 g; Fat 13 g; Carbohydrate 40 g;
Dietary Fibre 1.5 g; Cholesterol 50 mg;
1295 kJ (310 cal)

Buy the fresh rice noodle as a block and cut it into thin strips.

Mix together the garlic, ginger, oyster and soy sauces to marinate the beef.

Stir-fry the noodles until they are softened, then add the garlic chives.

LINGUINE WITH BACON, MUSHROOMS AND PEAS

Preparation time: 20 minutes
Total cooking time: 25 minutes
Serves 4
Fat per serve: 7 g

3 bacon rashers
2 teaspoons olive oil
2–3 cloves garlic, crushed
1 red onion, chopped
185 g (6 oz) field mushrooms, sliced
1/3 cup (20 g/3/4 oz) chopped fresh
    parsley

1 cup (155 g/5 oz) peas
11/2 cups (375 ml/12 fl oz) low-fat
    evaporated milk
2 teaspoons cornflour
325 g (11 oz) dried linguine
25 g (3/4 oz) Parmesan shavings

1 Remove the fat and rind from the bacon and chop roughly. Heat the oil in a medium pan, add the garlic, onion and bacon and cook over low heat for 5 minutes, stirring frequently, until the onion and bacon are soft. Add the sliced mushrooms and cook, stirring, for another 5 minutes, or until soft.
2 Add the parsley, peas and milk to

the pan. Mix the cornflour with 1 tablespoon of water until smooth, add to the mixture and stir over medium heat until slightly thickened.
3 Meanwhile, cook the pasta in a large pan of rapidly boiling, salted water for 8 minutes, or until *al dente*. Drain and serve with the hot sauce and Parmesan shavings.

NUTRITION PER SERVE
Protein 30 g; Fat 7 g; Carbohydrate 80 g;
Dietary Fibre 9 g; Cholesterol 25 mg;
2085 kJ (500 cal)

Discard the fat and rind from the bacon and chop the meat roughly into strips.

When the onion is softened, add the sliced mushrooms and stir while cooking.

Stir the vegetable mixture until the liquid has slightly thickened.

PENNE WITH RICOTTA AND BASIL SAUCE

Preparation time: 20 minutes
Total cooking time: 15 minutes
Serves 4
Fat per serve: 10 g

2 bacon rashers
2 teaspoons olive oil
2–3 cloves garlic, crushed
1 onion, finely chopped
2 spring onions, finely chopped
250 g (8 oz) ricotta
1/2 cup (30 g/1 oz) finely chopped
  fresh basil
325 g (11 oz) penne
8 cherry tomatoes, halved

1 Remove the fat and rind from the bacon and chop roughly. Heat the oil in a pan, add the bacon, garlic, onion and spring onion and stir over medium heat for 5 minutes, or until cooked. Remove from the heat, stir in the ricotta and chopped basil and beat until smooth.
2 Meanwhile, cook the pasta in a large pan of rapidly boiling salted water for 10 minutes, or until *al dente*. Just prior to draining the pasta, add about a cup of the pasta water to the ricotta mixture to thin the sauce. Add more water if you prefer an even thinner sauce. Season well.
3 Drain the pasta and stir the sauce and tomato halves into the pasta.

NUTRITION PER SERVE
Protein 20 g; Fat 10 g; Carbohydrate 65 g;
Dietary Fibre 5 g; Cholesterol 40 mg;
1885 kJ (450 cal)

Remove from the heat and stir in the ricotta and chopped basil.

Bring a large pan of salted water to a rapid boil before adding the pasta.

Thin the ricotta mixture with about a cup of the water from the cooked pasta.

PORK, BEER AND CHICKPEA STEW

Preparation time: 35 minutes
Total cooking time: 1 hour 30 minutes
Serves 4
Fat per serve: 10 g

2 teaspoons ground cumin
1 teaspoon ground coriander
1/2 teaspoon chilli powder
1/4 teaspoon ground cinnamon
400 g (13 oz) lean diced pork, trimmed
1 tablespoon plain flour
1 tablespoon olive oil
1 large onion, finely chopped
3 cloves garlic, finely chopped
2 large carrots, chopped
2 celery sticks, sliced
1/2 cup (125 ml/4 fl oz) chicken stock
1/2 cup (125 ml/4 fl oz) beer
2 ripe tomatoes, chopped
310 g (10 oz) can chickpeas, rinsed
2 tablespoons chopped fresh parsley

1 Cook the spices in a dry frying pan over low heat, shaking the pan, for 1 minute, or until aromatic.
2 Combine the pork, trimmed of all fat, with the spices and flour in a plastic bag and toss well. Remove the pork and shake off the excess flour. Heat the oil in a large heavy-based pan over high heat and cook the pork, tossing regularly, for 8 minutes, or until lightly browned.
3 Add the onion, garlic, carrot, celery and half the stock to the pan and toss well. Cover and cook for 10 minutes. Add the remaining stock, beer and tomato and season to taste. Bring to the boil, reduce the heat, cover with a tight-fitting lid, then simmer over low heat for 1 hour. Gently shake the pan

occasionally, but do not remove the lid during cooking. Stir in the chickpeas and fresh parsley. Simmer, uncovered, for 5 minutes and serve.

NUTRITION PER SERVE
Protein 40 g; Fat 10 g; Carbohydrate 35 g; Dietary Fibre 15 g; Cholesterol 50 mg; 1720 kJ (410 cal)

Chop the carrots into quite small pieces and thinly slice the celery sticks.

Dry-fry the spices over low heat, stirring the spices and shaking the pan.

Cook the flour-coated pork, tossing regularly, until lightly browned.

PORK ROLLS WITH ROASTED CAPSICUM

Preparation time: 40 minutes
Total cooking time: 30 minutes
Serves 4
Fat per serve: 5 g

SAUCE
3/4 cup (185 ml/6 fl oz) beef stock
2 teaspoons soy sauce
2 tablespoons red wine
2 teaspoons wholegrain mustard
2 teaspoons cornflour

1 red capsicum
4 x 150 g (5 oz) lean pork leg steaks
1/3 cup (90 g/3 oz) ricotta
2 spring onions, finely chopped
1 clove garlic, crushed
75 g (2 1/2 oz) rocket
4 small lean slices prosciutto (about
    35 g/1 1/4 oz)
cooking oil spray

1 To make the sauce, put the beef stock, soy sauce, red wine and mustard in a pan. Blend the cornflour with 1 tablespoon water and add to the pan. Stir until the mixture boils.
2 Cut the capsicum into quarters and remove the seeds and membrane. Grill until the skin blisters and blackens. Cool under a damp tea towel, peel and cut the flesh into thin strips.
3 Flatten each steak into a thin square between 2 sheets of plastic, using a rolling pin or mallet. Combine the ricotta, onion and garlic in a bowl, then spread evenly over the pork. Top with a layer of rocket and prosciutto. Place a quarter of the capsicum at one end and roll up to enclose the capsicum. Tie with string or secure with toothpicks at even intervals.

4 Spray a non-stick pan with oil and fry the pork rolls over medium heat for 5 minutes, or until well browned. Add the sauce to the pan and simmer over low heat for 10–15 minutes, or until the rolls are cooked. Remove the string or toothpicks. Slice and serve with the sauce.

NUTRITION PER SERVE
Protein 40 g; Fat 5 g; Carbohydrate 3.5 g;
Dietary Fibre 1 g; Cholesterol 95 mg;
925 kJ (220 cal)

Flatten the pork between two pieces of plastic wrap, using a rolling pin or mallet.

Secure the pork rolls with string or toothpicks at even intervals.

Add the sauce to the pan and simmer over low heat until cooked through.

PORK, BOK CHOY AND BLACK BEAN STIR-FRY

Preparation time: 20 minutes
Total cooking time: 20 minutes
Serves 4
Fat per serve: 3 g

400 g (13 oz) lean pork leg steaks
2 teaspoons sesame oil
2 onions, finely sliced
2 cloves garlic, finely chopped
2–3 teaspoons chopped fresh ginger
1 red capsicum, cut into strips

1 tablespoon canned salted black
   beans, rinsed, roughly chopped
500 g (1 lb) baby bok choy, shredded
1/2 cup (90 g/3 oz) water chestnuts,
   finely sliced
2 tablespoons oyster sauce
1 tablespoon soy sauce
2 teaspoons fish sauce

1 Slice the pork steaks into strips
across the grain.
2 Heat half the sesame oil in a large
non-stick frying pan or wok. Cook the
onion, garlic and ginger over high heat
for 3–4 minutes, add the capsicum and

cook for 2–3 minutes. Remove from
the pan. Heat the remaining sesame oil
and stir-fry the pork in batches over
high heat.
3 Return the pork to the pan with the
onion mixture, black beans, bok choy,
water chestnuts and oyster, soy and
fish sauces. Toss quickly, lower the
heat, cover and steam for 3–4 minutes,
or until the bok choy has just wilted.

NUTRITION PER SERVE
Protein 30 g; Fat 3 g; Carbohydrate 20 g;
Dietary Fibre 3.5 g; Cholesterol 55 mg;
910 kJ (215 cal)

Trim the ends from the bok choy, then separate
the leaves and shred them with a knife.

Stir-fry the pork strips in batches over high heat
until brown.

Toss all the ingredients quickly until combined,
then lower the heat.

HUNGARIAN-STYLE PORK AND LENTIL STEW

Preparation time: 20 minutes
Total cooking time: 1 hour
Serves 4
Fat per serve: 8 g

1 tablespoon olive oil
2 onions, chopped
500 g (1 lb) lean diced pork
2 teaspoons sweet Hungarian paprika
1 teaspoon hot paprika
1/2 teaspoon dried thyme

2 tablespoons tomato paste
2 teaspoons soft brown sugar
1/4 cup (60 g/2 oz) red lentils
1 1/2 cups (375 ml/12 fl oz) beef stock
1 tomato, to garnish
2 tablespoons low-fat natural yoghurt

1 Heat the olive oil in a large, deep saucepan over high heat. Add the onion, pork and paprika and stir for 3–4 minutes, until browned.
2 Add the thyme, tomato paste, sugar, lentils, stock and salt and pepper. Bring to the boil, reduce the heat to very low and cook, covered, for

20 minutes, stirring occasionally to prevent sticking. Uncover and cook for 15–20 minutes, or until thickened.
3 Remove from the heat and set aside for 10 minutes. To prepare the tomato, cut in half and scoop out the seeds. Slice the flesh into thin strips.
4 Just before serving, stir the yoghurt into the stew. Scatter with tomato. Serve with plain boiled rice.

NUTRITION PER SERVE
Protein 35 g; Fat 8 g; Carbohydrate 13 g; Dietary Fibre 4 g; Cholesterol 70 mg; 1110 kJ (265 cal)

Stir the onion, pork and paprika until the pork is browned on all sides.

Add the thyme, tomato paste, sugar, lentils and beef stock to the pan and bring to the boil.

To make the tomato garnish, remove the seeds and slice the flesh into thin strips.

PORK WITH SNAKE BEANS

Preparation time: 15 minutes
Total cooking time: 20 minutes
Serves 4
Fat per serve: 12 g

1 tablespoon oil
400 g (13 oz) pork fillet, cut into
    thick slices
2 onions, thinly sliced
150 g (5 oz) snake beans, diagonally
    sliced (see NOTE)
3 cloves garlic, finely chopped
1 tablespoon finely chopped
    fresh ginger
1 red capsicum, thinly sliced
6 spring onions, diagonally sliced
2 tablespoons sweet chilli sauce

1 Heat the wok until very hot, add half the oil and swirl it around to coat the side of the wok. Stir-fry the pork in two batches over high heat for 3–4 minutes, or until it is just cooked, adding a little more oil if necessary for the second batch. Remove all the pork from the wok.
2 Heat the remaining oil in the wok over medium heat and add the sliced onion. Cook for 3–4 minutes, or until the onion has softened slightly. Add the sliced snake beans and cook for 2–3 minutes. Add the garlic, ginger, capsicum and spring onion, and toss well. Increase the heat and cook for 3–4 minutes.
3 Return the pork to the wok, add the sweet chilli sauce and toss well. Remove from the heat and season with salt and pepper. Serve immediately.

NUTRITION PER SERVE
Protein 25 g; Fat 12 g; Carbohydrate 8 g; Dietary Fibre 4 g; Cholesterol 50 mg; 1005 kJ (240 cal)

NOTE: If you can't find snake beans you can use ordinary green beans in this recipe.

Top and tail the snake beans, then cut them into diagonal pieces.

BARBECUED PORK AND BROCCOLI

Preparation time: 25 minutes
Total cooking time: 10 minutes
Serves 6
Fat per serve: 15 g

1 tablespoon oil
1 large onion, thinly sliced
2 carrots, cut into matchsticks
200 g (6½ oz) broccoli, chopped
6 spring onions, diagonally sliced
1 tablespoon grated fresh ginger

3 cloves garlic, finely chopped
400 g (13 oz) Chinese barbecued pork, thinly sliced
2 tablespoons soy sauce
2 tablespoons mirin
2 cups (180 g/6 oz) bean sprouts

1 Heat the wok until very hot, add the oil and swirl it around to coat the side. Stir-fry the onion over medium heat for 3–4 minutes, or until slightly softened. Add the carrot, broccoli, spring onion, ginger and garlic and cook for 4–5 minutes, tossing the mixture constantly.

2 Increase the heat to high and add the barbecued pork. Toss constantly until the pork is well mixed with the vegetables and is heated through. Add the soy sauce and mirin, and toss until the ingredients are well coated. (The wok should be hot enough for the sauce to reduce into a glaze.) Add the bean sprouts and season well with salt and pepper. Serve immediately.

NUTRITION PER SERVE
Protein 20 g; Fat 15 g; Carbohydrate 6.5 g;
Dietary Fibre 6 g; Cholesterol 40 mg;
920 kJ (220 cal)

Peel the carrots, if necessary, and cut them into even-sized matchsticks.

Cut the pieces of Chinese barbecued pork into thin slices.

Add the pork to the wok and toss until it is well mixed with the vegetables.

BOSTON BAKED BEANS

Preparation time: 25 minutes +
    6 hours soaking
Total cooking time: 1 hour 35 minutes
Serves 6
Fat per serve: 5 g

1³/₄ cups (350 g/11 oz) dried
    cannellini beans (see NOTE)
1 whole ham hock
2 onions, chopped
2 tablespoons tomato paste
1 tablespoon Worcestershire sauce
1 tablespoon molasses
1 teaspoon French mustard
¹/₄ cup (45 g/1¹/₂ oz) brown sugar
¹/₂ cup (125 ml/4 fl oz) tomato juice

1 Cover the beans with cold water and soak for at least 6 hours or overnight (see NOTE).
2 Drain the beans, rinse them well and place in a large pan. Add the ham hock and cover with cold water. Bring to the boil, then reduce the heat and simmer, covered, for 25 minutes, or until the beans are tender. Preheat the oven to warm 160°C (315°F/Gas 2–3).
3 Remove the ham hock from the pan and set aside to cool. Drain the beans, reserving 1 cup (250 ml/8 fl oz) of the cooking liquid. Trim the ham of all skin, fat and sinew, then roughly chop the meat and discard the bone.
4 Transfer the meat and beans to a 2 litre casserole dish. Add the reserved liquid and all remaining ingredients. Mix gently, then cover and bake for 1 hour. Serve with toast.

NUTRITION PER SERVE
Protein 28 g; Fat 5 g; Carbohydrate 30 g;
Dietary Fibre 2 g; Cholesterol 60 mg;
1090 kJ (260 cal)

NOTE: Any type of dried bean can be used in this recipe.

If you don't have 6 hours to soak the beans, to quick-soak beans, place them in a pan, add hot water to cover, bring slowly to the boil, then remove from the heat. Leave to soak for 1 hour before draining and using.

Cooked beans can be frozen in small quantities.

Place the drained beans in a large pan. Add the ham hock and cover with cold water.

Trim the ham of all fat, skin and sinew, then roughly chop the meat.

Add the reserved liquid and remaining ingredients to the meat and beans.

PORK AND CORIANDER STEW

Preparation time: 15 minutes
  + overnight marinating
Total cooking time: 1 hour 20 minutes
Serves 6
Fat per serve: 12 g

1¹/₂ tablespoons coriander seeds
800 g (1 lb 10 oz) pork fillet, cubed
1 tablespoon plain flour
2 tablespoons olive oil
1 large onion, thinly sliced
1¹/₂ cups (375 ml/12 fl oz) red wine
1 cup (250 ml/8 fl oz) chicken stock
1 teaspoon sugar
fresh coriander sprigs, to garnish

1 Crush the coriander seeds in a mortar and pestle. Combine the pork, crushed seeds and ¹/₂ teaspoon cracked pepper in a bowl. Cover and marinate overnight in the fridge.
2 Toss the flour and pork. Heat the oil in a large frying pan and cook the pork in batches over high heat for 1–2 minutes, or until brown. Remove.
3 Add the onion to the frying pan and cook over medium heat for 2–3 minutes, or until just golden. Return the meat to the pan, add the red wine, stock and sugar, and season. Bring to the boil, then reduce the heat and simmer, covered, for 1 hour.
4 Remove the meat. Return the pan to the heat and boil over high heat for 3–5 minutes, or until reduced and slightly thickened. Pour over the meat and top with the coriander.

NUTRITION PER SERVE
Protein 30 g; Fat 12 g; Carbohydrate 2.5 g; Dietary Fibre 0 g; Cholesterol 65 mg; 1180 kJ (282 cal)

Coat the pork fillet pieces in the ground coriander and pepper.

Remove the meat from the pan and set aside to keep warm.

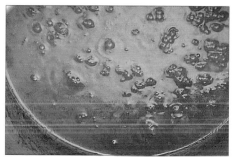

Boil the liquid until it has reduced and is slightly thickened.

PASTA AMATRICIANA

Preparation time: 45 minutes
Total cooking time: 20 minutes
Serves 6
Fat per serve: 9 g

6 thin slices pancetta or 3 bacon
    rashers
1 kg (2 lb) very ripe tomatoes
500 g (1 lb) pasta (see NOTE)
2 teaspoons olive oil
1 small onion, very finely chopped
2 teaspoons very finely chopped fresh
    chilli
Parmesan shavings, for serving

1 Finely chop the pancetta or bacon.
Score a cross in the base of each
tomato. Soak in boiling water for
10 seconds, then drain and plunge into
cold water briefly. Peel back the skin
from the cross. Halve, remove the

seeds and chop the flesh.
2 Add the pasta to a large pan of
rapidly boiling water and cook until
al dente. Drain and return to the pan.
3 Meanwhile, heat the oil in a heavy-
based frying pan. Add the pancetta or
bacon, onion and chilli and stir over
medium heat for 3 minutes. Add the
tomato and season to taste. Reduce the
heat and simmer for 3 minutes. Add
the sauce to the pasta and toss well.
Serve with shavings of Parmesan.

Remove the tomatoes from the cold water and
peel the skin down from the cross.

NUTRITION PER SERVE
Protein 15 g; Fat 9 g; Carbohydrate 60 g;
Dietary Fibre 6 g; Cholesterol 15 mg;
1640 kJ (390 cal)

NOTE: You can also use Roma (plum)
tomatoes in this recipe. They are firm-
fleshed, with few seeds and have a
rich flavour when cooked.
Traditionally, bucatini, as shown, is
used with this sauce, but you can use
any pasta you prefer.

Halve the tomatoes and use a teaspoon to
scrape out the seeds before chopping the flesh.

PENNE WITH PROSCIUTTO

Preparation time: 15 minutes
Total cooking time: 25 minutes
Serves 4
Fat per serve: 9 g

2 teaspoons olive oil
6 thin slices prosciutto, chopped
1 onion, finely chopped
1 tablespoon chopped fresh rosemary
825 g (1 lb 11 oz) can Italian
  tomatoes
500 g (1 lb) penne or macaroni
grated Parmesan, for serving

1 Heat the oil in a heavy-based frying pan. Add the prosciutto and onion and cook, stirring occasionally, over low heat for 5 minutes, or until golden.
2 Add the rosemary and tomato and season to taste. Simmer for 10 minutes.
3 Meanwhile, cook the pasta in a large pan of rapidly boiling water until *al dente*. Drain. Divide the pasta among serving bowls and top with the sauce. Sprinkle with a little grated Parmesan to serve.

NUTRITION PER SERVE
Protein 20 g; Fat 9 g; Carbohydrate 65 g; Dietary Fibre 6 g; Cholesterol 20 mg; 1725 kJ (410 cal)

NOTE: Rosemary is a herb commonly used in Mediterranean cooking and lends a distinctive flavour to the dish. Fresh basil or parsley could be used but dried rosemary is not suitable.

You can cut up the tomato with a pair of kitchen scissors while it is still in the can.

Cook the prosciutto and onion over low heat until they are golden.

Add the rosemary and tomatoes and leave to simmer for 10 minutes.

PORK AND APPLE BRAISE

Preparation time: 20 minutes
Total cooking time: 40 minutes
Serves 4
Fat per serve: 12 g

1 tablespoon oil
1 large onion, thinly sliced
1 clove garlic, chopped
2 teaspoons soft brown sugar
2 green apples, cut into wedges
4 pork loin steaks or medallions
2 tablespoons brandy

2 tablespoons seeded mustard
1 cup (250 ml/8 fl oz) chicken stock
1/2 cup (140 g/5 oz) pitted prunes
1/2 cup (125 ml/4 fl oz) light cream

1 Heat the oil in a large heavy-based pan. Cook the onion and garlic for 10 minutes over low heat, stirring often, until softened and golden brown. Add the sugar and apple and cook, stirring regularly, until the apple begins to brown. Remove the apple and onion from the pan.

2 Reheat the pan and lightly brown the pork steaks, two at a time, then return them all to the pan. Add the brandy and stir until it has nearly all evaporated. Add the mustard and stock. Simmer over low heat, covered, for 15 minutes.

3 Return the apple to the pan with the prunes and cream and simmer for 10 minutes, or until the pork is tender. Season to taste before serving.

NUTRITION PER SERVE
Protein 25 g; Fat 12 g; Carbohydrate 22 g;
Dietary Fibre 4 g; Cholesterol 55 mg;
1250 kJ (298 cal)

HINT: Take care not to overcook pork or it can become tough and dry.

Stir the apple regularly over the heat until it begins to brown.

Brown the pork steaks two at a time and then return them all to the pan.

Put the browned apple back in the pan with the prunes and cream.

PORK WITH PEAR AND CORIANDER SALSA

Preparation time: 35 minutes
Total cooking time: 10 minutes
Serves 4
Fat per serve: 7 g

3 beurre bosc pears
3–4 tablespoons lime juice
1 red onion, finely diced

3/4 cup (25 g/3/4 oz) coriander leaves, finely chopped
1/2 teaspoon chilli flakes
1 teaspoon finely grated lime rind
cooking oil spray
4 pork steaks, butterflied

1 Cut the pears into quarters, remove the cores and chop into small dice. Sprinkle with the lime juice.
2 Combine the pear, onion, coriander, chilli flakes and lime rind and season.

3 Lightly spray a frying pan with oil and cook the pork steaks for 5 minutes on each side, or until cooked through. Serve with the salsa.

NUTRITION PER SERVE
Protein 24 g; Fat 7 g; Carbohydrate 17 g; Dietary Fibre 3 g; Cholesterol 53 mg; 930 kJ (234 cal)

NOTE: Use pears that are just ready to eat, not overripe and floury fruit.

To dice an onion, slice it almost to the root, two or three times.

Then slice through vertically, leaving the root to hold it together. Then chop finely.

Cut the pears into quarters, then remove the cores and chop into dice.

GOAN PORK CURRY

Preparation time: 50 minutes
Total cooking time: 1 hour 50 minutes
Serves 6
Fat per serve: 12 g

2 teaspoons cumin seeds
2 teaspoons black mustard seeds
1 teaspoon cardamom seeds
   (see NOTE)
1 teaspoon ground turmeric
1 teaspoon ground cinnamon
1/2 teaspoon black peppercorns
6 whole cloves
5 small dried red chillies
1/3 cup (80 ml/2³/4 fl oz) white vinegar
1 tablespoon soft brown sugar
1 tablespoon oil
1 large onion, chopped
6–8 cloves garlic, crushed
1 tablespoon finely grated fresh ginger
1.5 kg (3 lb) pork leg, cut into cubes

1 Dry-fry the spices and chillies in a large frying pan for 2 minutes, or until fragrant. Place in a spice grinder or food processor and grind until finely ground. Transfer to a bowl and stir in the vinegar, sugar and 1 teaspoon salt to form a paste.

2 Heat half the oil in a large saucepan. Add the onion and cook for 5 minutes, or until lightly golden. Place the onion in a food processor with 2 tablespoons water and process until smooth. Stir into the spice paste.

3 Place the garlic and ginger in a small bowl, mix together well and stir in 2 tablespoons water.

4 Heat the remaining oil in the pan over high heat. Add the meat and cook in 3–4 batches for 8 minutes, or until well browned. Return all the meat to the pan and stir in the garlic and ginger mixture. Add the spice and onion mix and 1 cup (250 ml/8 fl oz) hot water. Simmer the curry, covered, for 1 hour, or until the pork is tender. Uncover, bring to the boil and cook, stirring frequently, for 10 minutes, or until the sauce has reduced and thickened slightly. Serve with rice.

NUTRITION PER SERVE
Protein 59 g; Fat 12 g; Carbohydrate 5 g; Dietary Fibre 1 g; Cholesterol 115 mg; 1643 kJ (392 cal)

NOTE: Crush cardamom pods with the blade of a heavy knife and open with your fingers to remove the seeds.

Place the dry-fried spices in a spice grinder and finely grind.

Process the fried onion with 2 tablespoons water and then stir into the spice paste.

Bring the curry to the boil and cook until the sauce reduces and thickens slightly.

BURMESE PORK CURRY

Preparation time: 30 minutes
Total cooking time: 1 hour
Serves 6
Fat per serve: 8.5 g

2 stems lemon grass, white part only,
  sliced
1 red onion, chopped
1 clove garlic
1 teaspoon grated fresh ginger
2 large red dried chillies
1 teaspoon fenugreek seeds, roasted
  and ground
1 teaspoon yellow mustard seeds,
  roasted and ground
2 teaspoons paprika
2 tablespoons Worcestershire sauce

750 g (1 1/2 lb) lean boneless shoulder
  pork, cut into cubes
2 tablespoons fish sauce
6 chat potatoes, peeled and sliced
2 small red onions, diced
1 tablespoon oil
2 tablespoons mango chutney

1 Put the lemon grass, onion, garlic, ginger, chillies, fenugreek seeds, yellow mustard seeds, paprika and Worcestershire sauce in a processor or blender and mix to a thick paste.
2 Place the pork in a bowl, sprinkle with the fish sauce and 1/4 teaspoon ground black pepper and toss to coat.
3 Place the potato and onion in another bowl, add 3 tablespoons of the paste and toss to coat. Add the remaining paste to the pork. Mix well.

4 Heat the oil in a saucepan or wok over medium heat. Add the pork and cook in batches, stirring, for 8 minutes, or until the meat begins to brown. Remove from the pan. Add the potato and onion and cook, stirring, for 5 minutes, or until soft and starting to brown.
5 Return the meat to the pan and stir in 3 cups (750 ml/24 fl oz) water, adding 1 cup (250 ml/8 fl oz) at a time. Stir in the mango chutney, then reduce the heat and simmer for 30 minutes, or until the meat and potatoes are tender.

NUTRITION PER SERVE
Protein 30 g; Fat 8.5 g; Carbohydrate 16 g;
Dietary Fibre 2.5 g; Cholesterol 60 mg;
1126 kJ (270 cal)

Process all the spice paste ingredients to make a thick paste.

Heat the oil in a saucepan or wok and brown the pork in batches.

Add the potato and onion and cook until they are starting to brown.

PASTA ALL' ARRABBIATA

Preparation time: 20 minutes
Total cooking time: 1 hour
Serves 4
Fat per serve: 12 g

4 slices double smoked bacon, rind
    removed
2 teaspoons olive oil
4 red chillies, seeded and chopped
2 large onions, finely chopped
3 cloves garlic, crushed
800 g (1 lb 10 oz) very ripe tomatoes,
    finely chopped
500 g (1 lb) lasagnette pasta
2 tablespoons chopped fresh parsley
grated Parmesan, to serve

1 Chop the bacon. Heat the olive oil
in a heavy-based pan and add the
bacon, chilli, onion and garlic. Cook
over medium heat for about 8 minutes,
stirring occasionally.
2 Add the tomato and 3 tablespoons
water to the pan and season to taste
with salt and pepper. Cover and
simmer for about 40 minutes, or until
the sauce is thick and rich.
3 Cook the pasta in a large pan of
rapidly boiling water until *al dente*.
Drain and rinse thoroughly in a
colander, then return the pasta to the
pan and keep warm.
4 Add the parsley to the sauce and
season again if necessary. Pour the
sauce over the pasta, tossing to coat
the pasta thoroughly. Serve sprinkled
with a little grated Parmesan.

NUTRITION PER SERVE
Protein 30 g; Fat 12 g; Carbohydrate 95 g;
Dietary Fibre 10 g; Cholesterol 30 mg;
2765 kJ (600 cal)

NOTE: Good-quality bacon and very
ripe, red, full-flavoured tomatoes are
essential to the flavour of this dish.

Cook the bacon, chilli, onion and garlic over
medium heat, stirring occasionally.

Simmer the tomato sauce until it becomes rich
and thick.

Drain and rinse the cooked pasta thoroughly in a
colander, then return to the pan.

Toss the pasta and sauce together with two
wooden spoons.

SPICY PORK SALAD

Preparation time: 20 minutes
  + 3 hours marinating
Total cooking time: 15 minutes
Serves 6
Fat per serve: 10 g

1 tablespoon oil
500 g (1 lb) pork mince
2 tablespoons fish sauce
1 tablespoon soy sauce
50 ml (1³/₄ fl oz) lime juice
1 tablespoon soft brown sugar

10 spring onions, finely chopped
3 stems lemon grass, white part only,
  finely chopped
2 red chillies, seeded and sliced
2 tablespoons each of chopped fresh
  coriander, mint and parsley
lettuce leaves, for serving

1 Heat the oil in a frying pan. Add the mince and cook over medium heat until well browned, breaking up any lumps with a fork as it cooks. Remove from the pan and leave to cool.
2 Combine the fish sauce, soy sauce, lime juice and brown sugar in a bowl.

Add the pork mince. Mix in the spring onion, lemon grass, chilli and herbs.
3 Cover and refrigerate for at least 3 hours, stirring occasionally, or overnight. To serve, lay a lettuce leaf on each plate and spoon in some of the pork mixture.

NUTRITION PER SERVE
Protein 20 g; Fat 10 g; Carbohydrate 5 g;
Dietary Fibre 0 g; Cholesterol 50 mg;
875 kJ (210 cal)

Chop the spring onions, lemon grass, chillies, coriander, mint and parsley.

Break up any lumps of the pork mince with a fork as you brown it.

Mix in the spring onion, lemon grass, chilli and herbs and leave to marinate.

THAI-SPICED PORK AND GREEN MANGO SALAD

Preparation time: 45 minutes +
   2 hours refrigeration
Total cooking time: 10 minutes
Serves 4
Fat per serve: 14 g

2 stems lemon grass (white part only),
   thinly sliced
1 clove garlic
2 red Asian shallots
1 tablespoon coarsely chopped fresh
   ginger
1 red bird's-eye chilli, seeded
1 tablespoon fish sauce
1/2 cup (15 g/1/2 oz) fresh coriander
1 teaspoon grated lime rind
1 tablespoon lime juice
2 tablespoons oil
2 pork tenderloins, trimmed

DRESSING
1 large red chilli, seeded and finely
   chopped
2 cloves garlic, finely chopped
3 fresh coriander roots, finely chopped
11/4 tablespoons grated palm sugar
2 tablespoons fish sauce
1/4 cup (60 ml) lime juice

SALAD
2 green mangoes or 1 small green
   papaya, peeled, pitted and cut into
   julienne strips
1 carrot, grated
1/2 cup (45 g/11/2 oz) bean sprouts
1/2 red onion, thinly sliced
3 tablespoons roughly chopped fresh
   mint
3 tablespoons roughly chopped fresh
   coriander leaves
3 tablespoons roughly chopped fresh
   Vietnamese mint

1 Place the lemon grass, garlic, shallots, ginger, chilli, fish sauce, coriander, lime rind, lime juice and oil in a blender or food processor and process until a coarse paste forms. Transfer to a non-metallic dish. Coat the pork in the marinade, cover and refrigerate for at least 2 hours, but no longer than 4 hours.
2 To make the salad dressing, mix all the ingredients together in a bowl.

3 Combine all the salad ingredients in a large bowl.
4 Preheat a grill or chargrill pan and cook the pork over medium heat for 4–5 minutes each side, or until cooked through. Remove from the heat, and then leave to rest for 5 minutes before slicing to serve.
5 Toss the dressing and salad together. Season to taste with salt and

cracked black pepper. Arrange the sliced pork in a circle in the centre of each plate and top with salad. Delicious with steamed jasmine rice.

NUTRITION PER SERVE
Protein 60 g; Fat 14 g; Carbohydrate 20 g;
Dietary Fibre 3 g; Cholesterol 122 mg;
1860 kJ (444 cal)

Mix the marinade ingredients to a coarse paste in a processor or blender.

Cook the pork under the grill or in a chargrill pan until it is cooked through.

SWEET AND SOUR PORK

Preparation time: 25 minutes
  + 30 minutes marinating
Total cooking time: 20 minutes
Serves 4
Fat per serve: 12 g

500 g (1 lb) pork fillet, thickly sliced
2 tablespoons cornflour
1 tablespoon sherry
1 tablespoon soy sauce
1 tablespoon sugar
oil, for cooking
1 large onion, thinly sliced
1 green capsicum, cut into cubes
2 small carrots, thinly sliced
1 small Lebanese cucumber, seeded
    and chopped
5 spring onions, cut into short lengths
440 g (14 oz) can pineapple pieces in
    juice, drained, juice reserved
1/4 cup (60 ml/2 fl oz) white vinegar
1/2 teaspoon salt

1 Place the pork in a shallow glass or ceramic bowl. Combine the cornflour with the sherry, soy sauce and half the sugar and add to the pork. Cover and refrigerate for 30 minutes.
2 Drain the pork, reserving the marinade. Heat the wok until very hot, add 1 tablespoon of oil and swirl to coat the side. Stir-fry half the pork over high heat for 4–5 minutes, or until the pork is golden brown and just cooked. Remove from the wok and cook the remaining pork, adding a little more oil if necessary. Remove all the pork from the wok.
3 Reheat the wok, add 1 tablespoon of oil and stir-fry the onion over high heat for 3–4 minutes, or until slightly softened. Add the capsicum and carrot, and cook for 3–4 minutes, or until tender. Stir in the marinade, cucumber, spring onion, pineapple, vinegar, salt, remaining sugar and 4 tablespoons of the reserved pineapple juice.
4 Bring to the boil and simmer for 2–3 minutes, or until the sauce has thickened slightly. Return the pork to the wok and toss until the pork is heated through. Serve immediately with steamed rice.

NUTRITION PER SERVE
Protein 25 g; Fat 12 g; Carbohydrate 25 g; Dietary Fibre 4 g; Cholesterol 50 mg; 1325 kJ (315 cal)

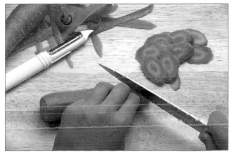
Peel the carrots, if necessary, and cut them into thin diagonal slices.

Halve the cucumber lengthways and scoop out the seeds with a teaspoon.

Stir-fry the pork until it is golden brown and just cooked through.

JAPANESE STIR-FRIED PORK AND NOODLES

Preparation time: 30 minutes
Total cooking time: 15 minutes
Serves 4
Fat per serve: 8 g

1 tablespoon oil
150 g (5 oz) pork loin, thinly sliced
5 spring onions, cut into short lengths
1 carrot, cut into thin strips
2 tablespoons Japanese soy sauce

200 g (6½ oz) Chinese cabbage, shredded
500 g (1 lb) Hokkien noodles, gently pulled apart to separate
1 tablespoon Worcestershire sauce
1 tablespoon mirin
2 teaspoons caster sugar
1 cup (90 g/3 oz) bean sprouts, scraggly ends removed
1 sheet toasted nori, shredded

1 Heat the oil in a large wok over medium heat. Stir-fry the pork, spring onion and carrot for 1–2 minutes, or until the pork just changes colour.

2 Add the soy sauce, cabbage, noodles, Worcestershire sauce, mirin, sugar and 2 tablespoons water. Cover and cook for 1 minute.

3 Add the bean sprouts and toss well to coat the vegetables and noodles in the sauce. Serve immediately, sprinkled with the shredded nori.

NUTRITION PER SERVE
Protein 25 g; Fat 8 g; Carbohydrate 93 g;
Dietary Fibre 5.5 g; Cholesterol 40 mg;
2300 kJ (550 cal)

Finely shred the Chinese cabbage with a large, sharp knife.

Use your fingers to remove the scraggly ends from the bean sprouts.

Stir-fry the pork, spring onion and carrot until the pork just changes colour.

NOODLES WITH MUSHROOMS AND BARBECUED PORK

Preparation time: 30 minutes
Total cooking time: 6 minutes
Serves 4
Fat per serve: 12 g

8 dried Chinese mushrooms
1 tablespoon oil
4 cloves garlic, chopped
5 cm (2 inch) piece fresh ginger, grated
1–2 teaspoons chopped red chillies
100 g (3½ oz) barbecued pork, cut into small pieces
200 g (6½ oz) fresh egg noodles
2 teaspoons fish sauce
2 tablespoons lime juice
2 teaspoons soft brown sugar
2 tablespoons crisp-fried garlic
2 tablespoons crisp-fried onion
chilli flakes

1 Soak the mushrooms in hot water for 20 minutes. Drain and cut them into quarters.
2 Heat the oil in a large wok. Add the garlic, ginger and chilli and stir-fry for 1 minute over high heat. Add the pork to the wok and stir for 1 minute.
3 Add the egg noodles and mushrooms and toss well. Sprinkle the fish sauce, lime juice and soft brown sugar over the pork and then toss quickly, cover and steam for 30 seconds. Sprinkle the crisp garlic and onion and chilli flakes over the top before serving.

NUTRITION PER SERVE
Protein 16 g; Fat 12 g; Carbohydrate 40 g;
Dietary Fibre 3 g; Cholesterol 32 mg;
1375 kJ (328 cal)

Drain the Chinese mushrooms and use a sharp knife to cut them into quarters.

Add the pork pieces to the wok and stir with a wooden spoon for a minute.

Cover the wok and allow the noodles to steam for 30 seconds.

HASH HAM CAKE

Preparation time: 30 minutes +
　1 hour refrigeration
Total cooking time: 50 minutes
Serves 6
Fat per serve: 10 g

500 g (1 lb) floury potatoes, quartered
200 g (6¹/₂ oz) ham, finely chopped
4 spring onions, finely chopped
1 small gherkin, finely chopped
2 tablespoons chopped fresh parsley
1 egg, lightly beaten
cooking oil spray

1 Cook the potato until tender. Drain and mash in a large bowl.
2 Mix in the ham, spring onion, gherkin, parsley, beaten egg and lots of black pepper. Spread on a plate, cover and refrigerate for at least 1 hour, or overnight, to firm.
3 Spray a heavy-based non-stick frying pan lightly with oil. Add the potato mixture, spread evenly into the pan and smooth the surface with the back of a spoon. Cook over moderate heat for 15 minutes, then slide out onto a plate. Spray the pan with oil again, carefully flip the cake back into the pan and cook for another 15–20 minutes, or until the outside forms a brown crust. Serve hot, cut into wedges.

NUTRITION PER SERVE
Protein 9 g; Fat 10 g; Carbohydrate 10 g;
Dietary Fibre 2 g; Cholesterol 70 mg;
730 kJ (175 cal)

Spread the mixture on a plate, cover and refrigerate for at least 1 hour.

Spread the mixture in a heavy-based frying pan and smooth the surface.

Slide the hash cake onto a plate, then flip back into the pan to cook the other side.

LAMB CUTLETS WITH CANNELLINI BEAN PUREE

Preparation time: 30 minutes +
  1 hour refrigeration
Total cooking time: 20 minutes
Serves 4
Fat per serve: 8 g

8 lamb cutlets
4 cloves garlic
1 tablespoon chopped fresh rosemary
2 teaspoons olive oil
2 x 400 g (13 oz) cans cannellini
  beans, drained
1 teaspoon ground cumin
1/2 cup (125 ml/4 fl oz) lemon juice
cooking oil spray
2 tablespoons balsamic vinegar

1 Trim the cutlets of excess fat from the outside edge and scrape the fat away from the bones. Place in a single layer in a shallow dish. Thinly slice 2 garlic cloves and mix with the rosemary, oil and 1/2 teaspoon salt and cracked black pepper. Pour over the meat, cover and refrigerate for 1 hour.

2 Rinse the beans and purée with the remaining garlic, the cumin and half the lemon juice in a food processor. Transfer to a pan, then set aside.

3 Lightly spray a non-stick frying pan with oil and cook the cutlets over medium heat for 1–2 minutes on each side. Add the vinegar and cook for 1 minute, turning to coat. Remove the cutlets and cover to keep warm. Add the remaining lemon juice to the pan and simmer for 2–3 minutes, or until the sauce thickens slightly. Warm the purée over medium heat and serve with the cutlets.

NUTRITION PER SERVE
Protein 30 g; Fat 8 g; Carbohydrate 45 g;
Dietary Fibre 3.5 g; Cholesterol 50 mg;
1560 kJ (375 cal)

Peel 2 of the garlic cloves and thinly slice with a sharp knife.

Trim all the excess fat from the cutlets, scraping any away from the bones.

After cooking the cutlets lightly on each side, add the vinegar to the pan.

MOUSSAKA

Preparation time: 30 minutes
Total cooking time: 1 hour 30 minutes
Serves 6
Fat per serve: 10 g

1 kg (2 lb) eggplants
cooking oil spray
400 g (13 oz) lean lamb mince
2 onions, finely chopped
2 cloves garlic, crushed
400 g (13 oz) can tomatoes
1 tablespoon chopped fresh thyme
1 teaspoon chopped fresh oregano
1 tablespoon tomato paste
1/3 cup (80 ml/2¾ fl oz) dry white
    wine
1 bay leaf
1 teaspoon sugar

CHEESE SAUCE
1¼ cups (315 ml/10 fl oz) skim milk
2 tablespoons plain flour
1/4 cup (30 g/1 oz) grated reduced-fat
    Cheddar
1 cup (250 g/8 oz) ricotta
pinch of cayenne pepper
1/4 teaspoon ground nutmeg

1 Cut the eggplant into 1 cm (1/2 inch) thick slices, place in a colander over a large bowl, layering with a generous sprinkling of salt, and leave to stand for 20 minutes. This is to draw out the bitter juices.
2 Lightly spray a non-stick frying pan with oil and brown the lamb mince, in batches if necessary, over medium-high heat. Once all the meat is browned, set aside.
3 Spray the pan again with oil, add the onion and stir continuously for 2 minutes. Add 1 tablespoon water to the pan to prevent sticking. Add the

garlic and cook for about 3 minutes, or until the onion is golden brown.
4 Push the undrained tomatoes through a sieve, then discard the contents of the sieve.
5 Return the meat to the pan with the onion. Add the herbs, tomato pulp, tomato paste, wine, bay leaf and sugar. Cover and simmer over low heat for 20 minutes. Preheat a grill.
6 Thoroughly rinse and pat dry the eggplant, place on a grill tray, spray lightly with oil and grill under high heat until golden brown. Turn over, spray lightly with oil and grill until golden brown. Arrange half the eggplant slices over the base of a 1.5 litre capacity baking dish. Top with half the meat mixture and then repeat the layers.
7 Preheat the oven to moderate 180°C (350°F/Gas 4). To make the cheese sauce, blend a little of the milk with the flour to form a paste in a small pan. Gradually blend in the remaining milk, stirring constantly over low heat until the milk starts to simmer and thicken. Remove from the heat and stir in the Cheddar, ricotta, cayenne and nutmeg. Pour over the moussaka and bake for 35–40 minutes, or until the cheese is golden brown and the moussaka heated through.

NUTRITION PER SERVE
Protein 10 g; Fat 10 g; Carbohydrate 15 g; Dietary Fibre 5.5 g; Cholesterol 25 mg; 735 kJ (175 cal)

STORAGE TIME: Freeze for up to 2 months. Thaw in the fridge, then heat in a moderate oven for 30–45 minutes.

Sprinkle a generous amount of salt on the eggplant slices and set aside.

Empty the can of tomatoes into a sieve and push the tomatoes through.

Stir the herbs, tomato pulp, tomato paste, wine, bay leaf and sugar into the meat.

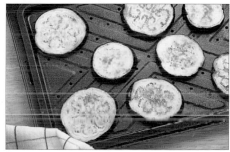

Rinse and dry the eggplant slices and grill on both sides until golden.

Layer the eggplant slices and meat evenly in the baking dish.

Remove from the heat before adding the Cheddar, ricotta, cayenne and nutmeg.

PEPPERED LAMB AND ASPARAGUS STIR-FRY

Preparation time: 35 minutes
  + 20 minutes marinating
Total cooking time: 20 minutes
Serves 4
Fat per serve: 12 g

400 g (13 oz) lamb fillets
2 teaspoons green peppercorns,
  finely chopped
3 cloves garlic, finely chopped
1 tablespoon oil
1 onion, cut into small wedges
1/3 cup (80 ml/2³/4 fl oz) dry sherry
1 green capsicum, cut into strips

1/2 teaspoon sugar
16 small asparagus spears, cut into
  bite-sized pieces, tough ends
  discarded
200 g (6¹/2 oz) broccoli florets
2 tablespoons oyster sauce
garlic chives, cut into short lengths, to
  garnish

1 Trim away any sinew from the lamb
and cut the lamb into bite-sized
pieces. Combine in a bowl with the
green peppercorns, garlic and oil, then
toss well and set aside for 20 minutes.
2 Heat a wok over high heat until
slightly smoking. Add the pieces
of lamb and stir-fry in batches until
brown and just cooked. Remove,

cover and keep warm.
3 Reheat the wok and stir-fry the
onion and 2 teaspoons of the sherry
for 1 minute. Add the capsicum, sugar
and a large pinch of salt. Cover, steam
for 2 minutes, add the asparagus,
broccoli, then remaining sherry, and
stir-fry for 1 minute. Cover and steam
for 3 minutes, or until the vegetables
are just tender. Return the lamb to the
pan, add the oyster sauce and stir to
combine with the vegetables. Serve
garnished with the chives.

NUTRITION PER SERVE
Protein 25 g; Fat 12 g; Carbohydrate 8 g;
Dietary Fibre 4 g; Cholesterol 65 mg;
1100 kJ (265 cal)

Trim the lamb of any excess fat or sinew, then cut into bite-sized pieces.

Stir-fry the lamb over high heat until brown and just cooked.

Add the asparagus and broccoli to the capsicum and onion.

TAGINE OF LAMB WITH QUINCE AND LEMON

Preparation time: 25 minutes
Total cooking time: 2 hours 10 minutes
Serves 4
Fat per serve: 15 g

1.5 kg (3 lb) boned shoulder of lamb,
    cut into 12 even pieces
1 onion, finely chopped
2 cloves garlic, crushed
1 cinnamon stick
1 teaspoon ground ginger
1/2 teaspoon saffron threads
1 large quince, peeled, seeded and
    cut into 12 pieces

1/4 cup (90 ml/3 fl oz) honey
1 teaspoon ground cinnamon
1/2 preserved lemon

1 Trim the lamb of excess fat and place in a large pan. Add the onion, garlic, cinnamon stick, ginger and saffron and enough cold water to cover. Slowly bring to the boil, stirring occasionally. Reduce the heat, cover and simmer for 45 minutes. Transfer the meat to a casserole dish.
2 Add the quince, honey and ground cinnamon to the cooking liquid and simmer for 15 minutes, or until the quince is tender. Discard the cinnamon, remove the quince and add to the meat, reserving the liquid.

3 Preheat the oven to moderate 180°C (350°F/Gas 4). Boil the cooking liquid for 30 minutes, or until reduced by half, then pour over the meat and quince. Remove and discard the flesh from the lemon. Slice the rind thinly, then add to the meat. Cover and bake for 40 minutes, or until the meat is tender.

NUTRITION PER SERVE
Protein 80 g; Fat 15 g; Carbohydrate 20 g; Dietary Fibre 3 g; Cholesterol 250 mg; 2160 kJ (515 cal)

HINT: As you work, place the peeled quince in water with a little lemon juice to prevent discolouring.

Add the onion, garlic, cinnamon stick, ginger, saffron and cold water to the lamb.

Add the quince, honey and ground cinnamon to the cooking liquid.

Remove and discard the flesh from the preserved lemon and slice the rind thinly.

LAMB WITH BORLOTTI BEANS

Preparation time: 20 minutes +
  overnight soaking
Total cooking time: 2 hours
Serves 6
Fat per serve: 8 g

1 cup (200 g /6¹/₂ oz) dried borlotti
  beans
1 tablespoon olive oil
12 lamb loin chops
1 onion, finely chopped
1 celery stick, chopped
1 carrot, chopped
3 cloves garlic, finely chopped

¹/₂ teaspoon dried chilli flakes
1 teaspoon cumin seeds
2 cups (500 ml/16 fl oz) lamb or
  chicken stock
2 bay leaves
3 tablespoons lemon juice
¹/₃ cup (20 g/³/₄ oz) chopped fresh
  parsley
1 tablespoon shredded fresh mint

1 Soak the beans overnight in cold water. Drain, rinse well and set aside.
2 Preheat the oven to moderate 180°C (350°F/Gas 4). Heat the oil in a large heavy-based pan. Brown the lamb over high heat in batches and transfer to a casserole dish.
3 Add the onion, celery and carrot to the pan and cook over low heat for about 10 minutes, or until soft and golden. Add the garlic, chilli and cumin seeds and cook for 1 minute, then transfer to the casserole dish.
4 Add the stock, beans and bay leaves. Cover tightly; bake for 1¹/₂–1³/₄ hours, or until the lamb is very tender and the beans are cooked. Season well and stir in the lemon juice, parsley and mint just before serving.

NUTRITION PER SERVE
Protein 30 g; Fat 8 g; Carbohydrate 20 g;
Dietary Fibre 5 g; Cholesterol 65 mg;
1185 kJ (280 cal)

When the oil is hot, brown the lamb over high heat in batches.

Add the onion, celery and carrot to the pan and cook until soft and golden.

Add the stock, drained borlotti beans and bay leaves to the casserole.

ROSEMARY-INFUSED LAMB AND LENTIL CASSEROLE

Preparation time: 20 minutes
Total cooking time: 2 hours 30 minutes
Serves 6
Fat per serve: 15 g

1 tablespoon olive oil
1 onion, finely sliced
2 cloves garlic, crushed
1 small carrot, finely chopped
2 teaspoons cumin seeds
1/4 teaspoon chilli flakes
2 teaspoons finely chopped fresh
   ginger
1 kg (2 lb) boned leg of lamb, cut into
   4 cm (11/2 inch) cubes
2 teaspoons fresh rosemary leaves,
   chopped
3 cups (750 ml/24 fl oz) chicken stock
1 cup (185 g/6 oz) green or brown
   lentils
3 teaspoons soft brown sugar
2 teaspoons balsamic vinegar

1 Preheat the oven to moderate 180°C (350°F/Gas 4). Heat half the oil in a large, heavy-based pan. Add the onion, garlic and carrot and cook over medium heat for about 5 minutes, or until soft and golden. Add the cumin seeds, chilli flakes and ginger, cook for 1 minute, then transfer to a large casserole dish.
2 Heat the remaining oil in the pan and brown the lamb in batches over high heat. Transfer to the casserole.
3 Add the rosemary to the pan and stir in 21/2 cups (625 ml/20 fl oz) of the stock. Heat until the stock is bubbling, then pour into the casserole dish. Cover the dish and bake in the oven for 1 hour.

4 Add the lentils, sugar and vinegar and cook for 1 hour more, or until the lentils are cooked. If the mixture is too thick, stir in the remaining stock. Season with salt and pepper to taste and serve.

NUTRITION PER SERVE
Protein 45 g; Fat 15 g; Carbohydrate 15 g; Dietary Fibre 5 g; Cholesterol 120 mg; 1618 kJ (385 cal)

When the oil is hot, add the onion, garlic and carrot and cook until soft and golden.

After browning the lamb, add the rosemary and stock to the pan.

Bake the casserole for 1 hour, then add the lentils, sugar and vinegar.

LAMB CHOP CASSEROLE

Preparation time: 15 minutes
Total cooking time: 1 hour 15 minutes
Serves 4
Fat per serve: 11 g

6–8 lamb chump chops (see NOTE)
1 tablespoon oil
1 large onion, finely chopped
1/3 cup (90 g/3 oz) redcurrant jelly
1 teaspoon grated lemon rind
1 tablespoon lemon juice
1 tablespoon barbecue sauce
1 tablespoon tomato sauce
1/2 cup (125 ml/4 fl oz) chicken stock

1 Trim any fat from the lamb. Preheat the oven to moderate180°C (350°F/ Gas 4). Heat the oil in a large heavy-based frying pan; add the chops and cook over medium-high heat for 2–3 minutes, turning once, until well browned. Remove from the pan and put in a casserole dish.
2 Add the onion to the frying pan and cook over medium heat, stirring frequently, for 5 minutes or until the onion is softened. Add the jelly, lemon rind and juice, barbecue and tomato sauces and stock. Stir for 2–3 minutes until heated through. Pour over the chops and stir well, cover and place in the oven. Cook for 1 hour, or until the meat is tender, turning 2–3 times. Lift out the chops onto a side plate and leave them to keep warm.
3 Pour the sauce into a pan and boil rapidly for 5 minutes until the sauce has thickened and reduced. Return the chops to the sauce before serving.

NUTRITION PER SERVE
Protein 30 g; Fat 11 g; Carbohydrate 13 g; Dietary Fibre 1 g; Cholesterol 95 mg; 1150 kJ (275 cal)

STORAGE TIME: Keep covered and refrigerated for up to 2 days. Suitable to freeze for up to 1 month.

NOTE: Other lamb chop cuts can be used instead of chump.

Once the chops have been well browned, put them in a casserole dish.

Pour the sauce over the chops in the dish and stir to combine.

Use a pair of tongs to turn the chops a couple of times during cooking.

NAVARIN OF LAMB

Preparation time: 20 minutes
Total cooking time: 1 hour 45 minutes
Serves 4
Fat per serve: 12 g

1.25 kg (2 lb 8 oz) boned shoulder or
    leg of lamb (ask your butcher to
    bone the meat)
1 tablespoon oil
1 small onion, quartered
1 clove garlic, crushed
2 rashers bacon, rind removed, finely
    chopped
12 large bulb spring onions, stems
    removed
1 tablespoon plain flour
1 cup (250 ml/8 fl oz) chicken stock

1 tablespoon tomato paste
1 turnip, swede or parsnip, peeled
    and cubed
1 large carrot, thickly sliced
4–6 new potatoes, halved
1/2 cup (60 g/2 oz) frozen peas

1 Remove any excess fat from the
lamb and cut the meat into bite-sized
cubes. Preheat the oven to slow 150°C.
(300°F/Gas 2). Heat the oil in a heavy-
based non-stick frying pan. Cook the
onion, garlic, bacon and spring onions
over medium heat for 5 minutes, or
until the onion is soft. Remove with a
slotted spoon to a large heatproof
casserole dish

2 Add the lamb to the frying pan and
brown quickly in batches. When all
the meat is browned return it to the
pan and sprinkle with the flour. Stir for
1 minute to combine, then pour on the
stock and tomato paste. Stir until
thickened and smooth and pour into
the casserole.

3 Stir in the turnip, swede or parsnip,
carrot and potato. Cover with a tight-
fitting lid and bake for 1¼ hours,
stirring a couple of times. Add the peas
and cook for another 15 minutes, or
until the lamb is tender. Season to taste
before serving.

NUTRITION PER SERVE
Protein 9 g; Fat 12 g; Carbohydrate 22 g;
Dietary Fibre 7 g; Cholesterol 30 mg;
970 kJ (235 cal)

STORAGE TIME: Keep covered and
refrigerated for up to 3 days.

Remove the onion, spring onion, garlic and
bacon to a casserole dish.

Return all the browned meat to the pan and
sprinkle with flour.

Add the turnip, carrot and potato to the meat in
the casserole dish.

SHEPHERD'S PIE

Preparation time: 40 minutes
Total cooking time: 40 minutes
Serves 4
Fat per serve: 7 g

cooking oil spray
2 onions, thinly sliced
1 large carrot, finely chopped
2 celery sticks, finely chopped
500 g (1 lb) lean lamb mince
2 tablespoons plain flour
2 tablespoons tomato paste
2 tablespoons Worcestershire sauce
1 beef or chicken stock cube
1.25 kg (2¼ lb) potatoes
½ cup (125 ml/4 fl oz) skim milk
⅓ cup (20 g/¾ oz) finely chopped
    fresh parsley
paprika, to sprinkle

1 Lightly spray a large non-stick frying pan with oil, then heat. Add the onion, carrot and celery and stir constantly over medium heat for 5 minutes, until the vegetables begin to soften. Add 1 tablespoon water to prevent sticking.

Remove from the pan and set aside. Spray the pan with a little more oil, add the lamb mince and cook over high heat until well browned.
2 Add the plain flour and stir for 2–3 minutes. Return the vegetables to the pan and add the tomato paste, Worcestershire sauce, stock cube and 2 cups (500 ml/16 fl oz) water. Stir and slowly bring to the boil. Reduce the heat, cover and simmer for 20 minutes, stirring occasionally.
3 Meanwhile, chop the potatoes and cook until tender. Drain and mash until smooth. Add the milk, season with salt and pepper, then beat well.
4 Stir the chopped parsley through

the mince and season well. Preheat a grill. Pour the mince into a 1.5 litre capacity baking dish. Spoon the potato over the top, spreading evenly with the back of the spoon. Use a fork to roughen up the potato and make the traditionally crunchy topping. Sprinkle lightly with paprika and grill until golden, watching carefully because the potato browns quickly.

NUTRITION PER SERVE
Protein 3 g; Fat 7 g; Carbohydrate 15 g; Dietary Fibre 2.5 g; Cholesterol 1 mg; 915 kJ (220 cal)

Add the tomato paste, Worcestershire sauce, stock cube and water.

Create a decorative effect by running the back of a fork across the potato.

LAMB WITH ROAST PUMPKIN AND CAPSICUM SAUCE

Preparation time: 30 minutes
Total cooking time: 1 hour 20 minutes
Serves 4
Fat per serve: 15 g

500 g (1 lb) pumpkin (jap, butternut or
   golden nugget)
2 cloves garlic, crushed
1 tablespoon olive oil
1 red capsicum
2 teaspoons cumin seeds
2 teaspoons coriander seeds
1 cup (250 ml/8 fl oz) vegetable stock
750 g (1 lb 8 oz) lamb backstrap

1 Preheat the oven to 200°C.
(400°F/Gas 6). Cut the pumpkin into
wedges and put in a baking dish.
Combine the garlic and oil and drizzle
over the pumpkin. Season well with
salt and pepper. Cook for 1 hour or
until tender. Cool slightly.
2 Cut the capsicum into large flat
pieces, removing the membranes and
seeds. Place, skin-side-up, under a hot
grill for 10 minutes, or until the skin
blackens and blisters. Cool under a tea
towel or in a plastic bag, peel away
the skin and cut the flesh into strips.
3 Put the cumin and coriander seeds
in a small frying pan and dry-fry for
5 minutes. Grind in a small food
processor or mortar and pestle.
Remove the skin from the pumpkin
and put the flesh, ground spices and
stock in a food processor. Purée the
mixture until smooth, then transfer to
a pan and heat through gently. Add
the capsicum strips and stir through.
3 Lightly spray a chargrill pan with
oil. Cook the lamb for 3–4 minutes on
each side. Leave to rest for 5 minutes
before slicing. Serve with the sauce.

NUTRITION PER SERVE
Protein 60 g; Fat 15 g; Carbohydrate 22 g;
Dietary Fibre 7 g; Cholesterol 210 mg;
2330 kJ (550 cal)

Drizzle the combined garlic and oil over the
pumpkin and season well.

Peel the blackened skin away from the capsicum
and cut the flesh into strips.

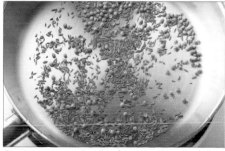

Put the cumin and coriander seeds in a dry frying
pan and toast for 5 minutes.

Purée the roast pumpkin, dry-fried spices and
stock until smooth.

LANCASHIRE HOTPOT

Preparation time: 20 minutes
Total cooking time: 2 hours
Serves 8
Fat per serve: 10 g

8 forequarter chops, cut 2.5 cm
    (1 inch) thick
4 lamb kidneys, cut into quarters,
    cores removed
3 tablespoons plain flour
30 g (1 oz) butter
4 potatoes, thinly sliced
2 large onions, sliced
2 celery sticks, chopped
1 large carrot, peeled and chopped
1³/₄ cups (440 ml/14 fl oz) chicken or
    beef stock
200 g (6¹/₂ oz) button mushrooms,
    sliced
2 teaspoons chopped fresh thyme
1 tablespoon Worcestershire sauce

1 Preheat the oven to warm 160°C (315°F/Gas 2–3). Lightly brush a large casserole dish with oil. Trim the meat of fat and sinew and toss the chops and kidneys in flour, shaking off the excess. Heat the butter in a large frying pan and brown the chops quickly on both sides. Remove the chops from the pan and brown the kidneys. Layer half the potato slices in the base of the dish and place the chops and kidneys on top of them.

2 Add the onion, celery and carrot to the pan and cook until the carrot begins to brown. Layer on top of the chops and kidneys. Sprinkle the remaining flour over the base of the pan and cook, stirring, until dark brown. Gradually pour in the stock and bring to the boil, stirring. Add the mushrooms, salt, pepper, thyme and Worcestershire sauce, reduce the heat and leave to simmer for 10 minutes. Pour into the casserole dish.

3 Layer the remaining potato over the top of the casserole, to cover the meat and vegetables. Cover and cook in the oven for 1¹/₄ hours. Remove the lid and cook for a further 30 minutes, or until the potatoes are brown.

NUTRITION PER SERVE
Protein 40 g; Fat 10 g; Carbohydrate 11 g; Dietary Fibre 3 g; Cholesterol 170 mg; 1227 kJ (295 cal)

Toss the kidneys in flour and then brown in the pan you used for browning the chops.

Stir in the mushrooms, seasoning, thyme and Worcestershire sauce.

Layer the remaining potato over the top of the casserole, covering the meat and vegetables.

MEDITERRANEAN LAMB CASSEROLE

Preparation time: 15 minutes
Total cooking time: 1 hour
Serves 4
Fat per serve: 12 g

1 tablespoon olive oil
750 g (1 1/2 lb) lamb from the bone, diced
1 large onion, sliced
2 cloves garlic, crushed
2 carrots, chopped
2 parsnips, chopped
400 g (13 oz) can chopped tomatoes
2 tablespoons tomato paste
2 teaspoons chopped fresh rosemary
1/2 cup (125 ml/4 fl oz) red wine
1 cup (250 ml/8 fl oz) chicken stock

1 Heat the oil in large saucepan and cook the lamb, in batches, for 3–4 minutes, or until browned. Remove from the pan and keep warm. Add the onion and garlic to the pan and cook for 2–3 minutes, or until the onion is soft.
2 Return the lamb and juices to the pan. Add the carrots, parsnips, tomatoes, tomato paste, rosemary, wine and stock and bring to the boil. Reduce the heat and cover the pan. Simmer the casserole for 50 minutes, or until the lamb is tender and the sauce has thickened. Serve with soft polenta or couscous.

NUTRITION PER SERVE
Protein 45 g; Fat 12 g, Carbohydrate 12 g; Dietary Fibre 4.5 g; Cholesterol 125 mg; 1517 kJ (362 cal)

Add the onion and garlic to the pan and cook until the onion is soft.

Simmer until the lamb is tender and the sauce has thickened.

SLOW-COOKED SHANKS

Preparation time: 20 minutes
Total cooking time: 3 hours
Serves 4
Fat per serve: 10 g

1 tablespoon oil
4 lamb shanks
2 red onions, sliced
10 cloves garlic, peeled
400 g (13 oz) can chopped tomatoes
1/2 cup (125 ml/4 fl oz) dry white wine
1 bay leaf
1 teaspoon grated lemon rind
1 large red capsicum, chopped
3 tablespoons chopped fresh parsley

1 Preheat the oven to warm 170°C (325°F/Gas 3). Heat the oil in a large flameproof casserole dish, add the shanks in batches and cook over high heat until browned on all sides. Return all the lamb to the casserole.
2 Add the onion and garlic to the casserole and cook until softened. Add the tomato, wine, bay leaf, lemon rind, capsicum and 1/2 cup (125 ml/4 fl oz) water and bring to the boil.
3 Cover the casserole and cook in the oven for 2–21/2 hours, or until the meat is tender and falling off the bone and the sauce has thickened. Season to taste. Sprinkle the parsley over the top before serving. Serve with couscous or soft polenta.

NUTRITION PER SERVE
Protein 35 g; Fat 10 g; Carbohydrate 9 g;
Dietary Fibre 4.5 g; Cholesterol 85 mg;
1275 kJ (305 cal)

Heat the oil in a pan and brown the lamb shanks in batches.

Add the onion and garlic to the casserole and cook until softened.

Add the tomato, wine, bay leaf, lemon rind, capsicum and water.

LAMB CASSEROLE WITH BEANS

Preparation time: 25 minutes +
  overnight soaking
Total cooking time: 2 hours 15 minutes
Serves 6
Fat per serve: 10 g

1¹/₂ cups (300 g/10 oz) borlotti or red
  kidney beans
1 kg (2 lb) boned leg lamb
1 tablespoon olive oil
2 rashers bacon, rind removed,
  chopped
1 large onion, chopped
2 cloves garlic, crushed
1 large carrot, chopped
2 cups (500 ml/16 fl oz) dry red wine

1 tablespoon tomato paste
1¹/₂ cups (375 ml/12 fl oz) beef stock
2 large sprigs fresh rosemary
2 sprigs fresh thyme

1 Put the beans in a bowl and cover
with plenty of water. Leave to soak
overnight, then drain well.
2 Preheat the oven to warm 160°C
(315°F/Gas 2–3). Trim any fat from the
lamb and cut into bite-sized cubes.
3 Heat the oil in a large flameproof
casserole and brown the lamb in two
batches over high heat for 2 minutes.
Remove all the lamb from the
casserole and set aside.
4 Add the bacon and onion to the
casserole. Cook over medium heat for
3 minutes, or until the onion is soft.
Add the garlic and carrot and cook for

1 minute, or until aromatic.
5 Return the lamb and any juices to
the pan, increase the heat to high and
add the wine. Bring to the boil and
cook for 2 minutes. Add the beans,
tomato paste, stock, rosemary and
thyme, bring to the boil, then cover
and cook in the oven for 2 hours, or
until the meat is tender. Stir
occasionally during cooking. Skim off
any fat from the surface and then
season and remove the herb sprigs
before serving.

NUTRITION PER SERVE
Protein 50 g; Fat 10 g; Carbohydrate 48 g;
Dietary Fibre 9 g; Cholesterol 117 mg;
2367 kJ (565 cal)

Remove the fat from the lamb then cut it into bite-sized cubes.

Heat the oil in the casserole and brown the lamb in two batches.

Return the meat and juices to the pan, add the wine, and bring to the boil.

ROGAN JOSH

Preparation time: 25 minutes
Total cooking time: 1 hour 40 minutes
Serves 6
Fat per serve: 13 g

1 kg (2 lb) boned leg of lamb
1 tablespoon oil
2 onions, chopped
1/2 cup (125 g/4 oz) low-fat natural
   yoghurt
1 teaspoon chilli powder
1 tablespoon ground coriander
2 teaspoons ground cumin
1 teaspoon ground cardamom
1/2 teaspoon ground cloves
1 teaspoon ground turmeric

3 cloves garlic, crushed
1 tablespoon grated fresh ginger
400 g (13 oz) can chopped tomatoes
1/4 cup (30 g/1 oz) slivered almonds
1 teaspoon garam masala
chopped fresh coriander leaves, for
   serving

1 Trim the lamb of any fat or sinew
and cut into small cubes.
2 Heat the oil in a large saucepan,
add the onion and cook, stirring, for
5 minutes, or until soft. Stir in the
yoghurt, chilli powder, coriander,
cumin, cardamom, cloves, turmeric,
garlic and ginger. Add the tomato and
1 teaspoon salt and simmer for
5 minutes.
3 Add the lamb and stir until coated.

Cover and cook over low heat, stirring
occasionally, for 1–11/2 hours, or until
the lamb is tender. Uncover and
simmer until the liquid thickens.
4 Meanwhile, toast the almonds in a
dry frying pan over medium heat for
3–4 minutes, shaking the pan gently,
until the nuts are golden brown.
Remove from the pan at once to
prevent them burning.
5 Add the garam masala to the curry
and mix through well. Sprinkle the
slivered almonds and coriander leaves
over the top and serve.

NUTRITION PER SERVE
Protein 40 g; Fat 13 g; Carbohydrate 5.5 g;
Dietary Fibre 2 g; Cholesterol 122 mg;
1236 kJ (295 cal)

Cook the onion in the oil for 5 minutes, or until it
is soft.

Remove the lid from the pan and simmer until the
liquid thickens.

Toast the almonds in a dry frying pan until they
are golden brown.

INDIAN-STYLE LAMB COUSCOUS SALAD

Preparation time: 25 minutes
Total cooking time: 35 minutes
Serves 6
Fat per serve: 10 g

250 g (8 oz) lamb backstrap
    (tender eye of the lamb loin)
1 tablespoon mild curry powder
2 tablespoons pepitas
    (pumpkin seeds)
2 tablespoons sesame seeds
2 teaspoons cumin seeds
2 teaspoons coriander seeds
1 tablespoon oil
2 tablespoons lemon juice
1 onion, chopped
1 carrot, chopped
125 g (4 oz) orange sweet potato,
    cubed
1 clove garlic, finely chopped
1 cup (185 g/6 oz) couscous
1/4 cup (50 g/1³/₄ oz) raisins

1 Sprinkle the lamb with the combined curry powder and a pinch of salt, then turn to coat well. Cover with plastic wrap and refrigerate while preparing the salad.

2 Place the pepitas and sesame seeds in a dry frying pan and cook, stirring, over medium-high heat until the seeds begin to brown. Add the cumin and coriander seeds and continue stirring until the pepitas are puffed and begin to pop. Remove from the heat and allow to cool.

3 Heat the oil in a pan, add the lamb and cook over medium-high heat for 5–8 minutes, or until browned and tender. Remove from the pan, drizzle with half the lemon juice and leave to cool to room temperature. Turn the

meat occasionally to coat in the lemon juice while cooling.

4 Using the same pan, stir the onion, carrot and sweet potato over high heat until the onion is translucent. Reduce the heat to medium, add 3 tablespoons water, cover and cook for about 3 minutes, or until the vegetables are tender. Stir in the chopped garlic and remaining lemon juice.

5 Pour 1 cup (250 ml/8 fl oz) boiling water into a heatproof bowl and add the couscous. Stir until combined. Leave for about 2 minutes, or until the water has been absorbed. Fluff gently with a fork to separate the grains. Add

the vegetable mixture, raisins and most of the toasted nuts and seeds, reserving some to sprinkle over the top, and toss until just combined. Spoon the mixture onto a serving plate. Slice the lamb thinly and arrange over the salad. Drizzle with any leftover lemon juice and sprinkle with the nuts and seeds.

NUTRITION PER SERVE
Protein 15 g; Fat 10 g; Carbohydrate 30 g;
Dietary Fibre 3 g; Cholesterol 30 mg;
1135 kJ (270 cal)

Sprinkle the lamb backstrap with the combined curry powder and salt.

Fry the seeds in a dry frying pan until the pepitas puff up.

When the water has been absorbed, fluff the couscous gently with a fork.

Vegetables

By using a minimal amount of oil, vegetables can be cooked your favourite way, taste good and still have a low fat content. And hold the mayonnaise—try low-fat natural yoghurt instead.

CRUNCHY WEDGES

Preheat the oven to 200°C (400°F/Gas 6). Cut 6 potatoes into 8 wedges each. Dry, then toss with 1 tablespoon oil. Combine 1/2 teaspoon vegetable stock powder, 1/4 cup (25 g/3/4 oz) dry breadcrumbs, 2 teaspoons chopped chives, 1 teaspoon celery salt, 1/4 teaspoon garlic powder and 1/2 teaspoon chopped fresh rosemary. Add the wedges and toss. Spread on lightly greased baking trays and bake for 40 minutes or until golden. Serves 6.

NUTRITION PER SERVE
Protein 3.5 g; Fat 1 g; Carbohydrate 20 g; Dietary Fibre 2 g; Cholesterol 0 mg; 515 kJ (125 cal)

BAKED HASH BROWNS

Preheat the oven to 200°C (400°F/Gas 6). Cut 3 potatoes in half and boil for 10 minutes—the potatoes will be just tender on the outside and firm in the centre. Cool, then coarsely grate and divide into 6 portions. Using wet hands, shape into flat patties. Spray a non-stick baking tray with oil. Arrange the hash browns on the tray and spray lightly with olive oil. Bake for 20 minutes, turn and bake for 5–10 minutes, or until crisp and golden. Serves 6.

NUTRITION PER SERVE
Protein 2.5 g; Fat 1 g; Carbohydrate 13 g; Dietary Fibre 1.5 g; Cholesterol 0 mg; 275 kJ (65 cal)

GRILLED POTATOES WITH GARLIC CREAM

Cook 4 potatoes until tender. Drain and cool. Cut into 1 cm (1/2 inch) slices. Brown both sides on a lightly greased griddle pan or barbecue. Serve hot with 1/4 cup (60 g/2 oz) light sour cream combined with 100 g (3 1/2 oz) low-fat natural yoghurt, 2 cloves crushed garlic, 1/4 teaspoon paprika and 1 tablespoon chopped garlic chives. Sprinkle with parsley and a little chopped red capsicum. Serves 4.

NUTRITION PER SERVE
Protein 5 g; Fat 3 g; Carbohydrate 20 g; Dietary Fibre 2 g; Cholesterol 10 mg; 525 kJ (125 cal)

SWEET POTATO CRISPS

Peel an orange sweet potato and cut it into very thin slices. Put the slices in a large bowl of iced water with 1 teaspoon of salt. Leave for 30 minutes, then drain, spread in a single layer on a lightly greased baking tray and spray lightly with cooking oil. Bake at moderately hot 200°C (400°F/Gas 6) for 30 minutes, turning after 15 minutes. Remove from the tray as soon as they are brown and crisp. Sprinkle while hot with 1 teaspoon dried parsley flakes combined with 1 teaspoon salt, 1/2 teaspoon paprika, a pinch of caster sugar and 1/4 teaspoon ground cumin. Toss well and store in an airtight container for 3–4 days. Serves 4.

NUTRITION PER SERVE
Protein 1 g; Fat 0 g; Carbohydrate 10 g; Dietary Fibre 1 g; Cholesterol 0 mg; 235 kJ (55 cal)

MUSHROOMS WITH LEEK AND CHEESE

Preheat the oven to moderately hot 200°C (400°F/Gas 6). Chop the stalks from 6 cap mushrooms. In a pan, cook the mushroom stalks and 1 finely sliced leek (white part only) with 2 teaspoons butter and 2 teaspoons water, stirring until very soft. Season and spoon into the mushroom caps. Sprinkle with a mixture of 1 1/2 tablespoons fresh breadcrumbs, 1 1/2 tablespoons grated Parmesan and 1 1/2 tablespoons chopped fresh parsley. Bake for 20 minutes, or until golden. Serves 6.

NUTRITION PER MUSHROOM
Protein 2.5 g; Fat 2 g; Carbohydrate 2 g; Dietary Fibre 1.5 g; Cholesterol 6.5 mg; 160 kJ (40 cal)

BAKED VEGETABLES

Preheat the oven to moderately hot 200°C (400°F/Gas 6). Cut 2 carrots and 2 parsnips in half lengthways, then crossways. Quarter 2 large potatoes. Cut 300 g (10 oz) pumpkin into chunks. Put the vegetables in a baking dish and spray lightly with cooking oil. Sprinkle with salt and pepper and bake for 20 minutes, turning occasionally. Cut 2 finger eggplants in half lengthways and make thin shallow cuts through the skin. Add to the dish and cook, turning occasionally, for 20 minutes, or until the vegetables are tender. Sprinkle with parsley. Serves 4.

NUTRITION PER SERVE
Protein 5.5 g; Fat 1 g; Carbohydrate 25 g; Dietary Fibre 6 g; Cholesterol 0 mg; 535 kJ (130 cal)

Clockwise from top left: Sweet potato crisps; Baked hash browns; Mushrooms with leek and cheese; Grilled potatoes with garlic cream; Baked vegetables; Crunchy wedges.

Chicken

CHICKEN AND VEGETABLE LASAGNE

Preparation time: 45 minutes
Total cooking time: 1 hour 20 minutes
Serves 8
Fat per serve: 10 g

500 g (1 lb) chicken breast fillets
cooking oil spray
2 cloves garlic, crushed
1 onion, chopped
2 zucchini, chopped
2 celery sticks, chopped
2 carrots, chopped
300 g (10 oz) pumpkin, diced
2 x 400 g (13 oz) cans
    tomatoes, chopped
2 sprigs fresh thyme
2 bay leaves
1/2 cup (125 ml/4 fl oz) white wine
2 tablespoons tomato paste
2 tablespoons chopped fresh basil
500 g (1 lb) English spinach
500 g (1 lb) reduced-fat cottage
    cheese
450 g (14 oz) ricotta
1/4 cup (60 ml/2 fl oz) skim milk
1/2 teaspoon ground nutmeg
1/3 cup (35 g/11/4 oz) grated
    Parmesan
300 g (10 oz) instant or fresh lasagne
    sheets

1 Preheat the oven to moderate 180°C (350°F/Gas 4). Trim any fat from the chicken breasts, then finely mince in a food processor. Heat a large, deep, non-stick frying pan, spray lightly with oil and cook the chicken mince in batches until browned. Remove.
2 Add the garlic and onion to the pan and cook until softened. Return the chicken to the pan and add the zucchini, celery, carrot, pumpkin, tomato, thyme, bay leaves, wine and tomato paste. Simmer, covered, for 20 minutes. Remove the bay leaves and thyme and stir in the fresh basil.
3 Shred the spinach and set aside. Mix the cottage cheese, ricotta, skim milk, nutmeg and half the Parmesan.
4 Spoon a little of the tomato mixture over the base of a casserole dish and top with a single layer of pasta. Top with half the remaining tomato mixture, then the spinach and spoon over half the cottage cheese mixture. Continue with another layer of pasta, the remaining tomato and another layer of pasta. Spread the remaining cottage cheese mixture on top and sprinkle with Parmesan. Bake for 40–50 minutes, or until golden. The top may puff up slightly but will settle on standing.

NUTRITION PER SERVE
Protein 40 g; Fat 10 g; Carbohydrate 35 g; Dietary Fibre 7 g; Cholesterol 70 mg; 1790 kJ (430 cal)

Cut any fat from the chicken fillets and then finely mince in a food processor.

Add the vegetables to the pan with the bay leaves, thyme, wine and tomato paste.

SWEET CHILLI CHICKEN

Preparation time: 15 minutes +
  2 hours refrigeration
Total cooking time: 20 minutes
Serves 6
Fat per serve: 4.5 g

1 kg (2 lb) chicken thigh fillets
2 tablespoons lime juice
1/2 cup (125 ml/4 fl oz) sweet chilli
  sauce
3 tablespoons kecap manis
  (see NOTE)

1 Trim any excess fat from the chicken thigh fillets and cut them in half. Put the chicken in a shallow non-metallic dish.
2 Place the lime juice, sweet chilli sauce and kecap manis in a bowl and whisk to combine.
3 Pour the marinade over the chicken, cover and refrigerate for 2 hours.
4 Chargrill or bake in a preheated moderately hot 200°C (400°F/Gas 6) oven for 20 minutes, or until the chicken is tender and cooked through and the marinade has caramelised.

NUTRITION PER SERVE
Protein 35 g; Fat 4.5 g; Carbohydrate 4 g;
Dietary Fibre 1 g; Cholesterol 85 mg;
880 kJ (210 cal)

NOTE: Kecap manis (ketjap manis) is a thick Indonesian sauce, similar to—but sweeter than—soy sauce, and is generally flavoured with garlic and star anise. Store in a cool, dry place and refrigerate after opening. If not available, use soy sauce sweetened with a little soft brown sugar.

Trim the excess fat from the thigh fillets and cut them in half.

To make the marinade, whisk together the lime juice, sweet chilli sauce and kecap manis.

Pour the marinade over the chicken, then cover and refrigerate.

SPICY GARLIC CHICKEN

Preparation time: 30 minutes
Total cooking time: 1 hour
Serves 6
Fat per serve: 13 g

1.4 kg (2 lb 13 oz) chicken pieces
1 small bunch coriander
1 tablespoon olive oil
4 cloves garlic, crushed
2 red onions, thinly sliced
1 large red capsicum, cut into squares
1 teaspoon ground ginger
1 teaspoon chilli powder
1 teaspoon caraway seeds, crushed
1 teaspoon ground turmeric
2 teaspoons ground coriander
2 teaspoons ground cumin
$^1/_2$ cup (60 g/2 oz) raisins
$^1/_2$ cup (90 g/3 oz) black olives
1 teaspoon finely grated lemon rind

1 Remove any fat and sinew from the chicken (if you prefer, remove the skin as well). Finely chop the bunch of coriander, including the roots.
2 Heat the oil in a large heavy-based pan. Add the garlic, onion, capsicum, ginger, chilli powder, caraway seeds, turmeric, coriander, cumin and coriander roots. Cook over medium heat for 10 minutes.
3 Add the chicken pieces and stir until combined. Add 1$^1/_2$ cups (375 ml/12 fl oz) water and bring to the boil. Reduce the heat and simmer for 45 minutes, or until the chicken is tender and cooked through.
4 Add the raisins, black olives and lemon rind and simmer for a further 5 minutes before serving.

NUTRITION PER SERVE
Protein 33 g; Fat 13 g; Carbohydrate 13 g; Dietary Fibre 2 g; Cholesterol 105 mg; 1236 kJ (295 cal)

VARIATION: You can use a whole chicken for this recipe and cut it into 12 pieces yourself.

Wash the coriander and finely chop the whole bunch, including the roots.

Heat the oil in a large pan and add the garlic, onion, capsicum and spices.

Add the chicken pieces to the pan and stir until combined.

Add the raisins, olives and lemon rind to the pan and simmer for 5 minutes.

LEMON CHILLI CHICKEN

Preparation time: 20 minutes
Total cooking time: 35 minutes
Serves 4
Fat per serve: 15 g

2 cloves garlic, chopped
1 tablespoon grated fresh ginger
2 tablespoons olive oil
600 g (1¼ lb) chicken thigh fillets
1 teaspoon ground coriander
2 teaspoons ground cumin
½ teaspoon ground turmeric

1 chopped red chilli
½ cup (125 ml/4 fl oz) lemon juice
¾ cup (185 ml/6 fl oz) white wine
1 cup (30 g/1 oz) fresh coriander
  leaves

1 Blend the garlic, ginger and
1 tablespoon water into a paste in a
small food processor or mortar and
pestle. Heat the olive oil in a heavy-
based pan and brown the chicken in
batches. Remove and set aside.
2 Add the garlic paste to the pan and
cook, stirring, for 1 minute. Add the
coriander, cumin, turmeric and chilli

and stir-fry for 1 minute more. Stir in
the lemon juice and wine.
3 Add the chicken pieces to the pan.
Bring to the boil, reduce the heat,
cover and cook for 20–25 minutes,
stirring occasionally, until the chicken
is tender. Uncover and cook the sauce
over high heat for 5 minutes to reduce
it by half. Stir in the coriander and
season to taste. Serve with rice.

NUTRITION PER SERVE
Protein 30 g; Fat 15 g; Carbohydrate 0 g;
Dietary Fibre 0 g; Cholesterol 105 mg;
1290 kJ (310 cal)

Brown the chicken in batches to stop the meat
from stewing.

Add the coriander, cumin, turmeric and chilli and
stir-fry for 1 minute.

Just before serving, stir in a cupful of fresh
coriander leaves.

CHICKEN CURRIED IN SPICY TOMATO SAUCE

Preparation time: 35 minutes
Total cooking time: 1 hour 40 minutes
Serves 10
Fat per serve: 11 g

1 tablespoon oil
2 x 1.5 kg (3 lb) chickens, jointed
1 onion, sliced
1/2 teaspoon ground cloves
1 teaspoon ground turmeric
2 teaspoons garam masala
3 teaspoons chilli powder
3 cloves garlic
1 tablespoon finely chopped fresh
    ginger
1 tablespoon poppy seeds
2 teaspoons fennel seeds
3 cardamom pods, seeds removed
    (see NOTE)
1 cup (250 ml/8 fl oz) light coconut
    milk
1 star anise
1 cinnamon stick
4 large tomatoes, roughly chopped
2 tablespoons lime juice

1 Heat the oil in a large frying pan, add the chicken in batches and cook for 5–10 minutes, or until browned, then transfer to a large saucepan.
2 Add the onion to the frying pan and cook, stirring, for 10–12 minutes, or until golden. Stir in the ground cloves, turmeric, garam masala and chilli powder, and cook, stirring, for 1 minute, then add to the chicken.
3 Place the garlic, ginger, poppy seeds, fennel seeds, cardamom seeds and 2 tablespoons of the coconut milk in a food processor or blender, and process until smooth. Add the spice mixture, remaining coconut milk, star

anise, cinnamon, tomato and 1/4 cup (60 ml/2 fl oz) water to the chicken.
4 Simmer, covered, for 45 minutes, or until the chicken is tender. Remove the chicken, cover and keep warm. Bring the cooking liquid to the boil and boil for 20–25 minutes, or until reduced by half. Mix the lime juice with the cooking liquid and pour over the chicken. Serve with low-fat yoghurt

NUTRITION PER SERVE
Protein 35 g; Fat 11 g; Carbohydrate 6.5 g; Dietary Fibre 1.5 g; Cholesterol 75 mg; 1027 kJ (245 cal)

NOTE: To remove the cardamom seeds from the cardamom pods, crush the pods with the flat side of a heavy knife, then peel away the pod with your fingers, scraping out the seeds.

Crush the cardamom pods with the back of a knife and then remove the seeds.

Brown the chicken for 5–10 minutes, a few pieces at a time.

Process the garlic, spices and coconut milk until the mixture is smooth.

CHICKEN MOLE

Preparation time: 25 minutes
Total cooking time: 1 hour
Serves 4
Fat per serve: 7 g

8 chicken drumsticks
plain flour, for dusting
cooking oil spray
1 large onion, finely chopped
2 cloves garlic, finely chopped
1 teaspoon ground cumin
1 teaspoon Mexican chilli powder
2 teaspoons cocoa powder
1 cup (250 ml/8 fl oz) chicken stock

440 ml (14 fl oz) can crushed
  tomatoes
440 g (14 oz) can tomatoes, roughly
  chopped
almonds and parsley, to garnish

1 Remove and discard the chicken skin. Wipe the chicken with paper towels and lightly dust with flour. Spray a large, deep, non-stick pan with oil. Cook the chicken for 8 minutes over high heat, turning until golden brown. Remove and set aside.
2 Add the onion, garlic, cumin, chilli powder, cocoa, 1 teaspoon salt, 1/2 teaspoon black pepper and 1/4 cup (60 ml/2 fl oz) water to the pan and

cook for 5 minutes, or until softened.
3 Stir in the stock, crushed tomatoes and tomatoes. Bring to the boil, add the chicken drumsticks, cover and simmer for 45 minutes, or until tender. Uncover and simmer for 5 minutes, until the mixture is thick. Garnish with the almonds and parsley.

NUTRITION PER SERVE
Protein 25 g; Fat 7 g; Carbohydrate 10 g;
Dietary Fibre 4 g; Cholesterol 100 mg;
910 kJ (220 cal)

NOTE: This Mexican dish is usually flavoured with a special type of dark chocolate rather than cocoa powder.

Pull the skin off the chicken drumsticks, then wipe the chicken with paper towels.

Turn the chicken until brown on all sides, then remove from the pan.

Stir in the onion, garlic, cumin, chilli powder, cocoa, salt, pepper and water.

LEMON GRASS CHICKEN SKEWERS

Preparation time: 20 minutes
  + overnight marinating
Total cooking time: 20 minutes
Serves 4
Fat per serve: 2.5 g

4 chicken thigh fillets
1¹/₂ tablespoons soft brown sugar
1¹/₂ tablespoons lime juice
2 teaspoons green curry paste
18 kaffir lime leaves
2 stems lemon grass

MANGO SALSA
1 small mango, finely diced
1 teaspoon grated lime rind
2 teaspoons lime juice
1 teaspoon soft brown sugar
¹/₂ teaspoon fish sauce

1 Cut the fat from the chicken and cut the fillets in half lengthways. Combine the brown sugar, lime juice, curry paste and 2 of the kaffir lime leaves, shredded, in a bowl. Add the chicken and mix well. Cover and refrigerate overnight, or for several hours.
2 Trim the lemon grass to measure about 20 cm (8 inches), leaving the root end intact. Cut each lengthways into four pieces. Cut a slit in each of the remaining lime leaves and thread one onto each skewer. Cut two slits in the chicken and thread onto the lemon grass, followed by another lime leaf. Repeat with the remaining lime leaves, chicken and lemon grass. Pan-fry or barbecue until cooked through.
3 To make the mango salsa, put all the ingredients in a bowl and stir gently to combine. Serve with the chicken skewers.

NUTRITION PER SERVE
Protein 25 g; Fat 2.5 g; Carbohydrate 15 g;
Dietary Fibre 1 g; Cholesterol 50 mg;
710 kJ (170 cal)

Discard any fat from the chicken thighs and cut them in half lengthways.

Cut each trimmed lemon grass stem longthways into four pieces.

Thread a lime leaf, then the chicken and another lime leaf onto the lemon grass.

CHICKEN WITH BAKED EGGPLANT AND TOMATO

Preparation time: 30 minutes
Total cooking time: 1¹/₂ hours
Serves 4
Fat per serve: 4.5 g

1 red capsicum
1 eggplant
3 tomatoes, cut into quarters
200 g (6¹/₂ oz) large button
    mushrooms, halved
1 onion, cut into thin wedges
cooking oil spray
1¹/₂ tablespoons tomato paste

¹/₂ cup (125 ml/4 fl oz) chicken stock
¹/₄ cup (60 ml/2 fl oz) white wine
2 lean bacon rashers, rind removed
4 chicken breast fillets
4 small sprigs fresh rosemary

1 Preheat the oven to moderately hot 200°C (400°F/Gas 6). Cut the capsicum and eggplant into bite-sized pieces and combine with the tomato, mushrooms and onion in a baking dish. Spray with oil and bake for 1 hour, or until starting to brown and soften, stirring once.
2 Pour the combined tomato paste, stock and wine into the dish and bake for 10 minutes, or until thickened.

3 Meanwhile, cut the bacon in half. Wrap a strip around each chicken breast and secure it underneath with a toothpick. Poke a sprig of fresh rosemary underneath the bacon. Pan-fry in a lightly oiled, non-stick frying pan, over medium heat, until golden on both sides. Cover and cook for 10–15 minutes, or until the chicken is cooked through. Remove the toothpicks. Serve the chicken on the vegetables, surrounded with sauce.

NUTRITION PER SERVE
Protein 35 g; Fat 4.5 g; Carbohydrate 8 g;
Dietary Fibre 5 g; Cholesterol 70 mg;
965 kJ (230 cal)

Spray the vegetables lightly with cooking oil before baking.

When the vegetables have softened, add the tomato paste, wine and stock.

Wrap a strip of bacon around the chicken and secure underneath with a toothpick.

SPICY CHICKEN PATTIES

Preparation time: 10 minutes +
  20 minutes refrigeration
Total cooking time: 10 minutes
Serves 4
Fat per serve: 12 g

500 g (1 lb) chicken mince
4 spring onions, finely chopped
1/3 cup (20 g/3/4 oz) finely chopped
  fresh coriander leaves
2 cloves garlic, crushed
3/4 teaspoon cayenne pepper
1 egg white, lightly beaten
1 tablespoon oil
1 lemon, halved

1 Preheat the oven to warm 170°C
(325°F/Gas 2–3). Mix together all the
ingredients except the oil and lemon,
season with salt and pepper and shape
the mixture into 4 patties. Refrigerate
for 20 minutes before cooking.
2 Heat the oil in a large frying pan
over medium heat, add the patties and
cook for about 5 minutes on each side,
or until browned and cooked through.
3 Squeeze the lemon on the cooked
patties and drain well on paper towels.
Serve with a salad or use to make
burgers with crusty rolls.

NUTRITION PER SERVE
Protein 25 g; Fat 12 g; Carbohydrate 1 g;
Dietary Fibre 1 g; Cholesterol 105 mg;
895 kJ (215 cal)

Mix together all the ingredients and then shape
into patties.

Cook the patties for about 5 minutes on each
side, or until cooked through.

Squeeze the lemon over the patties and drain on
paper towels before serving.

VIETNAMESE-STYLE CHICKEN AND CABBAGE SALAD

Preparation time: 15 minutes
Total cooking time: 10 minutes
Serves 4
Fat per serve: 3 g

3 chicken breast fillets
1 red chilli, seeded, finely chopped
1/4 cup (60 ml/2 fl oz) lime juice
2 tablespoons soft brown sugar
1/4 cup (60 ml/2 fl oz) fish sauce
1/2 Chinese cabbage, shredded
2 carrots, grated
1 cup (50 g/1 1/2 oz) shredded fresh
    mint

1 Put the chicken in a saucepan, cover with water and bring to the boil, then reduce the heat and simmer for 10 minutes, or until cooked through.
2 While the chicken is cooking, mix together the chilli, lime juice, sugar and fish sauce. Remove the chicken from the water. Cool slightly, then shred into small pieces.
3 Combine the chicken, cabbage, carrot, mint and dressing. Toss well and serve immediately.

NUTRITION PER SERVE
Protein 30 g; Fat 3 g; Carbohydrate 15 g;
Dietary Fibre 3.5 g; Cholesterol 62 mg;
900 kJ (215 cal)

Poach the chicken in the simmering water until it is cooked through.

Mix together the chilli, lime juice, sugar and fish sauce to make a dressing.

Mix together the chicken, cabbage, carrot, mint and dressing and toss well.

CHICKEN WITH SNOW PEA SPROUTS

Preparation time: 15 minutes
Total cooking time: 15 minutes
Serves 4
Fat per serve: 8.5 g

1 tablespoon oil
1 onion, finely sliced
3 kaffir lime leaves, shredded
3 chicken breast fillets, cubed
1 red capsicum, sliced
1/4 cup (60 ml/2 fl oz) lime juice
100 ml (3 1/2 fl oz) soy sauce
100 g (3 1/2 oz) snow pea sprouts
2 tablespoons chopped fresh
    coriander leaves

1 Heat a wok or frying pan over medium heat, add the oil and swirl to coat. Add the onion and kaffir lime leaves and stir-fry for 3–5 minutes, or until the onion begins to soften. Add the chicken and cook for a further 4 minutes. Add the capsicum and continue to cook for 2–3 minutes.
2 Stir in the lime juice and soy sauce and cook for 1–2 minutes, or until the sauce reduces slightly. Add the sprouts and coriander and cook until the sprouts have wilted slightly. Serve with steamed jasmine rice and extra coriander and chilli, if desired.

NUTRITION PER SERVE
Protein 38 g; Fat 8.5 g; Carbohydrate 5.5 g;
Dietary Fibre 2 g; Cholesterol 76 mg;
1075 kJ (250 cal)

VARIATION: Use the chicken, soy sauce and lime juice as a base, and add vegetables and herbs to your taste. For example, try fresh asparagus, or mint and basil instead of coriander.

Stir-fry the onion, lime leaves, chicken and capsicum in the wok.

Add the snow pea sprouts and coriander and cook until the sprouts have wilted slightly.

CHICKEN AND ASPARAGUS STIR-FRY

Preparation time: 15 minutes
Total cooking time: 10 minutes
Serves 4
Fat per serve: 12 g

1 tablespoon oil
1 clove garlic, crushed
10 cm (4 inch) piece fresh ginger, peeled and thinly sliced
3 chicken breast fillets, sliced
4 spring onions, sliced
200 g (6½ oz) fresh asparagus spears, cut into short pieces
2 tablespoons soy sauce
⅓ cup (40 g/1¼ oz) slivered almonds, roasted

1 Heat a wok or large frying pan over high heat, add the oil and swirl to coat. Add the garlic, ginger and chicken and stir-fry for 1–2 minutes, or until the chicken changes colour.
2 Add the spring onion and asparagus and stir-fry for a further 2 minutes, or until the spring onion is soft.
3 Stir in the soy sauce and ¼ cup (60 ml/2 fl oz) water, cover and simmer for 2 minutes, or until the chicken is tender and the vegetables are slightly crisp. Sprinkle with the almonds and serve over steamed rice.

NUTRITION PER SERVE
Protein 22 g; Fat 12 g; Carbohydrate 2 g; Dietary Fibre 2 g; Cholesterol 39 mg; 855 kJ (204 cal)

Stir-fry the garlic, ginger and chicken until the chicken changes colour.

Add the spring onion and asparagus and stir-fry until the spring onion is soft.

Stir in the soy sauce and water, cover and simmer for a couple of minutes.

PEPPERED CHICKEN STIR-FRY

Preparation time: 10 minutes
Total cooking time: 10 minutes
Serves 4
Fat per serve: 6.5 g

1 tablespoon oil
2 chicken breast fillets, cut into strips
2¹/₂ teaspoons seasoned
    peppercorns (see NOTE)
1 onion, cut into wedges
1 red capsicum, cut into strips
2 tablespoons oyster sauce
1 teaspoon soy sauce
1 teaspoon sugar

1 Heat a wok or frying pan over high heat, add the oil and swirl to coat. Add the chicken strips and stir-fry for 2–3 minutes, or until browned.
2 Add the peppercorns and stir-fry until fragrant. Add the onion and capsicum and stir-fry for 2 minutes, or until the vegetables have just softened slightly.
3 Reduce the heat and stir in the oyster sauce, soy and sugar. Serve hot with steamed rice.

NUTRITION PER SERVE
Protein 18 g; Fat 6.5 g; Carbohydrate 6 g; Dietary Fibre 1 g; Cholesterol 40 mg; 665 kJ (160 cal)

NOTE: Seasoned peppercorns are available in the herb and spice section of supermarkets.

Stir-fry the chicken strips for 2–3 minutes, or until they are browned.

Add the onion and capsicum and stir-fry until they soften slightly.

Reduce the heat and stir in the oyster sauce, soy sauce and sugar.

CHILLI CHICKEN STIR-FRY

Preparation time: 10 minutes
Total cooking time: 10 minutes
Serves 6
Fat per serve: 6.5 g

375 g (12 oz) Hokkien noodles
4 chicken thigh fillets,
    cut into small pieces (see NOTE)
1–2 tablespoons sweet chilli sauce
2 teaspoons fish sauce
1 tablespoon oil
100 g (3¹/₂ oz) baby sweet corn,
    halved lengthways
150 g (5 oz) sugar snap peas, topped
    and tailed
1 tablespoon lime juice

1 Place the noodles in a large bowl, cover with boiling water and gently break apart with a fork. Leave for 5 minutes, then drain.
2 Combine the chicken, sweet chilli sauce and fish sauce in a bowl.
3 Heat a wok or frying pan over high heat, add the oil and swirl to coat. Add the chicken pieces and stir-fry for 3–5 minutes, or until cooked through. Then add the corn and sugar snap peas and stir-fry for 2 minutes. Add the noodles and lime juice and serve.

NUTRITION PER SERVE
Protein 30 g; Fat 6.5 g; Carbohydrate 50 g; Dietary Fibre 4 g; Cholesterol 53 mg; 1593 kJ (380 cal)

NOTE: If thigh fillets are unavailable, use 3 breast fillets.

Cover the noodles with boiling water and then separate them gently with a fork.

Combine the chicken, sweet chilli sauce and fish sauce in a bowl.

Add the noodles and lime juice to the wok at the last minute before serving.

SMOKED CHICKEN AND SPINACH STIR-FRY

Preparation time: 10 minutes
Total cooking time: 10 minutes
Serves 4
Fat per serve: 13 g

300 g (10 oz) smoked chicken breast
    (see NOTE)
1 tablespoon olive oil
100 g (3¹/₂ oz) marinated chargrilled
    capsicum, cut into thin strips
¹/₃ cup (50 g/1¹/₂ oz) pine nuts
1 bunch (500 g/1 lb) English spinach,
    trimmed
1 tablespoon light sour cream
2 teaspoons wholegrain mustard
¹/₄ cup (7 g/¹/₄ oz) fresh basil leaves,
    finely shredded

1 Cut the chicken into thin strips.
2 Heat a wok or frying pan over high
heat, add the oil and swirl to coat the
base and side. Add the chicken,
capsicum and pine nuts and stir-fry for
3–4 minutes, or until the nuts are
golden. Add the spinach and stir-fry
for 2–3 minutes, or until wilted.
3 Stir through the sour cream,
mustard and basil. Season and serve
with noodles or rice.

NUTRITION PER SERVE
Protein 22 g; Fat 13 g; Carbohydrate 2.5 g;
Dietary Fibre 4.5 g; Cholesterol 45 mg;
900 kJ (215 cal)

NOTE: Smoked chicken breast and
marinated chargrilled capsicum are
available at speciality delicatessens.

Cut the smoked chicken breast into thin strips for
quick and even stir-frying.

Cook the chicken, capsicum and pine nuts until
the nuts are golden.

Stir in the sour cream, mustard and basil at the
end of the cooking time.

CHICKEN MEATBALLS

Preparation time: 15 minutes
Total cooking time: 30 minutes
Serves 6
Fat per serve: 8.5 g

500 g (1 lb) chicken mince
3 tablespoons fresh breadcrumbs
2 teaspoons finely chopped fresh
    thyme
1 tablespoon oil
1 onion, finely chopped
2 x 425 g (14 oz) cans diced tomatoes
2 teaspoons balsamic vinegar
1 cup (250 ml/8 fl oz) chicken stock
grated Parmesan, to serve

1 Combine the chicken mince, breadcrumbs and thyme in a large bowl and season well. Roll tablespoons of the mixture between your hands to make meatballs.
2 Heat the oil in a large non-stick frying pan and cook the meatballs in batches for 5–8 minutes, or until golden brown. Remove from the pan and drain well on paper towels.
3 Add the onion to the pan and cook for 2–3 minutes, or until softened. Add the tomato, vinegar and stock, return the meatballs to the pan, then reduce the heat and simmer for 10 minutes, or until the sauce thickens and the meatballs are cooked through. Serve with pasta and a little Parmesan.

NUTRITION PER SERVE
Protein 20 g; Fat 8.5 g; Carbohydrate 7.5 g;
Dietary Fibre 2 g; Cholesterol 42 mg;
812 kJ (194 cal)

Roll tablespoonfuls of the mixture between your hands to make meatballs.

Fry the meatballs in batches until golden brown, then drain well on paper towels.

Return the meatballs to the pan and simmer in the tomato sauce for 10 minutes.

CHICKEN WITH TOMATO AND MANGO CHUTNEY

Preparation time: 10 minutes +
  2 hours marinating
Total cooking time: 45 minutes
Serves 4
Fat per serve: 15 g

8 chicken drumsticks, scored
1 tablespoon mustard powder
2 tablespoons tomato sauce
1 tablespoon sweet mango chutney
1 teaspoon Worcestershire sauce
1 tablespoon Dijon mustard
1/4 cup (30 g/1 oz) raisins
1 tablespoon oil

1 Preheat the oven to moderately hot 200°C (400°F/Gas 6). Toss the chicken in the mustard powder and season.
2 Combine the tomato sauce, chutney, Worcestershire sauce, mustard, raisins and oil. Spoon over the chicken and toss well to coat evenly. Marinate for 2 hours, or overnight, turning once.
3 Put the chicken in a shallow baking tray and bake for 45 minutes, or until the meat comes away from the bone.

NUTRITION PER SERVE
Protein 25 g; Fat 15 g; Carbohydrate 3.5 g; Dietary Fibre 0.5 g; Cholesterol 103 mg; 1005 kJ (240 cal)

SERVING SUGGESTION: Serve with toasted Turkish bread and a mixture of yoghurt, cucumber and mint.

The cleanest way to toss the chicken in mustard powder is to put them in a plastic bag.

Marinate the chicken for at least 2 hours, turning it over once.

Bake the chicken for 45 minutes, or until the meat is coming away from the bone.

CHARGRILLED CHICKEN

Preparation time: 20 minutes +
  2 hours refrigeration
Total cooking time: 50 minutes
Serves 4
Fat per serve: 2.5 g

4 chicken breast fillets
2 tablespoons honey
1 tablespoon wholegrain mustard
1 tablespoon soy sauce
2 red onions, cut into wedges
8 Roma tomatoes, halved lengthways

2 tablespoons soft brown sugar
2 tablespoons balsamic vinegar
cooking oil spray
snow pea sprouts, for serving

1 Preheat the oven to moderate 180°C (350°F/Gas 4). Trim the chicken of any fat and place in a shallow dish. Combine the honey, mustard and soy sauce and pour over the chicken, tossing to coat. Cover and refrigerate for 2 hours, turning once.
2 Place the onion wedges and tomato halves on a baking tray covered with baking paper. Sprinkle with the sugar

and drizzle with the balsamic vinegar. Bake for 40 minutes.
3 Heat a chargrill pan and lightly spray with oil. Remove the chicken from the marinade and cook for 4–5 minutes on each side, or until cooked through. Slice and serve with the snow pea sprouts, tomato halves and onion wedges.

NUTRITION PER SERVE
Protein 25 g; Fat 2.5 g; Carbohydrate 30 g; Dietary Fibre 3 g; Cholesterol 50 mg; 990 kJ (235 cal)

Pour the marinade over the chicken and toss to coat thoroughly.

Drizzle the balsamic vinegar over the onion and tomato in the baking tray.

Cook the marinated chicken in a hot, lightly oiled chargrill pan.

GRILLED CHICKEN SKEWERS

Preparation time: 20 minutes +
  2 hours marinating
Total cooking time: 10 minutes
Serves 4
Fat per serve: 8 g

32 chicken tenderloins
24 (180 g/6 oz) cherry tomatoes
6 cap mushrooms, cut into quarters
2 cloves garlic, crushed
rind of 1 lemon, grated

2 tablespoons lemon juice
1 tablespoon olive oil
1 tablespoon fresh oregano leaves,
  chopped

1 Soak 8 wooden skewers for at least 30 minutes to prevent burning. Thread a piece of chicken onto each skewer, followed by a tomato, then a piece of mushroom. Repeat three times for each skewer.
2 Combine the garlic, lemon rind, lemon juice, olive oil and chopped oregano, pour over the skewers and toss well. Marinate for at least 2 hours.

3 Place the skewers on a grill plate and cook under high heat for 5 minutes each side, basting while cooking, or until the chicken is cooked and the tomatoes have shrivelled slightly. Serve hot with a green salad.

NUTRITION PER SERVE
Protein 34 g; Fat 8 g; Carbohydrate 1 g;
Dietary Fibre 1 g; Cholesterol 75 mg;
909 kJ (217 cal)

NOTE: The skewers can be made in advance and marinated for up to a day before cooking.

Thread the chicken, tomato and mushrooms onto the skewers.

Leave the skewers in the marinade for at least 2 hours and overnight if possible.

Grill the skewers, basting with the marinade as they cook.

CHICKEN PIES

Preparation time: 50 minutes
 + 30 minutes refrigeration
Total cooking time: 1 hour
Serves 4
Fat per serve: 10 g

300 g (10 oz) chicken breast fillet
1 bay leaf
2 cups (500 ml/16 oz) chicken stock
2 large potatoes, chopped
250 g (8 oz) orange sweet potato,
    chopped
2 celery sticks, chopped
2 carrots, chopped
1 onion, chopped
1 parsnip, chopped
1 clove garlic, crushed
1 tablespoon cornflour
1 cup (250 ml/8 fl oz) skim milk
1 cup (155 g/5 oz) frozen peas,
    thawed
1 tablespoon chopped fresh chives
1 tablespoon chopped fresh parsley
1 1/2 cups (185 g/6 oz) self-raising flour
20 g (3/4 oz) butter
1/3 cup (80 ml/2 3/4 fl oz) milk
1 egg, lightly beaten
1/2 teaspoon sesame seeds

1 Combine the chicken, bay leaf and
stock in a large, deep non-stick frying
pan and simmer over low heat for
about 10 minutes until the chicken is
cooked through. Remove the chicken,
set aside and, when cool, cut into
small pieces. Add the chopped potato,
orange sweet potato, celery and carrot
to the pan and simmer, covered, for
about 10 minutes, until just tender.
Remove the vegetables from the pan
with a slotted spoon.
2 Add the onion, parsnip and garlic to
the pan and simmer, uncovered, for

about 10 minutes, until very soft.
Discard the bay leaf. Purée in a food
processor until smooth.
3 Stir the cornflour into 2 tablespoons
of the skim milk until it forms a
smooth paste, stir into the puréed
mixture with the remaining milk and
then return to the pan. Stir over low
heat until the mixture boils and
thickens. Preheat the oven to
moderately hot 200°C (400°F/Gas 6).
4 Combine the puréed mixture with
the remaining vegetables, chicken and
herbs. Season with salt and pepper.
Spoon into four 1 3/4 cup (440 ml/
14 fl oz) capacity ovenproof dishes.
5 To make the pastry, sift the flour
into a large bowl, rub in the butter
with your fingertips, then make a well
in the centre. Combine the milk with
1/3 cup (80 ml/2 3/4 fl oz) water and
add enough to the dry ingredients to
make a soft dough. Turn out onto a
lightly floured surface and knead until
just smooth. Cut the dough into four
portions and roll each out so that it is
l cm (1/2 inch) larger than the top of
the dish. Brush the edge of the dough
with some of the egg and fit over the
top of each dish, pressing the edge
firmly to seal.
6 Brush the pastry tops lightly
with beaten egg and sprinkle with
the sesame seeds. Bake for about
30 minutes, until the tops are golden
and the filling is heated through.

NUTRITION PER SERVE
Protein 30 g; Fat 10 g; Carbohydrate 65 g;
Dietary Fibre 9.5 g; Cholesterol 100 mg;
2045 kJ (490 cal)

Cut the vegetables into even-sized pieces so that
they cook at the same rate.

Simmer the chicken and bay leaf in the stock until
the chicken is cooked through.

Purée the cooked onion, parsnip and garlic
together until smooth.

Stir the sauce constantly until the mixture boils and thickens.

Add enough liquid to the dry ingredients to make a soft dough.

Brush the edge of the dough with egg, then press over the top of each dish.

ASIAN BARBECUED CHICKEN

Preparation time: 10 minutes +
  2 hours marinating
Total cooking time: 25 minutes
Serves 6
Fat per serve: 8.5 g

2 cloves garlic, finely chopped
1/4 cup (60 ml/2 fl oz) hoisin sauce
3 teaspoons light soy sauce
3 teaspoons honey
1 teaspoon sesame oil
2 tablespoons tomato sauce
    or sweet chilli sauce
2 spring onions, finely sliced
1.5 kg (3 lb) chicken wings

1 To make the marinade, combine the garlic, hoisin sauce, soy, honey, sesame oil, tomato sauce and spring onion in a small bowl.
2 Pour over the chicken wings, cover and marinate in the refrigerator for at least 2 hours.
3 Place the chicken on a barbecue or chargrill and cook, in batches, turning once, for 20–25 minutes, or until cooked and golden brown. Baste with the marinade during cooking. Heat any remaining marinade in a pan until boiling and serve as a sauce.

NUTRITION PER SERVE
Protein 26 g; Fat 8.5 g; Carbohydrate 9 g;
Dietary Fibre 1.5 g; Cholesterol 111 mg;
916 kJ (219 cal)

NOTE: The chicken can also be baked in a moderate 180°C (350°F/Gas 4) oven for 30 minutes (turn once).

Mix together the garlic, hoisin, soy, honey, sesame oil, tomato sauce and spring onion.

Pour the marinade over the chicken wings and marinate in the fridge.

Cook the chicken wings in batches on a barbecue, or bake in the oven.

CHICKEN PROVENCALE

Preparation time: 15 minutes
Total cooking time: 1 hour 20 minutes
Serves 6
Fat per serve: 10 g

1 tablespoon olive oil
1.5 kg (3 lb) chicken pieces
1 onion, chopped
1 red capsicum, chopped
1/3 cup (80 ml/2¾ fl oz) white wine
1/3 cup (80 ml/2¾ fl oz) chicken stock
425 g (14 oz) can chopped tomatoes
2 tablespoons tomato paste
1/2 cup (90 g/3 oz) black olives
4 tablespoons shredded fresh basil

1 Heat the oil in a saucepan over high heat, add the chicken, in batches, and cook for 3–4 minutes, or until browned. Return all the chicken to the pan and add the onion and capsicum. Cook for 2–3 minutes, or until the onion is soft.

2 Add the wine, stock, tomatoes, tomato paste and olives and bring to the boil. Reduce the heat, cover and simmer for 30 minutes. Remove the lid, turn the chicken pieces over and cook for another 30 minutes, or until the chicken is tender and the sauce thickened. Season to taste, sprinkle with the basil and serve with rice.

NUTRITION PER SERVE
Protein 35 g; Fat 10 g; Carbohydrate 5 g; Dietary Fibre 2 g; Cholesterol 115 mg; 1133 kJ (270 cal)

Once the chicken is browned, return it all to the pan with the onion and capsicum.

Just before serving, season and sprinkle with the shredded basil.

BAKED CHICKEN AND LEEK RISOTTO

Preparation time: 10 minutes
Total cooking time: 40 minutes
Serves 6
Fat per serve: 15 g

1 tablespoon oil
1 leek, thinly sliced
2 chicken breast fillets, cubed
2 cups (440 g/14 oz) arborio rice
1/4 cup (60 ml/2 fl oz) white wine
5 cups (1.25) litres chicken stock
1/3 cup (30 g/1 oz) grated Parmesan
2 tablespoons fresh thyme leaves
fresh thyme leaves and Parmesan, for
    serving

1 Preheat the oven to slow 150°C (300°F/Gas 2) and place a 5 litre ovenproof dish with a lid in the oven to warm. Heat the oil in a saucepan over medium heat, add the leek and cook for 2 minutes, or until soft.
2 Add the chicken and cook, stirring, for 2–3 minutes, or until it colours. Add the rice and stir so that it is well coated. Cook for 1 minute.
3 Add the wine and stock and bring to the boil. Pour the mixture into the warm ovenproof dish and cover. Place in the oven and cook for 30 minutes, stirring halfway through. Remove from the oven and stir through the Parmesan and thyme leaves. Season to taste. Sprinkle with extra thyme leaves and a little Parmesan and serve.

NUTRITION PER SERVE
Protein 28 g; Fat 15 g; Carbohydrate 60 g;
Dietary Fibre 3 g; Cholesterol 75 mg;
2014 kJ (480 cal)

Cook the leek for a couple of minutes over medium heat until it is soft.

Add the arborio rice to the pan and stir until it is well coated.

Cook the risotto in the oven for 30 minutes, then remove and stir in the Parmesan and thyme.

CHILLI CON POLLO

Preparation time: 10 minutes
Total cooking time: 45 minutes
Serves 4
Fat per serve: 8.5 g

1 tablespoon olive oil
1 onion, finely chopped
500 g (1 lb) chicken mince
1–2 teaspoons mild chilli powder
440 g (14 oz) can chopped tomatoes
2 tablespoons tomato paste
1–2 teaspoons soft brown sugar
425 g (13 oz) can red kidney beans,
    rinsed and drained

1 Heat the oil in a large saucepan.
Add the onion and cook over medium
heat for 3 minutes, or until soft.
Increase the heat and add the chicken.
Cook until browned, breaking up any
lumps with a wooden spoon.
2 Add the chilli powder and cook for
1 minute. Add the tomato, tomato
paste and 1/2 cup (125 ml/4 fl oz)
water and stir well.
3 Bring to the boil, then reduce the
heat and simmer for 30 minutes. Stir
through the sugar to taste and the
kidney beans and heat through.
Season and serve with baked corn
chips and low-fat natural yoghurt.

NUTRITION PER SERVE
Protein 37 g; Fat 8.5 g; Carbohydrate 20 g;
Dietary Fibre 9 g; Cholesterol 60 mg;
1305 kJ (312 cal)

Cook the mince until it has browned, breaking up
any lumps with a wooden spoon.

Add the tomato, tomato paste and water and stir
well to combine.

Simmer for 30 minutes, then stir in the kidney
beans and heat through.

CHICKEN MEATLOAF

Preparation time: 15 minutes
Total cooking time: 1 hour 15 minutes
Serves 6
Fat per serve: 6 g

1 kg (2 lb) chicken mince
1 onion, grated
1 cup (90 g/3 oz) fresh white
    breadcrumbs (made from 2 slices
    of day-old bread)
2 eggs, lightly beaten

1/3 cup (80 ml/2 3/4 fl oz) barbecue
    sauce
2 tablespoons Worcestershire sauce
1/4 cup (60 ml/2 fl oz) canned crushed
    tomatoes
2 tablespoons finely chopped fresh
    flat-leaf parsley

1 Preheat the oven to moderate
180°C (350°F/Gas 4). Mix together
the mince, onion, breadcrumbs,
egg, 2 tablespoons barbecue sauce,
Worcestershire sauce, crushed
tomatoes, parsley, salt and pepper.

2 Press into a lightly greased 1.5 litre
loaf tin. Place on an oven tray to catch
any spills and bake for 1 hour.
3 Pour off any fat from the tin. Spread
the remaining barbecue sauce over the
top of the meatloaf and bake for a
further 15 minutes. Turn out the
meatloaf and serve in slices.

NUTRITION PER SERVE
Protein 40 g; Fat 6 g; Carbohydrate 15 g;
Dietary Fibre 1 g; Cholesterol 145 mg;
1175 kJ (280 cal)

Mix together all the ingredients with your hands
until they are well combined.

Press the mixture into a lightly greased loaf tin
and bake for 1 hour.

Pour off any fat from the meatloaf and spread the
remaining barbecue sauce over the top.

CHINESE BRAISED CHICKEN

Preparation time: 10 minutes
Total cooking time: 1 hour
Serves 6
Fat per serve: 10 g

1 cup (250 ml/8 fl oz) soy sauce
1 cinnamon stick
1/3 cup (90 g/3 oz) sugar
1/3 cup (80 ml/2³/4 fl oz) balsamic
   vinegar
2.5 cm (1 inch) piece fresh ginger,
   thinly sliced
4 garlic cloves
1/4 teaspoon chilli flakes
1.5 kg (3 lb) chicken pieces on the
   bone (skin removed)
1 tablespoon toasted sesame seeds,
   to garnish

1 Combine 1 litre water with the soy sauce, cinnamon, sugar, vinegar, ginger, garlic and chilli flakes in a saucepan. Bring to the boil, then reduce the heat and simmer for 5 minutes.
2 Add the chicken and simmer, covered, for 50 minutes, or until cooked through. Serve on a bed of steamed greens and sprinkle with toasted sesame seeds.

NUTRITION PER SERVE
Protein 45 g; Fat 10 g; Carbohydrate 16 g;
Dietary Fibre 0.5 g; Cholesterol 140 mg;
1420 kJ (339 cal)

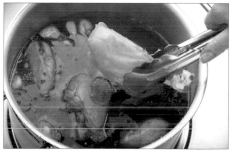

Poach the chicken in the Chinese-flavoured liquid until it is cooked through.

CHICKEN CHASSEUR

Preparation time: 20 minutes
Total cooking time: 1 hour 30 minutes
Serves 4
Fat per serve: 12 g

1 kg (2 lb) chicken thigh fillets
1 tablespoon oil
1 clove garlic, crushed
1 large onion, sliced
100 g (3½ oz) button mushrooms, sliced
1 teaspoon thyme leaves

400 g (13 oz) can chopped tomatoes
¼ cup (60 ml/2 fl oz) chicken stock
¼ cup (60 ml/2 fl oz) white wine
1 tablespoon tomato paste

1 Preheat the oven to moderate 180°C (350°F/Gas 4). Trim the chicken of any fat and sinew. Heat the oil in a heavy-based frying pan and brown the chicken in batches over medium heat. Drain on paper towels and then transfer to a casserole dish.
2 Add the garlic, onion and mushrooms to the pan and cook over medium heat for 5 minutes, or until

soft. Add to the chicken with the thyme and tomatoes.
3 Combine the stock, wine and tomato paste and pour over the chicken. Cover and bake for 1¼ hours, or until the chicken is tender and cooked through.

NUTRITION PER SERVE
Protein 60 g; Fat 12 g; Carbohydrate 6 g; Dietary Fibre 2 g; Cholesterol 125 mg; 1710 kJ (410 cal)

STORAGE TIME: Best cooked a day in advance to let the flavours develop.

Brown the chicken in the hot oil over medium heat and drain on paper towels.

Add the garlic, onion and mushrooms to the pan and cook until soft.

Pour the combined stock, wine and tomato paste over the chicken mixture.

CHICKEN CACCIATORE

Preparation time: 20 minutes
Total cooking time: 1 hour 15 minutes
Serves 6
Fat per serve: 10 g

1 tablespoon olive oil
1 kg (2 lb) chicken pieces
2 tablespoons plain flour
1 large onion, finely chopped
2 cloves garlic, chopped
2 x 425 g (13 oz) cans tomatoes
2 cups (500 ml/16 fl oz) chicken stock
1/2 cup (125 ml/4 fl oz) white wine

2 tablespoons tomato paste
1 teaspoon caster sugar
3 tablespoons black olives
2 tablespoons chopped fresh basil
2 tablespoons chopped fresh parsley

1 Heat the oil in a large heavy-based pan. Brown the chicken in batches over medium heat. Remove from the pan and sprinkle with flour.
2 Add the onion and garlic to the pan and cook for 10 minutes over low heat, stirring occasionally. Add the tomatoes and their juice, the chicken stock and wine. Bring to the boil and then reduce the heat and simmer for

15 minutes. Add the tomato paste, sugar and chicken and stir well.
3 Cover and simmer for 30 minutes over low heat. Add the olives and herbs, season and simmer for a further 15 minutes, stirring occasionally.

NUTRITION PER SERVE
Protein 30 g; Fat 10 g; Carbohydrate 10 g;
Dietary Fibre 3 g; Cholesterol 90 mg;
1100 kJ (265 cal)

VARIATION: It is traditional to add a few chopped anchovy fillets just before serving.

Remove the browned chicken from the pan and sprinkle with flour.

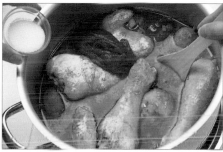

Add the chicken pieces, tomato paste and sugar to the pan.

Stir in the olives, basil and parsley and taste to check the seasoning.

ORANGE AND ROSEMARY GLAZED CHICKEN

Preparation time: 10 minutes +
 4 hours marinating
Total cooking time: 50 minutes
Serves 6
Fat per serve: 8.5 g

2 seedless oranges
1/2 cup (185 g/6 oz) honey
2 tablespoons Dijon mustard
1 1/2 tablespoons chopped fresh
 rosemary
4 cloves garlic, crushed
1.5 kg (3 lb) chicken pieces

1 Squeeze the juice from one orange into a bowl, add the honey, Dijon mustard, rosemary and garlic and mix together well. Cut the other orange in half and then cut it into slices.
2 Add the chicken and orange slices to the orange juice mixture. Season and mix well and leave to marinate for at least 4 hours. Preheat the oven to moderately hot 200°C (400°F/Gas 6). Line a large baking tray with foil. Arrange the chicken and the marinade in the baking tray.
3 Bake for 40–50 minutes, or until the chicken is golden, turning once and basting with the marinade.

NUTRITION PER SERVE
Protein 40 g; Fat 8.5 g; Carbohydrate 27 g;
Dietary Fibre 1 g; Cholesterol 138 mg;
1470 kJ (350 cal)

Mix together the orange juice, honey, Dijon mustard, rosemary and garlic.

Arrange the chicken and marinade in the large baking tray lined with foil.

Bake the chicken until it is golden, turning once and basting with the marinade.

COQ AU VIN

Preparation time: 15 minutes
Total cooking time: 1 hour 40 minutes
Serves 6
Fat per serve: 11 g

1 tablespoon olive oil
125 g (4 oz) bacon, rind removed,
   roughly chopped
1.5 kg (3 lb) skinless chicken pieces
350 g (12 oz) baby onions (use bulb or
   pickling onions)
2 tablespoons plain flour
3 cups (750 ml/24 fl oz) red wine
250 g (8 oz) field mushrooms, sliced
1 tablespoon fresh thyme leaves, to
   garnish

1 Preheat the oven to moderate 180°C
(350°F/Gas 4). Heat the oil in a large
ovenproof casserole dish. Add the
bacon and cook until golden, then
remove. Add the chicken and cook, in
batches, for 4–5 minutes, or until
browned. Remove. Add the onions
and cook for 2–3 minutes, or until
browned, then remove from the pan.
2 Add the flour to the pan and stir
well, remove from the heat and slowly
stir in the red wine. Return to the heat,
bring to the boil and return the bacon
and chicken to the pan. Cover and
cook in the oven for 1 hour. Return the
onions to the pan and add the
mushrooms. Cook for a further
30 minutes. Season to taste and
garnish with the thyme. Serve with
crusty bread or pasta.

NUTRITION PER SERVE
Protein 65 g; Fat 11 g; Carbohydrate 11 g;
Dietary Fibre 2 g; Cholesterol 150 mg;
2040 kJ (487 cal)

Cook the onions for a couple of minutes, or until
they are browned.

Bring the red wine to the boil, then return the
chicken and bacon to the pan.

LIME STEAMED CHICKEN

Preparation time: 15 minutes
Total cooking time: 15 minutes
Serves 4
Fat per serve: 12 g

2 limes, thinly sliced
4 chicken breast fillets
1 bunch (500 g/1 lb) bok choy
1 bunch (500 g/1 lb) choy sum
1 teaspoon sesame oil
1 tablespoon peanut oil
1/2 cup (125 ml/4 fl oz) oyster sauce
1/3 cup (80 ml/2³/4 fl oz) lime juice

1 Line the base of a bamboo steamer with the lime, place the chicken on top and season. Place over a wok with a little water in the base, cover and steam for 8–10 minutes, or until the chicken is cooked through. Cover the chicken and keep warm. Remove the water from the wok.
2 Wash and trim the greens. Heat the oils in the wok and cook the greens for 2–3 minutes, or until just wilted.
3 Combine the oyster sauce and lime juice and pour over the greens when they are cooked. Place the chicken on serving plates on top of the greens and serve with rice and lime slices.

NUTRITION PER SERVE
Protein 60 g; Fat 12 g; Carbohydrate 10 g; Dietary Fibre 4.5 g; Cholesterol 120 mg; 1665 kJ (398 cal)

NOTE: The Asian green vegetables used in this recipe, bok choy and choy sum, can be replaced by any green vegetables, such as broccoli, snow peas, or English spinach.

Lay the lime slices in the bamboo steamer, put the chicken on top and steam until cooked.

Heat the oils in the wok and stir-fry the greens until they are wilted.

Mix together the oyster sauce and lime juice and pour over the cooked greens.

TANDOORI CHICKEN

Preparation time: 10 minutes +
1 hour marinating
Total cooking time: 15 minutes
Serves 4
Fat per serve: 3.5 g

¹/₂ cup (125 g/4 oz) Greek-style
low-fat natural yoghurt
2 tablespoons tandoori paste
2 cloves garlic, crushed
2 tablespoons lime juice
1¹/₂ teaspoons garam masala
2 tablespoons finely chopped fresh
coriander leaves
6 chicken thigh fillets, fat removed

1 Combine the yoghurt, tandoori paste, garlic, lime juice, garam masala and coriander in a bowl and mix well.
2 Add the chicken, coat well, cover and refrigerate for at least 1 hour.
3 Preheat a barbecue or chargrill plate and lightly brush with oil. Cook the chicken, in batches if necessary, for 10–15 minutes on medium heat, turning once and basting with the remaining marinade until golden and cooked through. Serve with cucumber raita and naan bread.

NUTRITION PER SERVE
Protein 27 g; Fat 3.5 g; Carbohydrate 2 g;
Dietary Fibre 0 g; Cholesterol 60 mg;
635 kJ (150 cal)

Mix together the yoghurt, tandoori paste, garlic, lime juice, garam masala and coriander.

Add the chicken, coating well, and leave in the marinade for at least one hour.

Cook the chicken on a barbecue, turning once and basting with the remaining marinade.

CHICKEN WITH CORIANDER CHUTNEY AND SPICED EGGPLANT

Preparation time: 1 hour 10 minutes
+ overnight refrigeration +
30 minutes soaking
Total cooking time: 1 hour 10 minutes
Serves 4
Fat per serve: 15 g

1 cup (250 g/8 oz) low-fat natural
  yoghurt
1 tablespoon lemon juice
1/2 onion, roughly chopped
2 cloves garlic, finely chopped
2 teaspoons grated fresh ginger
1/2 teaspoon ground cumin
750 g (1 1/2 lb) chicken thighs, trimmed
  of fat, cut into large cubes
4 pieces naan bread
low-fat natural yoghurt, to serve

SPICED EGGPLANT
1 large eggplant
1 tablespoon oil
1 onion, finely chopped
3 teaspoons finely chopped fresh
  ginger
2 cloves garlic, crushed
1/2 teaspoon ground turmeric
1 teaspoon ground cumin
1 tomato, finely diced
2 teaspoons lemon juice

CORIANDER CHUTNEY
1/4 cup (60 ml/2 fl oz) lemon juice
2 cups (100 g/3 1/2 oz) roughly
  chopped fresh coriander leaves
  and stems
1/2 onion, finely chopped
1 tablespoon finely chopped fresh
  ginger
1/2 jalapeño pepper, seeded, diced
1 teaspoon sugar

1 Combine the yoghurt, lemon juice, onion, garlic, ginger and cumin in a large non-metallic bowl, add the chicken and toss. Cover and refrigerate overnight.

2 Preheat the oven to very hot 240°C (475°F/Gas 9). Soak eight wooden skewers in water for 30 minutes. To make the spiced eggplant, prick the eggplant a few times, put on a baking tray and bake for 35–40 minutes, or until soft and wrinkled. Cool. Reduce the oven to moderately hot 200°C (400°F/Gas 6).

3 To make the chutney, put the lemon juice, coriander and 3 tablespoons water in a food processor and process until smooth. Add the remaining ingredients and season.

4 Cut the eggplant in half, scoop out the flesh and coarsely chop. Heat the oil in a frying pan over medium heat. Add the onion and cook for 5 minutes, or until soft. Add the ginger and garlic and cook for 2 minutes, or until fragrant. Add the spices and cook for 1 minute, then add the tomato and 1/4 cup (60 ml/2 fl oz) water and simmer for 5 minutes, or until the tomato is soft and the mixture thick. Stir in the eggplant and lemon juice and season. Cook for 2 minutes, then remove from the heat and keep warm.

5 Thread the chicken onto skewers and chargrill over medium heat for 4–6 minutes each side, or until tender.

6 Heat the naan in the oven for 5 minutes. Put on a plate and spread some eggplant in the centre. Lay 2 chicken skewers on top and drizzle with chutney and yoghurt.

NUTRITION PER SERVE
Protein 50 g; Fat 15 g; Carbohydrate 26 g; Dietary Fibre 5.5 g; Cholesterol 105 mg; 1956 kJ (467 cal)

Combine the marinade ingredients in a bowl and add the chicken.

Roast the eggplant on a baking tray until very soft and wrinkled.

Process the coriander, lemon juice and water until you have a smooth paste.

Cut the eggplant in half, scoop out the flesh and coarsely chop.

Simmer until the tomato has softened and the mixture has thickened.

Chargrill the chicken skewers until they are tender and cooked through.

CHICKEN WITH BLACK BEAN SAUCE

Preparation time: 10 minutes
Total cooking time: 10 minutes
Serves 4
Fat per serve: 3.5 g

2 tablespoons salted black beans
1 tablespoon oil
1 small onion, finely chopped
1 tablespoon finely chopped fresh
    ginger
1 clove garlic, finely chopped
1 red chilli, seeded and finely chopped
1¼ cups (315 ml/10 fl oz) chicken
    stock
2 teaspoons cornflour
2 teaspoons sesame oil
4 chicken breast fillets

1 Rinse the black beans under cold water for 3–4 minutes to remove any excess saltiness. Drain well.
2 Heat the oil in a small pan and add the onion, ginger, garlic and chilli. Cook over low heat until the onion is soft but not browned. Add the chicken stock and bring to the boil. Reduce the heat and simmer for 5 minutes.
3 Mix the cornflour and 1 tablespoon of water in a small bowl and add to the pan. Keep stirring and the mixture will thicken. Allow to simmer for 3 minutes, then add the beans and sesame oil and mix together well.
4 Grill the chicken under a preheated grill for 5 minutes on each side, or until cooked through and tender. Serve with the sauce.

NUTRITION PER SERVE
Protein 26 g; Fat 3.5 g; Carbohydrate 2 g; Dietary Fibre 0 g; Cholesterol 55 mg; 580 kJ (140 cal)

NOTE: Black beans are available canned or in vacuum packs from Asian food stores. Do not confuse these Chinese black beans with Mexican black turtle beans that are available from health food shops. The two varieties are very different.

Rinse the black beans under running water to get rid of excess saltiness.

Cook until the onion is soft but not browned, then add the stock.

Simmer the sauce for 3 minutes, then stir in the beans and sesame oil.

STEAMED LEMON GRASS AND GINGER CHICKEN WITH ASIAN GREENS

Preparation time: 25 minutes
Total cooking time: 40 minutes
Serves 4
Fat per serve: 7.5 g

200 g (6½ oz) fresh egg noodles
4 chicken breast fillets
2 stems lemon grass
5 cm (2 inch) piece fresh ginger, cut
    into julienne strips
1 lime, thinly sliced
2 cups (500 ml/16 fl oz) chicken stock
1 bunch (350 g/12 oz) choy sum,
    cut into 10 cm (4 inch) lengths
800 g (1 lb 10 oz) Chinese broccoli,
    cut into 10 cm (4 inch) lengths
3 tablespoons kecap manis
3 tablespoons soy sauce
1 teaspoon sesame oil
toasted sesame seeds, to garnish

1 Cook the egg noodles in a saucepan of boiling water for 5 minutes, then drain and keep warm.
2 Cut each chicken breast fillet horizontally through the middle so that you are left with eight thin flat chicken fillets.
3 Cut the lemon grass into lengths that are about 5 cm (2 inches) longer than the chicken fillets, then cut in half lengthways. Place one piece of lemon grass onto one half of each chicken breast fillet, top with some ginger and lime slices, then top with the other half of the fillet.
4 Pour the stock into a wok and bring to a simmer. Place two of the chicken fillets in a paper lined bamboo steamer. Place the steamer over the wok and steam over the simmering

stock for 12–15 minutes, or until the chicken is tender. Remove the chicken from the steamer, cover and keep warm. Repeat with the other fillets.
5 Steam the greens in the same way for 3 minutes, or until tender. Bring the stock in the wok to the boil.
6 Place the kecap manis, soy sauce and sesame oil in a bowl and whisk together well.
7 Divide the noodles among four

serving plates and ladle the boiling stock over them. Top with a pile of Asian greens, then add the chicken and generously drizzle each serve with the sauce. Sprinkle with toasted sesame seeds and serve.

NUTRITION PER SERVE
Protein 65 g; Fat 7.5 g; Carbohydrate 37 g; Dietary Fibre 9 g; Cholesterol 119 mg; 2045 kJ (488 cal)

Cut each chicken breast in half horizontally through the middle.

Top the bottom half of each fillet with lemon grass, ginger and lime.

Steam the lemon grass chicken fillets until cooked and tender.

CHICKEN WITH PEACH, RED CAPSICUM AND GINGER SALSA

Preparation time: 20 minutes
Total cooking time: 10 minutes
Serves 4
Fat per serve: 2.5 g

cooking oil spray
4 chicken breast fillets
3 tablespoons white wine vinegar
2 tablespoons caster sugar

2 teaspoons grated fresh ginger
1 clove garlic, crushed
1/2 teaspoon ground cumin
1/4 cup (15 g/1/2 oz) chopped fresh coriander leaves
1/4 cup (15 g/1/2 oz) chopped fresh mint
1 red capsicum, diced
1 small red onion, finely diced
1 small red chilli, finely chopped
3 canned or fresh peaches, diced

1 Lightly spray a chargrill pan with oil and cook the chicken breasts for 5 minutes on each side or until tender and cooked through.
2 Combine the vinegar, sugar, ginger, garlic, cumin, coriander and mint.
3 Put the capsicum, onion, chilli and peaches in a large bowl. Gently stir through the vinegar herb mixture and serve at once with the chicken.

NUTRITION PER SERVE
Protein 27 g; Fat 2.5 g; Carbohydrate 24 g;
Dietary Fibre 3 g; Cholesterol 55 mg;
960 kJ (240 cal)

Use fresh peaches if they are in season, otherwise canned can be used.

Mix together the vinegar, sugar, ginger, garlic, cumin, coriander and mint.

Stir through the vinegar herb mixture and serve the salsa at once.

CHICKEN WITH TOMATOES, OLIVES AND CAPERS

Preparation time: 20 minutes
Total cooking time: 1 hour
Serves 4
Fat per serve: 11 g

2 tablespoons olive oil
1 red onion, cut into thin wedges
1 celery stick, sliced
150 g (5 oz) cap mushrooms, sliced
3–4 cloves garlic, thinly sliced
8 chicken thigh cutlets
plain flour, for dusting
1/2 cup (125 ml/4 fl oz) white wine
300 ml (10 fl oz) chicken stock
400 g (10 oz) can chopped tomatoes
1 tablespoon tomato paste
1/3 cup (60 g/2 oz) black olives
1 tablespoon capers

1 Heat half the oil in a large non-stick frying pan. Add the onion, celery, mushrooms and garlic and cook, stirring, for 5 minutes, or until the onion is soft. Remove from the pan.
2 Coat the chicken lightly in flour, shaking off any excess. Heat the remaining oil in the frying pan and cook the chicken, in batches, turning once, for 5 minutes, or until well browned. Add the wine and stock and cook for a further 2 minutes.
3 Return the vegetables to the pan and add the tomato and tomato paste. Simmer, partially covered, for 40 minutes, or until thickened. Add the olives and capers and season.

NUTRITION PER SERVE
Protein 11 g; Fat 11 g; Carbohydrate 11 g; Dietary Fibre 4.3 g; Cholesterol 14 mg; 874 kJ (210 cal)

Cook the onion, celery, mushrooms and garlic in a frying pan.

Cook the chicken, turning once, until it is well browned all over.

Add the tomato and tomato paste to the pan and simmer for 40 minutes.

CHICKEN STEW WITH WHITE BEANS AND ZUCCHINI

Preparation time: 15 minutes
Total cooking time: 1 hour
Serves 4
Fat per serve: 8 g

1 tablespoon olive oil
8 chicken thigh cutlets
1 onion, halved, thinly sliced
4 cloves garlic, finely chopped
3 tablespoons white wine
1 cup (250 ml/8 fl oz) chicken stock
1 tablespoon finely chopped fresh
 rosemary

1 teaspoon grated lemon rind
1 bay leaf
2 x 400 g (13 oz) cans cannellini
 beans, rinsed and drained
3 zucchini, halved lengthways, cut on
 the diagonal

1 Heat the oil in a large flameproof casserole dish. Add the chicken, in batches, and cook for 4 minutes each side or until browned. Remove.
2 Add the onion to the dish and cook for 5 minutes, or until soft. Add the garlic and cook for 1 minute, or until fragrant, then add the wine and chicken stock and bring to the boil, scraping the bottom of the pan to remove any sediment.

3 Return the chicken and any juices to the pan along with the rosemary, lemon rind and bay leaf. Reduce the heat and simmer, covered, for 40 minutes, or until the chicken is tender. Stir in the cannellini beans and zucchini and cook for 5 minutes more, or until the zucchini is tender.

NUTRITION PER SERVE
Protein 37 g; Fat 8 g; Carbohydrate 25 g; Dietary Fibre 15 g; Cholesterol 50 mg; 1394 kJ (334 cal)

STORAGE TIME: Can be frozen in snap-lock bags or an airtight container for up to 3 months.

Brown the chicken thigh cutlets in batches in a large casserole dish.

Stir in the rinsed and drained cannellini beans and the zucchini and cook for 5 minutes more.

If you want to freeze this dish, transfer to snap-lock bags or an airtight container.

CHICKEN WITH ROASTED RED CAPSICUM SAUCE

Preparation time: 30 minutes
Total cooking time: 1 hour 15 minutes
Serves 4
Fat per serve: 7.5 g

2 red capsicums
1 tablespoon olive oil
1 red onion, roughly chopped
1–2 cloves garlic, crushed
425 g (14 oz) can chopped tomatoes
1/2 cup (30 g/1 oz) chopped fresh
    parsley
1/2 cup (30 g/1 oz) chopped fresh
    basil leaves
1 tablespoon tomato paste
1 tablespoon caster sugar
4 chicken breast fillets

1 Cut the capsicums into quarters, remove the membrane and seeds and grill, skin-side-up, until blackened. Cool in a plastic bag for 10 minutes, peel away the skin and chop roughly.
2 Heat the oil in a pan and cook the onion and garlic for 2 minutes, or until soft but not brown. Add the tomatoes, parsley, basil, tomato paste, sugar and 1 1/2 cups (375 ml/12 fl oz) water.
3 Add the chopped capsicum and cook, stirring often, over very low heat for 45 minutes to 1 hour, or until thick. Leave to cool slightly, then purée in batches in a food processor. Season.
4 Grill the chicken under a preheated grill for 5 minutes on each side, or until cooked through and tender. Serve with the sauce.

NUTRITION PER SERVE
Protein 27 g; Fat 7.5 g; Carbohydrate 9 g; Dietary Fibre 2 g; Cholesterol 55 mg; 886 kJ (210 cal)

Once the capsicum skin has been blackened it should peel away easily.

Cook the onion and garlic until they are softened but not browned.

Add the chopped capsicum to the sauce and cook for up to 1 hour, or until thick.

Seafood

FISH BURGERS WITH TARTARE SAUCE

Preparation time: 30 minutes +
    1 hour refrigeration
Total cooking time: 25 minutes
Serves 4
Fat per serve: 15 g

500 g (1 lb) white fish fillets
2 tablespoons finely chopped
    fresh parsley
2 tablespoons finely chopped
    fresh dill
2 tablespoons lemon juice
1 tablespoon capers, finely chopped
2 finely chopped gherkins
350 g (11 oz) potatoes, cooked and
    mashed
plain flour, for dusting
2 teaspoons olive oil
4 hamburger buns
lettuce leaves
2 Roma tomatoes, sliced

TARTARE SAUCE
1/3 cup (90 g/3 oz) low-fat mayonnaise
1/2 finely chopped gherkin
2 teaspoons capers, finely chopped
1/2 teaspoon malt vinegar
2 teaspoons finely chopped
    fresh parsley
2 teaspoons lemon juice

1 Place the fish fillets in a frying pan and just cover with water. Slowly heat the water, making sure it doesn't boil. Cover and cook over low heat until the fish is just cooked. Drain the fish on paper towels, transfer to a large bowl and flake with a fork. Add the parsley, dill, lemon juice, capers, gherkin and mashed potato, season well and mix thoroughly. Divide into 4 portions and shape into patties, handling the mixture carefully as it is quite soft. Dust lightly with flour and refrigerate on a plate for 1 hour.
2 Meanwhile, make the tartare sauce by mixing all the ingredients thoroughly in a bowl.
3 Heat the olive oil in a large non-stick frying pan, carefully add the patties and cook for 5–6 minutes on each side, or until well browned and heated through.
4 Meanwhile, cut the hamburger buns in half and toast under a grill. Fill the buns with lettuce leaves, tomato slices, the patties and then a spoonful of tartare sauce. Serve with crunchy potato wedges (page 114).

NUTRITION PER SERVE
Protein 40 g; Fat 15 g; Carbohydrate 70 g;
Dietary Fibre 7 g; Cholesterol 95 mg;
2375 kJ (565 cal)

Pour in enough water to cover the fish fillets and slowly heat the water.

Mix the flaked fish with the herbs, potato, juice, capers, gherkin and seasoning.

TUNA WITH CORIANDER NOODLES

Preparation time: 15 minutes
Total cooking time: 10 minutes
Serves 4
Fat per serve: 10 g

1/4 cup (60 ml/2 fl oz) lime juice
2 tablespoons fish sauce
2 tablespoons sweet chilli sauce
2 teaspoons grated palm sugar
1 teaspoon sesame oil
1 clove garlic, finely chopped
1 tablespoon virgin olive oil
4 tuna steaks
200 g (6½ oz) dried thin wheat
　　noodles

6 spring onions, thinly sliced
3/4 cup (25 g/3/4 oz) chopped fresh
　　coriander leaves
lime wedges, to garnish

1 To make the dressing, place the lime juice, fish sauce, chilli sauce, sugar, sesame oil and garlic in a small bowl and mix together.
2 Heat the olive oil in a chargrill pan. Add the tuna steaks and cook over high heat for 2 minutes each side, or until cooked to your liking. Transfer the steaks to a warm plate, cover and keep warm.
3 Place the noodles in a large saucepan of lightly salted, rapidly boiling water and return to the boil. Cook for 4 minutes, or until the

noodles are tender. Drain well. Add half the dressing and half the spring onion and coriander to the noodles and gently toss together.
4 Either cut the tuna into even cubes or slice it.
5 Place the noodles on serving plates and top with the tuna. Mix the remaining dressing with the spring onion and coriander and drizzle over the tuna. Garnish with lime wedges.

NUTRITION PER SERVE
Protein 32 g; Fat 10 g; Carbohydrate 5 g;
Dietary Fibre 1 g; Cholesterol 105 mg;
1030 kJ (245 cal)

Cook the tuna steaks in a chargrill pan until cooked to your liking.

Cook the noodles in lightly salted water until they are tender.

Combine the remaining dressing with the spring onion and coriander.

LIME AND PRAWN SALAD

Preparation time: 35 minutes
Total cooking time: 2 minutes
Serves 4
Fat per serve: 8 g

200 g (6¹/₂ oz) baby green beans
2 Lebanese cucumbers, sliced
4 spring onions, finely chopped
1 tablespoon finely shredded kaffir
    lime leaves
¹/₄ cup (15 g/¹/₂ oz) flaked coconut
750 g (1¹/₂ lb) cooked prawns,
    peeled, tails intact
2 teaspoons shredded lime rind

DRESSING
1 tablespoon peanut oil
1 tablespoon nam pla (Thai fish sauce)
1 tablespoon grated palm sugar
1 tablespoon chopped fresh coriander
2 teaspoons soy sauce
1–2 teaspoons sweet chilli sauce
¹/₄ cup (60 ml/2 fl oz) lime juice

1 Cook the beans in a small pan of boiling water for 2 minutes. Drain and cover with cold water, then drain again and pat dry with paper towels.
2 To make the dressing, whisk the ingredients in a bowl.
3 Combine the beans, cucumber, spring onion, lime leaves, flaked coconut and prawns in a large bowl. Add the dressing and toss gently to combine. Place the salad in a large serving bowl and garnish with the shredded lime rind.

NUTRITION PER SERVE
Protein 45 g; Fat 8 g; Carbohydrate 7 g;
Dietary Fibre 3 g; Cholesterol 350 mg;
1200 kJ (285 cal)

NOTE: Young lemon leaves can be used in place of the kaffir lime leaves if they are not available.

Soft brown or dark brown sugar may be substituted for the palm sugar.

Cut the cucumbers in half lengthways, then cut into slices.

Lower the beans into a small pan of boiling water and cook for 2 minutes.

Whisk the dressing ingredients in a small bowl until combined.

SARDINES WITH CHARGRILLED CAPSICUM AND EGGPLANT

Preparation time: 25 minutes
Total cooking time: 35 minutes
Serves 4
Fat per serve: 15 g

2 large red capsicums, quartered and
    seeded
4 finger eggplants, cut into quarters
    lengthways
cooking oil spray

DRESSING
1 tablespoon olive oil
1 tablespoon balsamic vinegar
1/2 teaspoon soft brown sugar
1 clove garlic, crushed
1 tablespoon chopped fresh chives

16 fresh sardines, butterflied
    (about 300 g/10 oz)
1 slice white bread, crusts removed
1/3 cup (7 g/1/4 oz) fresh parsley
1 clove garlic, crushed
1 teaspoon grated lemon rind

1 Preheat the oven to moderate 180°C
(350°F/Gas 4). Lightly grease a large
baking dish with oil. Preheat the grill
and line with foil.
2 Grill the capsicum until the skin is
blistered and blackened. Cool under a
damp tea towel, peel and slice thickly
lengthways. Lightly spray the eggplant
with oil and grill each side for
3–5 minutes, until softened.
3 Combine the dressing ingredients in
a jar and shake well. Put the capsicum
and eggplant in a bowl, pour the
dressing over, toss well and set aside.
4 Place the sardines on a baking tray
in a single layer, well spaced. Finely

chop the bread, parsley, garlic and
lemon rind together in a food
processor. Sprinkle over each sardine.
Bake for 10–15 minutes, until cooked
through. Serve the capsicum and
eggplant topped with sardines.

NUTRITION PER SERVE
Protein 20 g; Fat 15 g; Carbohydrate 15 g;
Dietary Fibre 3 g; Cholesterol 85 mg;
1185 kJ (285 cal)

When the capsicum has cooled enough to
handle, peel away the skin.

Pour the dressing over the capsicum and
eggplant, then toss.

Sprinkle the chopped bread, parsley, garlic and
lemon rind over the sardines.

TUNA KEBABS

Preparation time: 20 minutes
Total cooking time: 20 minutes
Serves 4
Fat per serve: 15 g

1 tablespoon olive oil
2–3 small red chillies,
    seeded and finely chopped
3–4 cloves garlic, crushed
1 red onion, finely chopped
3 tomatoes, seeded and chopped
1/4 cup (60 ml/2 fl oz) white wine or
    water
2 x 300 g (10 oz) cans chickpeas

1/4 cup (7 g/1/4 oz) chopped fresh
    oregano
1/3 cup (20 g/3/4 oz) chopped fresh
    parsley

TUNA KEBABS
1 kg (2 lb) tuna fillet, cut into 4 cm
    (11/2 inch) cubes
8 stalks of rosemary, about 20 cm
    (8 inches) long, with leaves
cooking oil spray
lemon wedges, to serve

1 Heat the oil in a large pan, add the
chilli, garlic and red onion and stir for
5 minutes, or until softened. Add the
tomato and wine or water. Cook over
low heat for 10 minutes, or until the
mixture is soft, pulpy and the liquid
has evaporated. Stir in the rinsed
chickpeas, oregano and parsley
Season with salt and pepper.
2 Heat a grill or barbecue plate.
Thread the tuna onto the rosemary
stalks, lightly spray with oil, then cook,
turning, for 3 minutes. Do not
overcook or the tuna will fall apart.
Serve with the chickpeas and lemon.

NUTRITION PER SERVE
Protein 75 g; Fat 15 g; Carbohydrate 25 g;
Dietary Fibre 10 g; Cholesterol 110 mg;
2355 kJ (565 cal)

Stir the chopped chilli, red onion and the crushed garlic until softened.

Drain the chickpeas and rinse well before adding to the pan.

Thread the tuna pieces onto the long rosemary stalks and grill or barbecue.

CRUMBED FISH WITH WASABI CREAM

Preparation time: 25 minutes +
  15 minutes refrigeration
Total cooking time: 20 minutes
Serves 4
Fat per serve: 6 g

3/4 cup (60 g/2 oz) fresh breadcrumbs
3/4 cup (25 g/3/4 oz) cornflakes
1 sheet nori, torn roughly
1/4 teaspoon paprika
4 x 150 g (5 oz) pieces firm white fish
  fillets
plain flour, for dusting
1 egg white
1 tablespoon skim milk
1 spring onion, thinly sliced

WASABI CREAM
1/2 cup (125 g/4 oz) low-fat natural
  yoghurt
1 teaspoon wasabi (see NOTE)
1 tablespoon low-fat mayonnaise
1 teaspoon lime juice

1 Preheat the oven to moderate 180°C
(350°F/Gas 4). Combine the crumbs,
cornflakes, nori and paprika in a food
processor and process until the nori is
finely chopped.
2 Dust the fish lightly with plain flour,
dip into the combined egg white and
milk, then into the breadcrumb
mixture. Press the crumb mixture on
firmly, then refrigerate for 15 minutes.
3 Line a baking tray with non-stick
baking paper and put the fish on the
paper. Bake for 15–20 minutes, or until
the fish flakes easily with a fork.
4 To make the wasabi cream, mix the
ingredients thoroughly in a bowl.
Serve with the fish and sprinkle with a
little spring onion.

NUTRITION PER SERVE
Protein 35 g; Fat 6 g; Carbohydrate 25 g;
Dietary Fibre 1 g; Cholesterol 105 mg;
1270 kJ (305 cal)

NOTE: Wasabi paste (a pungent paste,
also known as Japanese horseradish)
and nori (sheets of paper-thin dried
seaweed) are both available from
Japanese food stores.

Process the breadcrumbs, cornflakes, nori and
paprika together.

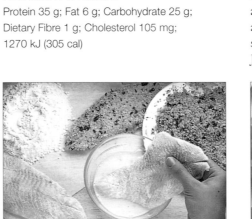

Dust the fish with flour, dip in the egg and milk,
then press in the breadcrumbs.

Thoroughly mix the wasabi cream ingredients in a
bowl and then serve with the fish.

STEAMED TROUT WITH GINGER AND CORIANDER

Preparation time: 20 minutes
Total cooking time: 30 minutes
Serves 2
Fat per serve: 10 g

2 whole rainbow trout (about 330 g/
    11 oz each), cleaned and scaled
2 limes, thinly sliced
5 cm (2 inch) piece ginger, cut into
    matchsticks
1/4 cup (60 g/2 oz) caster sugar
1/4 cup (60 ml/2 fl oz) lime juice
rind of 1 lime, cut in thin strips
1/3 cup (10 g/1/4 oz) fresh coriander
    leaves

1 Preheat the oven to moderate 180°C (350°F/Gas 4). Fill the fish cavities with the lime slices and some of the ginger, then place the fish on a large piece of greased foil. Wrap the fish and bake on a baking tray for 20–30 minutes, until the flesh flakes easily when tested with a fork.
2 Combine the sugar and lime juice with 250 ml (8 fl oz) water in a small pan and stir without boiling until the sugar dissolves. Bring to the boil, reduce the heat and simmer for 10 minutes, or until syrupy. Stir in the remaining ginger and lime strips. Put the fish on a plate. Top with coriander leaves and pour the hot syrup over it.

NUTRITION PER SERVE
Protein 50 g; Fat 10 g; Carbohydrate 30 g; Dietary Fibre 1 g; Cholesterol 120 mg; 1715 kJ (410 cal)

NOTE: You can ask the fishmonger to remove the bones from the fish.

Peel the fresh ginger with a potato peeler and cut it into fine, short matchsticks.

Fill the cavities of the trout with the lime slices and some of the ginger.

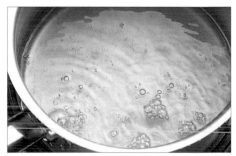
Simmer the sugar, lime juice and water until you have a syrupy sauce.

JAPANESE KING PRAWN AND NOODLE SALAD

Preparation time: 35 minutes
Total cooking time: 15 minutes
Serves 6
Fat per serve: 8 g

500 g (1 lb) fresh udon noodles
2 teaspoons sesame oil
3 cloves garlic, finely chopped
4 cm (1¹/₂ inch) piece fresh ginger, finely chopped
200 g (6¹/₂ oz) broccoli, cut into small pieces
2 carrots, cut into matchsticks
100 g (3¹/₂ oz) snow peas, sliced into long, thin strips
1 cup (90 g/3 oz) bean sprouts
¹/₄ cup (15 g/¹/₂ oz) chopped fresh coriander
2 tablespoons mirin
3 tablespoons low-salt soy sauce
8 cooked king prawns, peeled and deveined, tails intact
2 teaspoons sesame seeds, toasted
sliced spring onions, to garnish

1 Cook the udon noodles in a large pan of boiling water for 5 minutes, or until tender. Drain and rinse in cold water to prevent them sticking together. Transfer to a large bowl and cut into small pieces, using scissors. Toss 1 teaspoon of the sesame oil through, cover and set aside.
2 Heat the remaining sesame oil in a small pan, add the garlic and ginger and cook over low heat for 5 minutes, stirring occasionally. Remove from the heat, cool and add to the noodles.
3 Bring a large pan of water to the boil and add the broccoli, carrot and snow peas. Return to the boil, reduce the heat and simmer for 1 minute.

Drain under cold water until the vegetables are cold. Drain.
4 Add the blanched vegetables, bean sprouts, coriander, mirin, soy sauce and prawns to the noodles. Toss together until well combined. Transfer to a serving bowl and sprinkle with sesame seeds and spring onion. Serve immediately.

NUTRITION PER SERVE
Protein 20 g; Fat 8 g; Carbohydrate 65 g; Dietary Fibre 8 g; Cholesterol 35 mg; 1690 kJ (405 cal)

NOTE: Udon noodles and mirin are available from Japanese or Asian food stores and some supermarkets.

Use scissors to cut the udon noodles into pieces so they are easier to eat.

Cook the chopped garlic and ginger in the sesame oil for about 5 minutes.

Blanch the broccoli, carrot and snow peas, then rinse under water until completely cold.

FUSILLI WITH TUNA, CAPERS AND PARSLEY

Preparation time: 15 minutes
Total cooking time: 10 minutes
Serves 4
Fat per serve: 13 g

425 g (14 oz) can tuna in spring water, drained
2 tablespoons olive oil
2 cloves garlic, finely chopped
2 small red chillies, finely chopped
3 tablespoons capers (see HINT)

1/2 cup (30 g/1 oz) finely chopped fresh parsley
3 tablespoons lemon juice
375 g (12 oz) fusilli

1 Place the tuna in a bowl and flake lightly with a fork. Combine the oil, garlic, chilli, capers, parsley and lemon juice. Pour over the tuna and mix lightly. Season well.
2 Meanwhile, cook the pasta in a large pan of rapidly boiling salted water for 10 minutes, or until *al dente*. Reserve 1/2 cup (125 ml/4 fl oz) of the cooking water, then drain the pasta.

Toss the tuna mixture through the pasta, adding enough of the reserved water to give a moist consistency. Serve immediately.

NUTRITION PER SERVE
Protein 35 g; Fat 13 g; Carbohydrate 65 g; Dietary Fibre 5 g; Cholesterol 55 mg; 2270 kJ (545 cal)

HINT: Generally, the smaller the caper the tastier, so use baby ones if you can find them.

Finely chop the chillies. Remove the seeds if you prefer a milder taste.

Break the tuna into flakes with a fork and then mix with the dressing.

Cook the pasta in a large pan of rapidly boiling salted water.

SEAFOOD AND HERB RISOTTO

Preparation time: 40 minutes
Total cooking time: 50 minutes
Serves 4
Fat per serve: 5 g

150 g (5 oz) white boneless fish fillet
    such as sea perch
8 black mussels (200 g/6^{1}/$_{2}$ oz)
8 raw prawns (250 g/8 oz)
7 cups (1.75 litres) chicken stock
cooking oil spray
2 onions, finely chopped
2 cloves garlic, finely chopped
1 celery stick, finely chopped
2 cups (440 g/14 oz) arborio rice (see
    NOTE)
2 tablespoons chopped fresh parsley
1 tablespoon chopped fresh oregano
1 tablespoon chopped fresh thyme
    leaves
2 tablespoons grated Parmesan

1 Cut the fish fillet into small cubes. Scrub the mussels well and remove the beards. Discard any musssels that are broken or open and do not close when tapped. Peel and devein the prawns, leaving the tails intact. Put the seafood in a bowl and refrigerate until required.
2 Put the stock in a saucepan and bring to the boil, then reduce the heat until just gently simmering.
3 Lightly spray a large saucepan with cooking oil and heat over medium heat. Add the onion, garlic and celery and cook for 2–3 minutes. Add 2 tablespoons water, cover and cook for 5 minutes, or until the vegetables have begun to soften. Add the arborio rice and 2 tablespoons water and stir over medium heat for 3–4 minutes, or

until the rice grains are well coated.
4 Gradually add ^{1}/$_{2}$ cup (125 ml/ 4 fl oz) of the hot stock to the rice mixture, stirring constantly over low heat with a wooden spoon, until all the stock has been absorbed. Repeat the process, adding ^{1}/$_{2}$ cup of liquid each time until all but a small amount of stock is left and the rice is just tender.
5 Meanwhile, bring a small amount of water to the boil in a saucepan. Add the mussels, cover and cook for about 3 minutes, shaking the pan occasionally, until the mussels have opened. Drain the mussels and discard any that have not opened in the cooking time.
6 Add the fish and prawns and the remaining hot stock to the rice. Stir well and continue to cook for about 5–10 minutes, or until the seafood is just cooked and the rice is tender and creamy. Remove from the heat, add the cooked mussels, cover and set aside for 5 minutes. Stir the herbs and Parmesan through the risotto, then season well. Serve immediately.

NUTRITION PER SERVE
Protein 40 g; Fat 5 g; Carbohydrate 90 g; Dietary Fibre 4 g; Cholesterol 175 mg; 2395 kJ (570 cal)

NOTE: Arborio has a fatter and shorter grain than other short-grain rice. The chief ingredient of risotto, arborio has a high starch content which gives the dish its creamy texture. This is the reason you can't successfully use another type of rice.

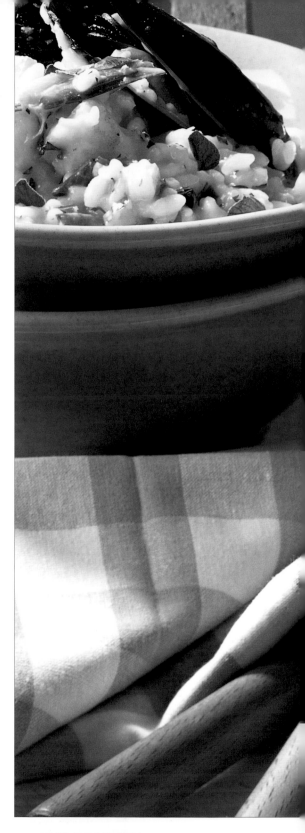

Scrub the mussels thoroughly and pull off the beards. Discard any open mussels.

Add the arborio rice to the pan and stir over the heat until the rice is well coated.

Stir in the stock a little at a time, not adding any more until the last portion has been absorbed.

Risotto is ready when the rice has absorbed all the hot stock.

Put the mussels in a pan of boiling water, cover and cook for 3 minutes to open them.

Stir the chopped herbs and grated Parmesan through the risotto.

CALAMARI WITH SPICY SAUCE

Preparation time: 50 minutes +
    3 hours marinating
Total cooking time: 7 minutes
Serves 4
Fat per serve: 6.5 g

500 g (l lb) calamari tubes, cleaned
2 stems lemon grass, white part only,
    finely chopped
3 teaspoons grated fresh ginger
3 cloves garlic, finely chopped
$^1/_2$ teaspoon chopped fresh red chilli
1 tablespoon vegetable oil
2 very ripe tomatoes
150 g (5 oz) mixed lettuce
$^1/_4$ cup (7 g/$^1/_4$ oz) fresh coriander
    leaves
2 tablespoons lime juice
1 teaspoon finely grated lime rind
1 red capsicum, cut into strips

LIME, CHILLI AND GARLIC SAUCE
$^1/_4$ cup (60 ml/2 fl oz) lime juice
1 tablespoon lemon juice
2 tablespoons fish sauce
1 tablespoon caster sugar
2 teaspoons chopped fresh red chilli
2 cloves garlic, finely chopped
1 tablespoon finely chopped fresh
    coriander

1 Cut the calamari tubes open, wash and pat dry. Cut shallow slashes about 5 mm ($^1/_4$ inch) apart on the soft inside, in a diamond pattern, then cut into 3 cm (1$^1/_4$ inch) strips. Mix in a bowl with the lemon grass, ginger, garlic, chilli and oil. Cover with plastic wrap and refrigerate for 3 hours.
2 Cut the tomatoes in half, scoop out the membrane and seeds and finely chop them, retaining all the juices. Cut the flesh into small cubes and set aside. Arrange the lettuce and coriander leaves in serving bowls.
3 Just before serving, lightly grease and heat a solid barbecue plate or large, heavy non-stick pan until very hot. Quickly cook the calamari in batches, tossing for 2–3 minutes, until just tender and curled, sprinkling the lime juice and rind over the top. Remove the calamari, toss with the chopped tomato seeds and arrange on the salad. Scatter the tomato and capsicum over the top. Season well.
4 Stir the sauce ingredients together until the sugar dissolves. Drizzle over the calamari.

NUTRITION PER SERVE
Protein 25 g; Fat 6.5 g; Carbohydrate 5 g;
Dietary Fibre 3 g; Cholesterol 250 mg;
755 kJ (180 cal)

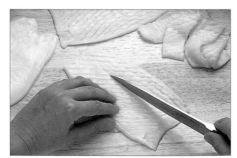

Score a shallow diamond pattern on the soft insides of the calamari tubes.

Scoop out the tomato membrane and seeds and finely chop the flesh.

Don't overcook the calamari or it will be tough, and don't crowd the pan.

JAPANESE-STYLE SALMON PARCELS

Preparation time: 40 minutes
Total cooking time: 15 minutes
Serves 4
Fat per serve: 14 g

2 teaspoons sesame seeds
4 x 150 g (5 oz) salmon cutlets or
  steaks
2.5 cm (1 inch) piece fresh ginger
2 celery sticks
4 spring onions
1/4 teaspoon dashi granules
3 tablespoons mirin
2 tablespoons tamari

1 Cut 4 squares of baking paper large enough to enclose the salmon steaks. Preheat the oven to very hot 230°C (450°F/Gas 8). Lightly toast the sesame seeds under a hot grill for 1 minute.
2 Wash the salmon and dry with paper towels. Place a salmon cutlet in the centre of each paper square.
3 Cut the ginger into paper-thin slices. Slice the celery and spring onions into short lengths, then lengthways into fine strips. Arrange a bundle of celery and spring onion and several slices of ginger on each salmon steak.
4 Combine the dashi granules, mirin and tamari in a small saucepan. Heat gently until the granules dissolve. Drizzle over each parcel, sprinkle with

sesame seeds and carefully wrap the salmon, folding in the sides to seal in all the juices. Arrange the parcels on a baking tray and cook for about 12 minutes, or until tender. (The paper will puff up when the fish is cooked.) Do not overcook or the salmon will dry out. Serve immediately, as standing time can spoil the fish.

NUTRITION PER SERVE
Protein 20 g; Fat 14 g; Carbohydrate 0 g;
Dietary Fibre 0.5 g; Cholesterol 85 mg;
935 kJ (225 cal)

NOTE: Dashi, mirin and tamari are all available from Japanese food stores.

Cut the celery sticks into short lengths, then lengthways into thin julienne strips.

Arrange celery and spring onion strips on the fish and top with ginger slices.

Wrap the salmon in baking paper, folding the sides to seal in the juices.

SPICED FISH WRAPPED IN BANANA LEAVES

Preparation time: 20 minutes
Total cooking time: 35 minutes
Serves 6
Fat per serve: 15 g

SPICE PASTE
1 red onion, finely chopped
3 small red chillies, seeded and
    chopped
1 teaspoon dried shrimp paste
1 cm (1/2 inch) piece fresh galangal,
    finely chopped
1 stem lemon grass, white part only,
    finely sliced
5 blanched almonds, chopped
4 kaffir lime leaves, finely shredded

2 teaspoons sesame oil
1 tablespoon vegetable oil
1 teaspoon soy sauce
1 banana leaf, (about 50 cm x
    30 cm/20 x 12 inches)
1 whole trout or silver bream (about
    750 g/1 1/2 lb), cleaned and scaled

1 To make the spice paste, grind all
the ingredients except the kaffir lime
leaves in a food processor with
2 tablespoons water until smooth.
Transfer to a bowl and mix in the kaffir
lime leaves. Set aside.

2 Preheat the oven to moderate 180°C
(350°F/Gas 4). Heat the sesame oil and
vegetable oil in a small frying pan and
gently fry the spice paste for
5 minutes. Mix in the soy sauce.
Remove from the heat and cool.

3 Cut a large rectangle from the
banana leaf and brush with oil. Wash
the fish well under running water and
pat dry. Score the fish several times on
both sides and rub in the spice paste,
pushing it well into the slits.

4 Place the fish on the banana leaf
and fold over to make a parcel. Wrap
again in foil to secure. Bake for
25–30 minutes, or until the flesh flakes
easily when tested with a fork. Unwrap
the fish to serve.

NUTRITION PER SERVE
Protein 30 g; Fat 15 g; Carbohydrate 3 g;
Dietary Fibre 1 g; Cholesterol 75 mg;
1050 kJ (250 cal)

Mix the spice paste until smooth and then add
the shredded kaffir lime leaves.

Stir the soy sauce into the fried spice paste and
mix well.

Score the fish several times on both sides with a
sharp knife.

Wrap the fish in the banana leaf, folding in the
ends securely.

PRAWN, PAWPAW AND CHILLI SALAD

Preparation time: 35 minutes
Total cooking time: Nil
Serves 4
Fat per serve: 15 g

3 tablespoons olive oil
3 tablespoons lime juice
1 tablespoon fish sauce
2 teaspoons grated palm sugar
1 teaspoon seeded, finely chopped
   red jalapeno chilli
1 teaspoon seeded, finely chopped
   green jalapeno chilli

800 g (1 lb 10 oz) cooked king prawns
400 g (13 oz) pawpaw
1 small red onion, finely sliced
2 tablespoons shredded fresh mint
2 tablespoons finely chopped fresh
   coriander

1 Combine the olive oil, lime juice, fish sauce, palm sugar and chilli in a large mixing bowl and set aside to allow the flavours to combine.
2 Meanwhile, peel and devein the prawns, leaving the tails intact. Peel and discard the seeds from the pawpaw and cut the flesh into bite-sized pieces.
3 Add the prawns, pawpaw, onion

mint and coriander to the bowl. Very gently, using two spoons, toss the salad to combine. Add the chilli dressing and toss gently again to coat just before serving.

NUTRITION PER SERVE
Protein 25 g; Fat 15 g; Carbohydrate 10 g; Dietary Fibre 3 g; Cholesterol 190 mg; 1175 kJ (280 cal)

NOTE: Palm sugar is a very dark brown sugar used in Asian cooking. If it is not available, you can use soft brown sugar instead.

Combine the oil, juice, fish sauce, palm sugar and chilli in a large mixing bowl.

Peel and devein the prawns with your fingers, leaving the tails intact.

Gently toss the mixture to combine all the ingredients, using two spoons.

PRAWNS WITH JASMINE RICE

Preparation time: 15 minutes
Total cooking time: 30 minutes
Serves 4
Fat per serve: 12 g

1 tablespoon peanut oil
8 spring onions, sliced
1 tablespoon finely chopped fresh
    ginger
1 tablespoon finely sliced lemon grass,
    white part only
2 teaspoons crushed coriander seeds
    (see NOTE)
2 cups (400 g/13 oz) jasmine rice
4 cups (1 litre) vegetable stock
1 tablespoon shredded lime rind
1 kg (2 lb) raw prawns, peeled,
    deveined and chopped
2 tablespoons lime juice
1 cup (30 g/1 oz) fresh coriander
    leaves
fish sauce, for serving

1 Heat the oil in a saucepan, add the spring onion and cook over low heat for 4 minutes, or until soft. Add the ginger, lemon grass, coriander seeds and rice, and stir for 1 minute.
2 Add the stock and lime rind and bring to the boil while stirring. Reduce the heat to very low and cook, covered, for 15–20 minutes, or until the rice is tender.
3 Remove the pan from the heat and stir in the prawns. Cover and leave for 4–5 minutes, or until the prawns are cooked. Add the lime juice and coriander leaves and flake the rice with a fork. Sprinkle with a few drops of fish sauce to serve.

NUTRITION PER SERVE
Protein 59 g; Fat 12 g; Carbohydrate 80 g;
Dietary Fibre 3 g; Cholesterol 373 mg;
2850 kJ (681 cal)

NOTE: To crush coriander seeds, place in a small plastic bag and, using a rolling pin, crush until fine.

Peel and devein the prawns and chop them into small pieces.

Add the ginger, lemon grass, coriander seeds and rice to the saucepan.

Add the lime juice and coriander leaves and flake the rice with a fork.

SMOKED SALMON PIZZAS

Preparation time: 20 minutes
Total cooking time: 15 minutes
Serves 6
Fat per serve: 8 g

250 g (8 oz) low-fat ricotta
6 small oval pitta breads
125 g (4 oz) sliced smoked salmon
1 small red onion, sliced

1 tablespoon baby capers
small dill sprigs, to garnish
1 lemon, cut into thin wedges,
    for serving

1 Preheat the oven to moderate 180°C (350°F/Gas 4). Put the ricotta in a bowl, season well with salt and pepper and stir until smooth. Spread the ricotta over the breads, leaving a clear border around the edge.
2 Top each pizza with some smoked

salmon slices, then some onion pieces. Scatter baby capers over the top and bake on a baking tray for 15 minutes, or until the bases are slightly crispy around the edges. Garnish with a few dill sprigs and serve with lemon wedges.

NUTRITION PER SERVE
Protein 20 g; Fat 8 g; Carbohydrate 60 g;
Dietary Fibre 4 g; Cholesterol 30 mg;
1650 kJ (395 cal)

Peel the small red onion and then cut it into thin slices.

Spread the seasoned ricotta over the pitta breads, leaving a border around the edge.

Put some smoked salmon slices over the ricotta, followed by onion and capers.

TUNA WITH CHILLI SPICED MANGO SAUCE

Preparation time: 35 minutes
Total cooking time: 25 minutes
Serves 4
Fat per serve: 8 g

1 large ripe mango
1 tablespoon oil
1 red onion, finely sliced
3 cloves garlic, finely chopped
4 cm (1½ inch) piece fresh ginger,
    finely chopped
2–3 red chillies, seeded and chopped
1 tablespoon honey
¼ teaspoon ground cinnamon
pinch of ground cardamom
pinch of ground nutmeg
pinch of ground cloves
¼ cup (60 ml/2 fl oz) dark rum
¼ cup (60 ml/2 fl oz) lime juice
¼ cup (7 g/¼ oz) coriander leaves,
    chopped
cooking oil spray
4 tuna steaks

1 Peel the mango and dice the flesh. Heat the oil in a frying pan and add the onion, garlic, ginger and chilli. Cook for 3 minutes, or until soft.
2 Add the mango, honey, cinnamon, cardamom, nutmeg and cloves. Mix well and bring to the boil. Simmer gently for 5 minutes. Add the rum and simmer for a further 5 minutes. Add the lime juice, coriander and season.
3 Lightly spray a chargrill pan and cook the tuna for 2 minutes each side. Serve with the sauce.

NUTRITION PER SERVE
Protein 27 g; Fat 8 g; Carbohydrate 19 g;
Dietary Fibre 3 g; Cholesterol 45 mg;
1200 kJ (300 cal)

Peel the large ripe mango and cut the flesh into small cubes.

Fry the onion, garlic, ginger and chilli until the onion is soft.

Add the rum to the simmering sauce and cook for a further 5 minutes.

THAI-STYLE WHOLE SNAPPER

Preparation time: 10 minutes
Total cooking time: 30 minutes
Serves 6
Fat per serve: 2 g

2 garlic cloves, crushed
1 tablespoon fish sauce
2 tablespoons lemon juice
1 tablespoon grated fresh ginger
2 tablespoons sweet chilli sauce
2 tablespoons chopped fresh
    coriander
1 tablespoon rice wine vinegar
2 tablespoons white wine
600 g (1¼ lb) whole snapper, cleaned
    and scaled (ask your fishmonger to
    do this)
2 spring onions, cut into thin strips

1 Preheat the oven to 190°C (375°F/Gas 5). Place the garlic, fish sauce, lemon juice, ginger, chilli sauce, coriander, rice wine vinegar and wine in a jug and mix together well.

2 Place the snapper on a large piece of foil on a baking tray. Pour the marinade over the fish and sprinkle with the spring onion.

3 Wrap some foil around the fish like a parcel and place in the oven. Bake for 20–30 minutes or until the flesh flakes easily when tested with a fork. Serve immediately with steamed rice.

NUTRITION PER SERVE
Protein 20 g; Fat 2 g; Carbohydrate 5 g;
Dietary Fibre 0 g; Cholesterol 60 mg;
495 kJ (120 cal)

Put the ingredients for the marinade in a jug and mix together well.

Pour the marinade over the snapper after you have placed it on the aluminium foil.

Cook the fish until the flesh flakes easily when tested with a fork.

MARINATED FISH SALAD WITH CHILLI AND BASIL

Preparation time: 30 minutes +
  3 hours marinating
Total cooking time: Nil
Serves 4
Fat per serve: 5 g

500 g (1 lb) firm white fish fillets,
  skinned
3 tomatoes, diced
3 Lebanese cucumbers, diced
5 spring onions, finely sliced

2 red chillies, seeded and sliced
2 cloves garlic, crushed
1 teaspoon grated fresh ginger
1/2 cup (15 g/1/2 oz) fresh basil leaves,
  torn
mixed salad leaves, to serve

MARINADE
1/4 cup (60 ml/2 fl oz) lime juice
1/4 cup (60 ml/2 fl oz) coconut milk
1 teaspoon salt
1/4 teaspoon cracked pepper

1 Slice the fish into thin strips and place in a glass or ceramic bowl.

2 To make the marinade, combine the lime juice, coconut milk, salt and pepper in a jug. Pour over the fish. Cover and refrigerate for at least 3 hours, turning once or twice.
3 Add the tomato, cucumber, spring onion, chilli, garlic, ginger and basil to the fish. Mix together well and serve spooned over salad leaves.

NUTRITION PER SERVE
Protein 30 g; Fat 5 g; Carbohydrate 10 g;
Dietary Fibre 5 g; Cholesterol 90 mg;
920 kJ (220 cal)

On a chopping board, bunch the 5 spring onions together and finely slice.

Slice the firm white fish fillets into thin strips with a sharp knife.

Pour the marinade over the fish and place in the refrigerator for several hours.

COD WITH PAPAYA AND BLACK BEAN SALSA

Preparation time: 25 minutes
Total cooking time: 5 minutes
Serves 4
Fat per serve: 6 g

1 small red onion, finely chopped
1 papaya (about 500 g/1 lb), peeled, seeded and cubed
1 bird's-eye chilli, seeded and finely chopped
1 tablespoon salted black beans, rinsed and drained
4 blue-eyed cod cutlets
2 teaspoons peanut oil
1 teaspoon sesame oil
2 teaspoons fish sauce
1 tablespoon lime juice
1 tablespoon chopped fresh coriander leaves
2 teaspoons shredded fresh mint

1 Toss together the onion, papaya, chilli and black beans.
2 Cook the cod cutlets in a lightly oiled chargrill pan for 2 minutes each side, or until cooked to your liking.
3 Whisk together the peanut oil, sesame oil, fish sauce and lime juice. Pour over the papaya and black bean salsa and toss. Add the coriander and mint and serve immediately, at room temperature, with the fish.

NUTRITION PER SERVE
Protein 18 g; Fat 6 g; Carbohydrate 5 g; Dietary Fibre 1 g, Cholesterol 40 mg; 540 kJ (130 cal)

NOTE: Black beans have a distinctive taste, so if you are not familiar with them, taste them before adding to the salsa. If you prefer not to add them, the salsa is equally delicious without.

VARIATION: Pawpaw can be used instead of papaya. It is a larger fruit from the same family, with yellower flesh and a less sweet flavour.

Cut the papaya in half and scoop out the seeds with a spoon.

The best way to toss the salsa, without breaking up the fruit, is with your hands.

Whisk together the oil dressing and add to the salsa just before serving.

CRAB CURRY

Preparation time: 25 minutes
Total cooking time: 20 minutes
Serves 6
Fat per serve: 7 g

4 raw large blue swimmer or mud
   crabs
1 tablespoon oil
1 large onion, finely chopped
2 cloves garlic, crushed
1 stem lemon grass, white part only,
   finely chopped
1 teaspoon sambal oelek
1 teaspoon ground cumin
1 teaspoon ground turmeric

1 teaspoon ground coriander
270 ml (9 fl oz) light coconut cream
2 cups (500 ml/16 fl oz) chicken stock
1/3 cup (20 g/3/4 oz) firmly packed
   fresh basil leaves

1 Pull back the apron and remove the
top shell from the crabs. Remove the
intestines and grey feathery gills. Cut
each crab into four pieces. Use a
cracker to crack the claws open; this
will make it easier to eat later and will
also allow the flavours to get into the
crab meat.
2 Heat the oil in a large saucepan or
wok. Add the onion, garlic, lemon
grass and sambal oelek and cook for
2–3 minutes, or until softened.

3 Add the cumin, turmeric, coriander
and 1/2 teaspoon salt, and cook for a
further 2 minutes, or until fragrant.
4 Stir in the coconut cream and stock.
Bring to the boil, then reduce the heat,
add the crab pieces and cook, stirring
occasionally, for 10 minutes, or until
the liquid has reduced and thickened
slightly and the crabs are cooked
through. Stir in the basil and serve
with steamed rice.

NUTRITION PER SERVE
Protein 0.5 g; Fat 7 g; Carbohydrate 1.5 g;
Dietary Fibre 0.5 g; Cholesterol 20 mg;
290 kJ (70 cal)

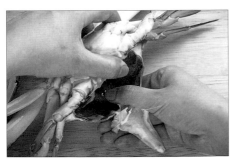

Pull back the apron and remove the top shell
from the crab.

Remove the intestines and grey feathery gills from
the crab.

Crack the claws open to allow the flavours to get
into the crab meat while it is cooking.

PRAWN CURRY

Preparation time: 25 minutes
Total cooking time: 15 minutes
Serves 6
Fat per serve: 12 g

1 tablespoon butter
1 onion, finely chopped
1 clove garlic, crushed
1½ tablespoons curry powder
2 tablespoons plain flour
2 cups (500 ml/16 fl oz) skim milk

1 kg (2 lb) raw prawns, peeled and deveined
1½ tablespoons lemon juice
2 teaspoons sherry
1 tablespoon finely chopped fresh parsley

1 Heat the butter in a large saucepan. Add the onion and garlic, and cook for 5 minutes, or until softened. Add the curry powder and cook for 1 minute, then stir in the flour and cook for a further 1 minute.
2 Remove from the heat and stir in the milk until smooth. Return to the heat and stir constantly until the sauce has thickened. Simmer for 2 minutes and then stir in the prawns. Continue to simmer for 5 minutes, or until the prawns are just cooked.
3 Stir in the lemon juice, sherry and parsley and serve immediately with rice.

NUTRITION PER SERVE
Protein 38 g; Fat 12 g; Carbohydrate 9 g; Dietary Fibre 1.5 g, Cholesterol 280 mg; 1247 kJ (298 cal)

Add the garlic and onion to the butter and cook until softened.

Return the saucepan to the heat and stir the curry constantly until thickened.

Add the prawns and continue to simmer until they are just cooked.

CLAMS IN ROASTED CHILLI PASTE

Preparation time: 15 minutes
Total cooking time: 15 minutes
Serves 4
Fat per serve: 15 g

ROASTED CHILLI PASTE
2 tablespoons oil
2 spring onions, sliced
2 cloves garlic, sliced
1/4 cup (90 g/3 oz) small dried shrimps
6 small red chillies, seeded
2 teaspoons palm sugar
2 teaspoons fish sauce
2 teaspoons tamarind concentrate
pinch of salt

3 cloves garlic, finely sliced
3 small red chillies, seeded and sliced
    lengthways
1 tablespoon light soy sauce
1 cup (250 ml/8 fl oz) chicken stock
1 kg (2 lb) clams, scrubbed
1/2 cup (25 g/3/4 oz) Thai basil leaves

1 To make the roasted chilli paste, heat the oil in a wok and fry the spring onion, garlic, dried shrimps and chillies until golden brown. Remove with a slotted spoon and keep the oil.
2 Place the onion, garlic, shrimps, chillies and sugar in a mortar and pestle or small food processor and grind until the mixture is well blended. Add the fish sauce, tamarind concentrate and salt. Blend or grind to

a fine paste. Transfer to a bowl.
3 Heat the reserved oil in the wok. Add the garlic, chilli, roasted chilli paste and soy sauce. Mix well, then add the chicken stock and bring just to the boil. Add the clams and cook over medium-high heat for 2–3 minutes. Discard any unopened clams. Stir in the basil and serve immediately with steamed jasmine rice.

NUTRITION PER SERVE
Protein 30 g; Fat 15 g; Carbohydrate 90 g;
Dietary Fibre 5 g; Cholesterol 280 mg;
2490 kJ (700 cal)

Use a slotted spoon to remove the onion, garlic, shrimps and chillies from the wok.

Blend or grind the mixture to obtain a finely textured paste.

Remove any clams that have not opened during the cooking time.

CRAB, CHILLI AND CORIANDER NOODLES

Preparation time: 15 minutes
Total cooking time: 10 minutes
Serves 4
Fat per serve: 12 g

1 tablespoon oil
4 spring onions, finely sliced
3 cloves garlic, crushed
2 green chillies, seeded and finely sliced
400 g (13 oz) fresh crab meat
3 tablespoons lime juice
3 teaspoons grated lime rind
1 teaspoon caster sugar
2 teaspoons sambal oelek
375 g (12 oz) thin dried egg noodles
1 teaspoon sesame oil
2 tablespoons sweet chilli sauce
4 tablespoons chopped fresh coriander

1 Heat the oil in a large frying pan and add the spring onion, garlic and chilli. Cook for 1–2 minutes over low heat, until soft. Add the crab meat, lime juice and rind, caster sugar and sambal oelek. Stir until heated through and season to taste with salt.
2 Cook the noodles in boiling salted water for 2–3 minutes until tender.
Drain well and toss with sesame oil.
3 Add the crab mixture, sweet chilli sauce and coriander to the noodles and gently toss. Serve immediately.

NUTRITION PER SERVE
Protein 25 g; Fat 12 g; Carbohydrate 75 g; Dietary Fibre 5 g; Cholesterol 100 mg; 2340 kJ (560 cal)

NOTE: You can also use canned crab meat instead of fresh, but you will need 4 x 200 g (6½ oz) cans, as a lot of weight will be lost when the meat is drained.

Add the crab meat, lime juice and rind, caster sugar and sambal oelek to the pan.

Cook the egg noodles in a large pan of boiling salted water.

After draining, toss the noodles with the sesame oil to prevent them sticking together.

SMOKED COD AND LENTIL SALAD

Preparation time: 25 minutes
Total cooking time: 45 minutes
Serves 6
Fat per serve: 4 g

250 g (8 oz) brown lentils
1 onion, finely chopped
1 bay leaf
500 g (1 lb) smoked cod
1/4 cup (15 g/1/2 oz) chopped fresh dill
3 spring onions, chopped
100 g (31/2 oz) sweet spiced gherkins, chopped
100 g (31/2 oz) sun-dried capsicum, chopped

DRESSING
2 cloves garlic, crushed
2 tablespoons low-fat mayonnaise
1/4 cup (60 g/2 oz) low-fat natural yoghurt
2 tablespoons chopped chives

1 Place the lentils, onion and bay leaf in a pan, cover with water and bring to the boil. Reduce the heat and simmer for 25–30 minutes, or until the lentils are just tender. Drain and set aside to cool. Do not overcook the lentils or they will become mushy.
2 Half fill a frying pan with water. Bring to the boil and add the smoked cod. Reduce the heat and simmer gently for 10 minutes, or until it flakes when tested with a fork. Drain and

cool slightly. Break into large pieces.
3 Add the dill, spring onion, gherkin and capsicum to the lentils, then gently fold in the cod pieces.
4 To make the dressing, combine the ingredients in a bowl and whisk until smooth. Pour over the salad and lightly toss to coat.

NUTRITION PER SERVE
Protein 25 g; Fat 4 g; Carbohydrate 25 g; Dietary Fibre 7 g; Cholesterol 45 mg; 1005 kJ (240 cal)

NOTE: Smoked cod is available from most supermarkets or fish markets. You can make this salad up to 3 hours ahead but don't add the dressing until you are ready to serve.

Cover the lentils, onion and bay leaf with water, and bring to the boil.

Gently simmer the smoked cod for 10 minutes, or until it flakes with a fork.

Add the dill, spring onion, gherkin and capsicum to the lentils and onion.

THAI PRAWN AND NOODLE SALAD

Preparation time: 25 minutes
Total cooking time: 5 minutes
Serves 4
Fat per serve: 15 g

DRESSING
2 tablespoons grated fresh ginger
2 tablespoons soy sauce
2 tablespoons sesame oil
1/3 cup (80 ml/2³/4 fl oz) red wine
    vinegar
3–4 teaspoons sweet chilli sauce
2 cloves garlic, crushed
1/3 cup (80 ml/2³/4 fl oz) kecap manis
    (see NOTE)

250 g (8 oz) fine instant noodles
5 spring onions, sliced
2 tablespoons chopped fresh
    coriander
1 red capsicum, chopped
100 g (3¹/2 oz) snow peas, sliced
500 g (1 lb) cooked king prawns,
    peeled, halved and deveined

1 To make the dressing, whisk together the ingredients with a fork.
2 Cook the noodles in a large pan of boiling water for 2 minutes and drain well. Add to the dressing and toss to combine. Leave to cool.
3 Add the remaining ingredients to the noodles and toss gently. Serve at room temperature.

NUTRITION PER SERVE
Protein 35 g; Fat 15 g; Carbohydrate 60 g;
Dietary Fibre 3 g; Cholesterol 235 mg;
2275 kJ (540 cal)

NOTE: Kecap manis (sweet soy sauce) is available from Asian food stores.

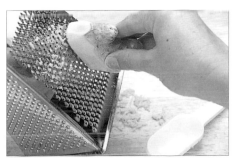

Peel and finely grate the fresh ginger on the fine side of the grater.

Add the kecap manis to the other ingredients and mix to combine.

Add the noodles to a large pan of boiling water and cook until tender.

185

TUNA WITH LIME AND CHILLI SAUCE

Preparation time: 15 minutes
Total cooking time: 5 minutes
Serves 4
Fat per serve: 5 g

1/2 cup (25 g/3/4 oz) chopped and firmly packed fresh mint leaves
1/2 cup (25 g/3/4 oz) chopped fresh coriander leaves
1 teaspoon grated lime rind
1 tablespoon lime juice
1 teaspoon grated fresh ginger
1 jalapeno chilli, seeded and finely chopped
1 cup (250 g/8 oz) low-fat natural yoghurt
4 tuna steaks

1 Mix together the mint, coriander, lime rind, lime juice, ginger and chilli. Fold in the yoghurt and season.
2 Cook the tuna in a lightly oiled chargrill pan for 2 minutes each side. Serve with the sauce.

NUTRITION PER SERVE
Protein 28 g; Fat 5 g; Carbohydrate 4 g; Dietary Fibre 1 g; Cholesterol 55 mg; 800 kJ (200 cal)

NOTE: Jalapeno chillies are smooth and thick-fleshed and are available both red and green. They are quite fiery and you can use a less powerful variety of chilli if you prefer.

It's a good idea to wear gloves to remove the seeds from chillies, to prevent skin irritation.

Mix together the mint, coriander, lime rind, juice, ginger and chilli.

Check the taste of the sauce before seasoning with salt and black pepper.

SWORDFISH WITH PINEAPPLE SALSA

Preparation time: 20 minutes
  + 2 hours standing
Total cooking time: 5 minutes
Serves 4
Fat per serve: 1 g

375 g (12 oz) pineapple, diced
1 small red onion, chopped
1 red capsicum, chopped
1 jalapeno chilli, seeded
1 tablespoon grated fresh ginger
finely grated rind of 1 lime
1 tablespoon lime juice
1/2 cup (15 g/1/2 oz) fresh coriander
  leaves, chopped
4 swordfish steaks

1 Put the diced pineapple, roughly chopped onion, capsicum, chilli and ginger in a food processor and mix, using the pulse button, until coarsely chopped. Stir in the lime rind and juice and the coriander leaves. Season with salt and pour into a small bowl.

2 Cover and leave the salsa for 2 hours (meanwhile, soak 4 wooden skewers in water). Drain off any excess liquid from the salsa.

3 Cut the swordfish into cubes and thread onto the skewers. Grill under a hot grill for 3 minutes each side, or until cooked through. Serve the skewers with the salsa.

NUTRITION PER SERVE
Protein 21 g; Fat 1 g; Carbohydrate 7 g;
Dietary Fibre 2 g; Cholesterol 55 mg;
390 kJ (120 cal)

Cut away the skin from the pineapple with a sharp knife.

Use the knife to cut out the tough eyes from the flesh of the pineapple.

Process the salsa until coarsely chopped and then stir in the remaining ingredients.

PAELLA

Preparation time: 25 minutes
Total cooking time: 45 minutes
Serves 6
Fat per serve: 14.5 g

500 g (1 lb) raw prawns
300 g (10 oz) skinless firm white fish
    fillets (see NOTE)
250 g (8 oz) black mussels
200 g (6½ oz) calamari rings
2 tablespoons olive oil
1 large onion, diced
3 cloves garlic, finely chopped
1 small red capsicum, thinly sliced
1 small red chilli, seeded and chopped
2 teaspoons paprika
1 teaspoon ground turmeric
2 tomatoes, peeled and diced
1 tablespoon tomato paste
2 cups (400 g/12 oz) long-grain rice
½ cup (125 ml/4 fl oz) white wine
5 cups (1.25 litres) fish stock
3 tablespoons chopped fresh
    flat-leaf parsley, for serving
lemon wedges, for serving

1 Peel the prawns, leaving the tails intact. Gently pull out the dark vein from each prawn back, starting at the head end. Cut the fish fillets into cubes. Scrub the mussels and pull out the hairy beards. Discard any broken mussels or any that don't close when tapped. Refrigerate the seafood, covered, until ready to use.
2 Heat the oil in a paella pan or a large deep frying pan with a lid. Add the onion, garlic, capsicum and chilli to the pan and cook over medium heat for 2 minutes, or until the onion and capsicum are soft. Add the paprika, turmeric and 1 teaspoon salt and stir-fry for 1–2 minutes, or until aromatic.

3 Add the tomato and cook for 5 minutes, or until softened. Add the tomato paste. Stir in the rice until it is well coated.
4 Pour in the wine and simmer until almost absorbed. Add all the fish stock and bring to the boil. Reduce the heat and simmer for 20 minutes, or until almost all the liquid is absorbed into the rice. There is no need to stir the rice, but you may occasionally wish to fluff it up with a fork.
5 Add the mussels to the pan, poking the shells into the rice, cover and cook for 2–3 minutes over low heat. Add the prawns and cook for 2–3 minutes. Add the fish, cover and cook for 3 minutes. Finally, add the calamari rings and cook for 1–2 minutes. By this time, the mussels should have opened—discard any unopened ones. The prawns should be pink and the fish should flake easily when tested with a fork. The calamari should be white, moist and tender. Cook for another 2–3 minutes if the seafood is not quite cooked, but avoid overcooking as the seafood will toughen and dry out.
6 Serve with parsley and lemon wedges and a green salad.

NUTRITION PER SERVE
Protein 44.5 g; Fat 14.5 g; Carbohydrate 60 g;
Dietary Fibre 3.5 g; Cholesterol 217 mg;
2360 kJ (560 cal)

NOTE: You can use just fish, or other seafood such as scampi, octopus and crabs. If using just fish, choose one with few bones and chunky flesh, such as ling, blue-eye or warehou.

Protect your hands with rubber gloves when seeding the chilli.

Peel and pull out the dark vein from along the back of each prawn.

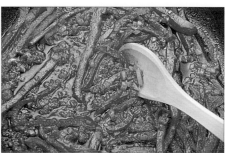
Add the paprika and turmeric to the pan and stir until aromatic.

Add the rice to the pan and stir with a wooden spoon until well coated.

Simmer the mixture until almost all the liquid is absorbed into the rice.

Cook the calamari rings for 1–2 minutes. Don't overcook or they will be tough.

MUSSELS IN CHUNKY TOMATO SAUCE

Preparation time: 15 minutes
Total cooking time: 30 minutes
Serves 6
Fat per serve: 12 g

1.5 kg (3 lb) black mussels
1 tablespoon olive oil
1 large onion, diced
4 cloves garlic, finely chopped
2 x 400 g (13 oz) cans diced tomatoes
1/4 cup (60 g/2 oz) tomato paste
1/4 cup (30 g/1 oz) pitted black olives
1 tablespoon capers
1/2 cup (125 ml/4 fl oz) fish stock
3 tablespoons chopped fresh
    flat-leaf parsley

1 Scrub the mussels with a stiff brush and pull out the hairy beards. Discard any damaged mussels, or any that don't close when tapped.

2 In a large saucepan, heat the olive oil and cook the onion and garlic over medium heat for 1–2 minutes, until softened. Add the tomato, tomato paste, olives, capers and fish stock. Bring to the boil, then reduce the heat and simmer, stirring occasionally, for 20 minutes, or until the sauce is thick.

3 Stir in the mussels and cover the saucepan. Shake or toss the mussels occasionally and cook for 4–5 minutes, or until the mussels begin to open. Remove the pan from the heat and discard any mussels that haven't opened in the cooking time.

4 Just before serving, toss the chopped parsley through.

NUTRITION PER SERVE
Protein 17 g; Fat 12 g; Carbohydrate 11 g;
Dietary Fibre 3 g; Cholesterol 35 mg;
973 kJ (233 cal)

Simmer the chunky tomato sauce, stirring occasionally, until thick.

Cook the mussels until they open. Discard any that don't open in the time.

SPAGHETTI WITH CHILLI CALAMARI

Preparation time: 15 minutes
Total cooking time: 30 minutes
Serves 4
Fat per serve: 15 g

500 g (1 lb) calamari, cleaned
500 g (1 lb) spaghetti
1 tablespoon olive oil
1 leek, chopped
2 cloves garlic, crushed
1–2 teaspoons chopped chilli
1/2 teaspoon cayenne pepper
425 g (14 oz) can crushed tomatoes
1/2 cup (125 ml/4 fl oz) fish stock
1 tablespoon chopped fresh basil
2 teaspoons chopped fresh sage
1 teaspoon chopped fresh marjoram

1 Pull the tentacles from the body of the calamari. Using your fingers, pull the quill from the pouch of the calamari. Pull the skin away from the flesh and discard. Use a sharp knife to slit the tubes up one side. Lay out flat and score one side in a diamond pattern. Cut each tube into four.
2 Cook the spaghetti in a large pan of rapidly boiling salted water until *al dente*. Drain and keep warm.
3 Heat the oil in a large frying pan. Add the leek and cook for 2 minutes. Add the garlic and stir over low heat for 1 minute. Stir in the chilli and cayenne. Add the tomato, stock and herbs and bring to the boil. Reduce the heat and simmer for 5 minutes.
4 Add the calamari to the pan. Simmer for another 5–10 minutes, or until tender. Serve the chilli calamari over the spaghetti.

NUTRITION PER SERVE
Protein 35 g; Fat 15 g; Carbohydrate 90 g;
Dietary Fibre 10 g; Cholesterol 250 mg;
2670 kJ (640 cal)

Pull the clear quill from the pouch of the calamari and then pull the skin away from the flesh.

Add the calamari to the pan and simmer for another few minutes, until tender.

191

PASTA PUTTANESCA

Preparation time: 20 minutes
Total cooking time: 20 minutes
Serves 4
Fat per serve: 15 g

500 g (1 lb) pasta
1 tablespoon olive oil
3 cloves garlic, crushed
2 tablespoons chopped fresh parsley
1/4–1/2 teaspoon chilli flakes or powder
2 x 425 g (14 oz) cans chopped
    tomatoes
1 tablespoon capers
3 anchovy fillets, thinly sliced
1/4 cup (45 g/1 1/2 oz) black olives
grated Parmesan, for serving

1 Cook the pasta in a large pan of rapidly boiling salted water until *al dente*. Drain and return to the pan.

2 While the pasta is cooking, heat the oil in a large heavy-based frying pan. Add the garlic, parsley and chilli flakes and stir constantly for about 1 minute, over medium heat.
3 Add the tomato to the pan and bring to the boil. Reduce the heat and simmer, covered, for 5 minutes.
4 Add the capers, anchovies and olives and stir for another 5 minutes. Season with black pepper. Add the

sauce to the pasta and toss gently. Serve with a little Parmesan.

NUTRITION PER SERVE:
Protein 20 g; Fat 15 g; Carbohydrate 95 g;
Dietary Fibre 9 g; Cholesterol 8 mg;
2510 kJ (595 cal)

NOTE: Traditionally, spaghetti is used with the sauce, but the pasta shown here is lasagnette.

Squash each clove of garlic with the flat side of a knife, pressing with the palm of your hand.

Roughly chop the garlic, with a little salt, then scrape the knife at an angle to finely crush.

SPAGHETTI MARINARA

Preparation time: 30 minutes
Total cooking time: 30 minutes
Serves 4
Fat per serve: 10 g

2 teaspoons olive oil
1 onion, chopped
2 cloves garlic, crushed
1/2 cup (125 ml/4 fl oz) red wine
2 tablespoons tomato paste
425 g (14 oz) can chopped tomatoes
1 cup (250 ml/8 fl oz) bottled tomato
    pasta sauce
1 tablespoon each of chopped fresh
    basil and oregano
12 mussels, beards removed, and
    scrubbed
30 g (1 oz) butter
125 g (4 oz) small calamari tubes,
    sliced
125 g (4 oz) boneless firm white fish
    fillets, cubed
200 g (6½ oz) raw prawns, peeled
    and deveined, leaving the tails
    intact
500 g (1 lb) spaghetti

1 Heat the olive oil in a large pan. Add the onion and garlic and cook over low heat for 2–3 minutes. Increase the heat to medium and add the wine, tomato paste, tomato and pasta sauce. Simmer, stirring occasionally, for 5–10 minutes or until the sauce reduces and thickens slightly. Stir in the herbs and season to taste. Keep warm.
2 While the sauce is simmering, heat ½ cup (125 ml/4 fl oz) water in a pan. Add the mussels (discarding any that are broken or already open and don't close when tapped.) Cover and steam for 3–5 minutes, or until the mussels have changed colour and opened.

Remove from the pan, discarding any mussels that haven't opened, and stir the liquid into the tomato sauce.
3 Heat the butter in a pan and sauté the calamari, fish and prawns, in batches, for 1–2 minutes, or until cooked. Add the seafood to the warm tomato sauce and stir gently.
4 Cook the pasta in a large pan of rapidly boiling salted water until *al dente* and then drain. Toss the seafood sauce with the pasta.

NUTRITION PER SERVE:
Protein 40 g; Fat 10 g; Carbohydrate 100 g; Dietary Fibre 10 g; Cholesterol 205 mg; 2840 kJ (675 cal)

Pull the beards away from the mussels and scrub the shells to remove any dirt or grit.

Remove the quills from inside the calamari tubes and slice the tubes into thin rings.

193

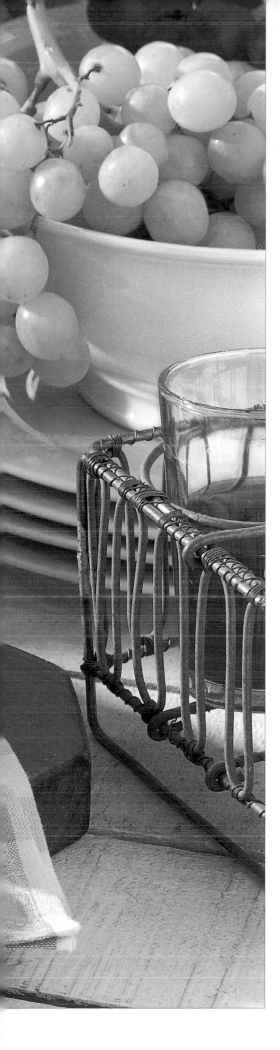

Vegetarian

MUSHROOM, RICOTTA AND OLIVE PIZZA

Preparation time: 30 minutes + proving
Total cooking time: 1 hour
Serves 6
Fat per serve: 7.5 g

4 Roma tomatoes, quartered
3/4 teaspoon caster sugar
7 g (1/4 oz) dry yeast or
　　15 g (1/2 oz) fresh yeast
1/2 cup (125 ml/4 fl oz) skim milk
13/4 cups (220 g/7 oz) plain flour
2 teaspoons olive oil
2 cloves garlic, crushed
1 onion, thinly sliced
750 g (1 1/2 lb) mushrooms, sliced
1 cup (250 g/8 oz) low-fat ricotta
2 tablespoons sliced black olives
small fresh basil leaves

1 Preheat the oven to hot 210°C (415°F/Gas 6–7). Put the tomato on a baking tray covered with baking paper, sprinkle with salt, cracked black pepper and 1/2 teaspoon sugar and bake for 20 minutes, or until the edges are starting to darken.
2 Stir the yeast and remaining sugar with 3 tablespoons warm water until the yeast dissolves. Cover and leave in a warm place until foamy. Warm the milk. Sift the flour into a large bowl and stir in the yeast and milk. Mix to a soft dough, then turn onto a lightly floured surface and knead for 5 minutes. Leave, covered, in a lightly oiled bowl in a warm place for 40 minutes, or until doubled in size.
3 Heat the oil in a pan and fry the garlic and onion until soft. Add the mushrooms and stir until they are soft and the liquid has evaporated. Leave to cool.
4 Turn the dough out onto a lightly floured surface and knead lightly. Roll out to a 36 cm (15 inch) circle and transfer to a lightly greased oven or pizza tray. Spread with the ricotta, leaving a border to turn over the filling. Top with the mushrooms, leaving a circle in the centre, and arrange the tomato and olives in the circle. Fold the dough edge over onto the mushroom and dust the edge with flour. Bake for 25 minutes, or until the crust is golden. Garnish with basil.

NUTRITION PER SERVE
Protein 15 g; Fat 7.5 g; Carbohydrate 30g;
Dietary Fibre 6 g; Cholesterol 20 mg;
1100 kJ (265 cal)

The yeast mixture is ready when it starts to foam—this shows the yeast is active.

Spread the ricotta over the pastry, leaving a border to turn over the filling.

ASIAN MUSHROOM RISOTTO

Preparation time: 20 minutes +
20 minutes soaking
Total cooking time: 45 minutes
Serves 4
Fat per serve: 15 g

10 g (¼ oz) dried Chinese
mushrooms
2 cups (500 ml/16 fl oz) vegetable
stock
2 tablespoons soy sauce
⅓ cup (80 ml/2¾ fl oz) mirin
150 g (5 oz) Swiss brown mushrooms
150 g (5 oz) oyster mushrooms
100 g (3½ oz) fresh shiitake
mushrooms
150 g (5 oz) shimeji mushrooms
1 tablespoon butter
1 tablespoon olive oil
1 onion, finely chopped
3 cloves garlic, crushed
1 tablespoon finely chopped fresh
ginger
2 cups (440 g/14 oz) arborio rice
100 g (3½ oz) enoki mushrooms,
trimmed
2 tablespoons snipped fresh chives
shaved Parmesan, to garnish

1 Put the Chinese mushrooms in a bowl, cover with 2½ cups (625 ml/ 20 fl oz) hot water and soak for 20 minutes, then drain, reserving the liquid. Remove the stems and thinly slice the caps.
2 Heat the vegetable stock, soy sauce, mirin, reserved mushroom liquid and 1 cup (250 ml/8 fl oz) water in a large saucepan. Bring to the boil, then keep at a low simmer, skimming off any scum that forms on the surface.
3 Trim and slice the Swiss brown, oyster and shiitake mushrooms, discarding any woody ends. Trim the shimeji and pull apart into small clumps. Melt the butter in a large saucepan over medium heat, add all the mushrooms except the Chinese and enoki and cook, stirring, for 3 minutes, or until wilted, then remove from the pan.
4 Add the oil to the pan, then add the chopped onion and cook, stirring, for 4–5 minutes, or until soft and just

starting to brown. Add the garlic and ginger and stir well until fragrant. Add the rice and stir for 1 minute, or until it is well coated in the oil mixture.
5 Gradually add ½ cup (125 ml/4 fl oz) of the hot stock to the rice. Stir constantly over medium heat until nearly all the liquid has been absorbed. Continue adding more stock, a little at a time, stirring for

20–25 minutes, until all the stock has been absorbed and the rice is tender.
6 Add all the mushrooms and stir well. Season and garnish with the chives and shaved Parmesan.

NUTRITION PER SERVE
Protein 17 g; Fat 15 g; Carbohydrate 92 g;
Dietary Fibre 8 g; Cholesterol 28 mg;
2397 kJ (573 cal)

Divide the shimeji and slice the Swiss brown, oyster and shiitake mushrooms.

Stir the rice constantly until nearly all the liquid has been absorbed.

POTATOES IN MEDITERRANEAN SAUCE

Preparation time: 30 minutes
Total cooking time: 50 minutes
Serves 6
Fat per serve: 10 g

1 kg (2 lb) chats or baby potatoes,
  unpeeled, halved
1 tablespoon olive oil
2 onions, finely chopped
3 cloves garlic, crushed
1 teaspoon sweet paprika
425 g (14 oz) can chopped tomatoes
2 tablespoons lemon juice

1/2 teaspoon grated lemon rind
2 teaspoons soft brown sugar
3 teaspoons tomato paste
1/2 teaspoon dried thyme
12 Kalamata olives
1 tablespoon capers, rinsed and
  roughly chopped
150 g (5 oz) feta cheese, cubed
1 tablespoon roughly chopped fresh
  flat-leaf parsley

1 Boil the potato until just tender. Heat the olive oil in a large saucepan, add the onion and cook until soft and golden. Add the garlic and paprika and cook for another minute.
2 Stir in the tomato, lemon juice, lemon rind, sugar, tomato paste and thyme. Simmer, covered, for 5 minutes and then add the potato and toss to coat. Simmer, covered, for 20 minutes, or until the potato is cooked through. Stir occasionally to prevent burning.
3 Remove the pan from the heat and, just before serving, stir through the olives, capers and feta. Season to taste and scatter the parsley over the top before serving.

NUTRITION PER SERVE
Protein 10 g; Fat 10 g; Carbohydrate 30 g;
Dietary Fibre 5 g; Cholesterol 15 mg;
1120 kJ (270 cal)

Stir in the tomato, lemon juice and rind, sugar, tomato paste and thyme.

Add the potato to the tomato sauce. Toss to coat well and then leave to simmer.

Stir in the olives, capers and cubes of feta just before serving.

SPINACH PIE

Preparation time: 25 minutes
Total cooking time: 45 minutes
Serves 6
Fat per serve: 10 g

1.5 kg (3 lb) English spinach
2 teaspoons olive oil
1 onion, chopped
4 spring onions, chopped
750 g (1½ lb) reduced-fat
   cottage cheese
2 eggs, lightly beaten
2 cloves garlic, crushed
pinch of ground nutmeg
¼ cup (15 g/½ oz) chopped fresh
   mint
8 sheets filo pastry
30 g (1 oz) butter, melted
½ cup (40 g/1¼ oz) fresh
   breadcrumbs

1 Preheat the oven to moderate 180°C (350°F/Gas 4). Lightly spray a square 1.5 litre capacity ovenproof dish with oil. Trim and wash the spinach, then place in a large pan. Cover and cook for 2–3 minutes, until the spinach is just wilted. Drain, cool then squeeze dry and chop.

2 Heat the oil in a small pan. Add the onion and spring onion and cook for 2–3 minutes, until softened. Combine in a bowl with the chopped spinach. Stir in the cottage cheese, egg, garlic, nutmeg and mint. Season and mix together thoroughly.

3 Brush a sheet of filo pastry with a little butter. Fold in half widthways and line the base and sides of the dish. Repeat with 3 more sheets. Keep the unused sheets moist by covering with a damp tea towel.

4 Sprinkle the breadcrumbs over the pastry. Spread the filling into the dish. Fold over any overlapping pastry. Brush and fold another sheet and place on top. Repeat with 3 more sheets. Tuck the pastry in at the sides. Brush the top with any remaining butter. Score squares or diamonds on top using a sharp knife. Bake for 40 minutes, or until golden. Cut the pie into squares to serve.

NUTRITION PER SERVE
Protein 35 g; Fat 10 g; Carbohydrate 30 g;
Dietary Fibre 8 g; Cholesterol 75 mg;
1500 kJ (360 cal)

Use your hands to squeeze the water out of the cooled spinach.

Line the base and sides of the dish with the greased and folded filo.

When you have covered the top with pastry, tuck it in at the sides.

MIDDLE EASTERN POTATO CASSEROLE

Preparation time: 10 minutes
Total cooking time: 30 minutes
Serves 4
Fat per serve: 6 g

1/4 teaspoon saffron threads
1 kg (2 lb) potatoes, cut into large
    cubes
1 teaspoon olive oil
1 small onion, sliced
1/2 teaspoon ground turmeric
1/2 teaspoon ground coriander

1 cup (250 ml/8 fl oz) vegetable stock
1 clove garlic, crushed
1/4 cup (30 g/1 oz) raisins
1 teaspoon chopped fresh
    flat-leaf parsley
1 teaspoon chopped fresh coriander
    leaves

1 Put the saffron to soak in 1 table-spoon of hot water. Place the potato in a saucepan of cold, salted water. Bring to the boil and cook until tender but still firm. Drain and set aside.
2 Heat the oil in a separate saucepan, add the onion, turmeric and ground coriander and cook over low heat for

5 minutes, or until the onion is soft.
3 Add the potato, vegetable stock and garlic. Bring to the boil, then reduce the heat and simmer for 10 minutes.
4 Add the saffron with its soaking water and the raisins, and cook for 10 minutes, or until the potato is soft and the sauce has reduced and thickened. Stir in the parsley and coriander. Delicious with couscous.

NUTRITION PER SERVE
Protein 10 g; Fat 6 g; Carbohydrate 65 g;
Dietary Fibre 8 g; Cholesterol 0.5 mg;
1500 kJ (358 cal)

Soak the saffron threads in 1 tablespoon hot water while you cook the potatoes.

Cook the onion, turmeric and ground coriander until the onion is soft.

Add the potato, stock and garlic to the saucepan and bring to the boil.

CHICKPEA CURRY

Preparation time: 10 minutes +
    overnight soaking
Total cooking time: 1 hour 15 minutes
Serves 6
Fat per serve: 9 g

1 cup (220 g/7 oz) dried chickpeas
1 tablespoon oil
2 onions, finely chopped
2 large ripe tomatoes, chopped
1/2 teaspoon ground coriander
1 teaspoon ground cumin
1 teaspoon chilli powder
1/4 teaspoon ground turmeric
1 tablespoon channa masala (see
    NOTE)
1 small white onion, sliced
mint and coriander leaves, to garnish

1 Place the chickpeas in a bowl, cover with water and leave to soak overnight. Drain, rinse and place in a large saucepan. Cover with plenty of water and bring to the boil, then reduce the heat and simmer for 40 minutes, or until soft. Drain.
2 Heat the oil in a large saucepan, add the onion and cook over medium heat for 15 minutes, or until golden brown. Add the tomato, ground coriander and cumin, chilli powder, turmeric and channa masala, and 2 cups (500 ml/ 16 fl oz) water and cook for 10 minutes, or until the tomato is soft. Add the chickpeas, season and cook for 7–10 minutes, or until the sauce thickens. Garnish with sliced onion and fresh mint and coriander leaves.

NUTRITION PER SERVE
Protein 8 g; Fat 9 g; Carbohydrate 17 g;
Dietary Fibre 6 g; Cholesterol 8.5 mg;
835 kJ (200 cal)

NOTE: Channa (chole) masala is a spice blend available at Indian grocery stores. Garam masala can be used as a substitute but the flavour will be a little different.

Cook the onion over medium heat for 15 minutes, or until golden brown.

Add the soaked chickpeas and cook until the sauce thickens.

ASIAN BARLEY PILAU

Preparation time: 10 minutes +
  15 minutes standing
Total cooking time: 35 minutes
Serves 4
Fat per serve: 8.5 g

15 g (¹/₂ oz) dried sliced mushrooms
2 cups (500 ml/16 fl oz) vegetable
  stock
¹/₂ cup (125 ml/4 fl oz) dry sherry
1 tablespoon oil
3 large French shallots, thinly sliced
2 large cloves garlic, crushed
1 tablespoon grated fresh ginger
1 teaspoon Sichuan peppercorns,
  crushed (see NOTE)
1¹/₂ cups (330 g/11 oz) pearl barley
500 g (1 lb) choy sum, cut into short
  lengths
3 teaspoons kecap manis
1 teaspoon sesame oil

1 Place the mushrooms in a bowl and
cover with boiling water, then leave
for 15 minutes. Strain, reserving
¹/₂ cup (125 ml/4 fl oz) of the liquid.
2 Bring the stock and sherry to the
boil in a saucepan, then reduce the
heat, cover and simmer until needed.
3 Heat the oil in a large saucepan and
cook the shallots over medium heat
for 2–3 minutes, or until soft. Add the
garlic, ginger and peppercorns and
cook for 1 minute. Add the barley and
mushrooms and mix well. Stir in the
stock and mushroom liquid, then
reduce the heat and simmer, covered,
for 25 minutes, or until the liquid
has evaporated.
4 Meanwhile, steam the choy sum
until wilted. Add to the barley mixture.
Stir in the kecap manis and sesame oil
to serve.

NUTRITION PER SERVE
Protein 13 g; Fat 8.5 g; Carbohydrate 52 g;
Dietary Fibre 13 g; Cholesterol 0 mg;
1552 kJ (370 cal)

NOTE: You can buy Sichuan
peppercorns at Asian food stores.

French shallots are like small onions. Peel them and then slice thinly.

Use a mortar and pestle to crush the Sichuan peppercorns.

Strain the mushrooms, reserving some of the liquid for flavouring the pilau.

Reduce the heat and simmer the pilau until the liquid has evaporated.

STUFFED EGGPLANTS

Preparation time: 20 minutes
Total cooking time: 1 hour
Serves 4
Fat per serve: 10 g

1/3 cup (60 g/2 oz) brown lentils
2 large eggplants
cooking oil spray
1 red onion, chopped
2 cloves garlic, crushed
1 red capsicum, finely chopped
1/4 cup (40 g/1 1/4 oz) pine nuts, toasted
3/4 cup (140 g/4 1/2 oz) cooked short-grain rice

440 g (14 oz) can chopped tomatoes
2 tablespoons chopped fresh coriander
1 tablespoon chopped fresh parsley
2 tablespoons grated Parmesan

1 Simmer the brown lentils in a pan of water for 25 minutes, or until soft; drain. Slice the eggplants in half lengthways and scoop out the flesh, leaving a 1 cm (1/2 inch) shell. Chop the flesh finely.

2 Spray a deep, large non-stick frying pan with oil, add 1 tablespoon water to the pan, then add the onion and garlic and stir until softened. Add the cooked lentils to the pan with the capsicum, pine nuts, rice, tomato and eggplant flesh. Stir over medium heat for 10 minutes, or until the eggplant has softened. Add the fresh coriander and parsley. Season, then toss until well mixed.

3 Cook the eggplant shells in boiling water for 4–5 minutes, or until tender, or microwave on High (100%) for 8 minutes. Spoon the filling into the eggplant shells and sprinkle with the Parmesan. Grill for 5–10 minutes, or until golden. Serve immediately.

NUTRITION PER SERVE
Protein 15 g; Fat 10 g; Carbohydrate 50 g;
Dietary Fibre 8.5 g; Cholesterol 9.5 mg;
1490 kJ (355 cal)

Scoop out the flesh, leaving a shell on the inside of the eggplant halves.

Stir in the chopped fresh coriander and parsley and season.

Cook the eggplant halves in boiling water for about 5 minutes, or until tender.

FETTUCINE BOSCAIOLA

Preparation time: 20 minutes
Total cooking time: 25 minutes
Serves 6
Fat per serve: 10 g

500 g (1 lb) button mushrooms
1 large onion
1 tablespoon olive oil
2 cloves garlic, finely chopped
2 x 425 g (14 oz) cans tomatoes,
   roughly chopped
500 g (1 lb) fettucine
2 tablespoons chopped fresh parsley

1 Wipe the mushrooms with a damp paper towel and then slice finely, including the stems.
2 Chop the onion roughly. Heat the oil in a heavy-based frying pan and cook the onion and garlic over medium heat, stirring occasionally, for about 6 minutes, or until the vegetables are light golden. Add the tomato including the juice, along with the mushrooms, to the pan and bring the mixture to the boil. Reduce the heat, cover the pan and simmer for 15 minutes.
3 While the sauce is cooking, cook the fettucine in a large pan of rapidly boiling salted water until *al dente*. Drain and return to the pan.
4 Stir the parsley into the sauce and season well with salt and pepper. Toss the sauce through the pasta.

NUTRITION PER SERVE
Protein 15 g; Fat 10 g; Carbohydrate 65 g; Dietary Fibre 10 g; Cholesterol 0 mg; 1640 kJ (390 cal)

Wipe the mushrooms with a damp paper towel to remove any dirt.

Use a large sharp knife to roughly chop the onion and then cook until golden.

Add the chopped tomatoes and sliced mushrooms to the pan.

203

VEGETABLE CASSEROLE WITH HERB DUMPLINGS

Preparation time: 30 minutes
Total cooking time: 50 minutes
Serves 4
Fat per serve: 10 g

1 tablespoon olive oil
1 large onion, chopped
2 cloves garlic, crushed
2 teaspoons sweet paprika
1 large potato, chopped
1 large carrot, sliced
400 g (13 oz) can chopped tomatoes
1¹/₂ cups (375 ml/12 fl oz) vegetable
    stock
400 g (13 oz) orange sweet potato,
    cubed
150 g (5 oz) broccoli, cut into florets
2 zucchini, thickly sliced
1 cup (125 g/4 oz) self-raising flour
20 g (³/₄ oz) cold butter, cut into small
    cubes
2 teaspoons chopped fresh flat-leaf
    parsley
1 teaspoon fresh thyme
1 teaspoon chopped fresh rosemary
¹/₃ cup (80 ml/2³/₄ fl oz) milk
2 tablespoons light sour cream

1 Heat the oil in a large saucepan and add the onion. Cook over low heat, stirring occasionally, for 5 minutes, or until soft. Add the garlic and paprika and cook, stirring, for 1 minute.
2 Add the potato, carrot, tomato and stock to the pan. Bring to the boil, then reduce the heat and simmer, covered, for 10 minutes. Add the sweet potato, broccoli and zucchini and simmer for 10 minutes, or until tender. Preheat the oven to moderately hot 200°C (400°F/Gas 6).
3 To make the dumplings, sift the

flour and a pinch of salt into a bowl and add the butter. Rub the butter into the flour with your fingertips until it resembles fine breadcrumbs. Stir in the herbs and make a well in the centre. Add the milk, and mix with a flat-bladed knife, using a cutting action, until the mixture comes together in beads. Gather up the dough and lift onto a lightly floured surface, then divide into eight portions. Shape each portion into a ball.

4 Add the sour cream to the casserole. Pour into a 2 litre ovenproof dish and top with the dumplings. Bake for 20 minutes, or until the dumplings are golden and a skewer comes out clean when inserted in the centre.

NUTRITION PER SERVE
Protein 8 g; Fat 10 g; Carbohydrate 27 g;
Dietary Fibre 7.5 g; Cholesterol 16 mg;
967 kJ (230 cal)

Add the remaining vegetables and simmer for 10 minutes, or until they are tender.

Rub the butter into the flour until the mixture resembles fine breadcrumbs.

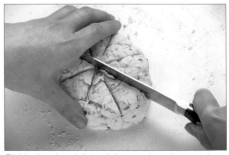

Divide the dough into eight equal portions and shape each portion into a dumpling.

VEGETABLE CURRY

Preparation time: 20 minutes
Total cooking time: 30 minutes
Serves 6
Fat per serve: 8.5 g

250 g (8 oz) potatoes, diced
250 g (8 oz) pumpkin, diced
200 g (6¹/₂ oz) cauliflower, broken into florets
150 g (5 oz) yellow squash, cut into quarters
1 tablespoon oil
2 onions, chopped
3 tablespoons curry powder

400 g (13 oz) can crushed tomatoes
1 cup (250 ml/8 fl oz) vegetable stock
150 g (5 oz) green beans, cut into short lengths
¹/₃ cup (90 g/3 oz) natural yoghurt
¹/₄ cup (30 g/1 oz) sultanas

1 Bring a saucepan of water to the boil, add the potato and pumpkin, and cook for 6 minutes, then remove. Add the cauliflower and squash, cook for 4 minutes, then remove.
2 Heat the oil in a large saucepan, add the onion and cook, stirring, over medium heat for 8 minutes, or until starting to brown.
3 Add the curry powder and stir for

1 minute, or until fragrant. Stir in the crushed tomato and vegetable stock.
4 Add the parboiled potato, pumpkin, cauliflower and squash and cook for 5 minutes, then add the green beans and cook for a further 2–3 minutes, or until the vegetables are just tender.
5 Add the yoghurt and sultanas, and stir to combine. Simmer for 3 minutes, or until thickened slightly. Season to taste and serve with lemon wedges.

NUTRITION PER SERVE
Protein 7 g; Fat 8.5 g; Carbohydrate 20 g;
Dietary Fibre 7 g; Cholesterol 2.5 mg;
805 kJ (192 cal)

Cook the onion over medium heat until it is starting to brown.

Add the beans and cook until the vegetables are just tender.

Add the yoghurt and sultanas and simmer until thickened slightly.

PASTA POMODORO

Preparation time: 15 minutes
Total cooking time: 15 minutes
Serves 4
Fat per serve: 10 g

500 g (1 lb) pasta
1 tablespoon olive oil
1 onion, finely chopped
2 x 400 g (13 oz) cans Italian
   tomatoes, chopped
1/4 cup (7 g/1/4 oz) fresh basil leaves

1 Cook the pasta in a large pan of rapidly boiling salted water until *al dente*. Drain, return to the pan and keep warm.
2 Heat the oil in a large frying pan. Add the onion and cook over medium heat until softened. Stir in the chopped tomato and simmer for 5–6 minutes, or until the sauce has reduced slightly and thickened. Season with salt and pepper. Stir in the basil leaves and cook for another minute.
3 Pour the sauce over the warm pasta and gently toss through. Serve immediately.

NUTRITION PER SERVE
Protein 20 g; Fat 10 g; Carbohydrate 95 g;
Dietary Fibre 10 g; Cholesterol 0 mg;
2295 kJ (545 cal)

To finely chop an onion, cut in half, then slice horizontally, without cutting all the way through.

Next, make cuts close together across one way, and then in the opposite direction.

PASTA NAPOLITANA

Preparation time: 20 minutes
Total cooking time: 1 hour
Serves 6
Fat per serve: 7 g

1 tablespoon olive oil
1 onion, finely chopped
1 carrot, finely chopped
1 celery stick, finely chopped
500 g (1 lb) ripe tomatoes, chopped
2 tablespoons chopped fresh parsley
2 teaspoons sugar
500 g (1 lb) pasta

1 Heat the oil in a heavy-based pan. Add the onion, carrot and celery. Cover and cook for 10 minutes over low heat, stirring occasionally.

2 Add the tomato to the vegetables with the parsley, sugar and 1/2 cup (125 ml/4 fl oz) of water. Bring to the boil, reduce the heat to low, cover and simmer for 45 minutes, stirring occasionally. Season with salt and pepper. If necessary, add a little more water to thin the sauce.
3 Add the pasta to a large pan of rapidly boiling salted water and cook until *al dente*. Drain and return to the pan. Pour the sauce over the pasta and gently toss.

NUTRITION PER SERVE
Protein 10 g; Fat 7 g; Carbohydrate 65 g;
Dietary Fibre 6 g; Cholesterol 0 mg;
1540 kJ (365 cal)

Chop the vegetables into small even pieces before adding to the oil.

Add the chopped tomatoes, parsley, sugar and water to the cooked vegetables.

TWO-TONED POTATO GNOCCHI

Preparation time: 1 hour 30 minutes
Total cooking time: 45 minutes
Serves 6
Fat per serve: 7 g

450 g (14 oz) floury potatoes,
    chopped
200 g (6¹/₂ oz) orange sweet potato,
    chopped
1¹/₂ cups (185 g/6 oz) plain flour
Parmesan shavings, to garnish

TOMATO AND CORIANDER SAUCE
1 tablespoon olive oil
3 cloves garlic, sliced thickly
1 onion, chopped
1 kg (2 lb) ripe tomatoes, peeled and
    chopped
1 small red chilli, seeded and diced
¹/₃ cup (10 g/¹/₃ oz) fresh coriander
    leaves

1 Steam or boil the chopped potato and sweet potato until tender and mash them in separate bowls. Add 1 cup (125 g/4 oz) of flour with 1 teaspoon of salt to the plain potato and bring together to make a smooth dough. Add enough of the remaining flour to the sweet potato to gently bring together. The mixtures should be slightly sticky to touch. On a lightly floured surface, press the two doughs together gently until they have a two-tone appearance.

2 Divide the mixture into four and roll each, on a lightly floured surface, into a log about 2.5 cm (1 inch) thick. Slice the logs into 2 cm (³/₄ inch) pieces. Shape each piece into an oval and roll the gnocchi ovals onto the prongs of a floured fork. You should have about 40 pieces. Put on a lightly floured tray and cover.

3 To make the tomato and coriander sauce, heat the oil in a heavy-based pan, add the garlic and cook over low heat for 2 minutes, or until it just begins to brown slightly. Remove with a slotted spoon and discard. Add the onion and cook until softened. Add the tomato and bring to the boil. Reduce the heat and simmer for 30–35 minutes, stirring occasionally.

Add the chilli and coriander leaves.
4 Cook the gnocchi in boiling water in batches for 2 minutes, or until they float to the surface. Remove each batch with a slotted spoon. Serve on the sauce. Garnish with Parmesan.

NUTRITION PER SERVE
Protein 7 g; Fat 7 g; Carbohydrate 40 g;
Dietary Fibre 4 g; Cholesterol 2 mg;
1060 kJ (255 cal)

Press the two doughs together gently until they take on a two-tone appearance.

Roll the gnocchi over the back of a fork to give the characteristic indentations.

VEGETARIAN CHILLI

Preparation time: 15 minutes
Total cooking time: 40 minutes
Serves 8
Fat per serve: 10 g

3/4 cup (150 g/5 oz) burghul (cracked wheat)
1 tablespoon olive oil
1 large onion, finely chopped
2 cloves garlic, crushed
1 teaspoon chilli powder
2 teaspoons ground cumin
1 teaspoon cayenne pepper
1/2 teaspoon ground cinnamon
2 x 400 g (13 oz) cans crushed tomatoes
3 cups (750 ml/24 fl oz) vegetable stock
440 g (14 oz) can red kidney beans, rinsed and drained
2 x 300 g (10 oz) cans chickpeas, rinsed and drained
310 g (10 oz) can corn kernels, drained
2 tablespoons tomato paste
corn chips and light sour cream, for serving

1 Soak the burghul in 1 cup (250 ml/ 8 fl oz) of hot water for 10 minutes. Heat the oil in a large heavy-based pan and cook the onion for 10 minutes, stirring often, until soft and golden.
2 Add the garlic, chilli powder, cumin, cayenne and cinnamon and cook, stirring, for a further minute.
3 Add the tomatoes, stock and burghul. Bring to the boil and simmer for 10 minutes. Stir in the beans, chickpeas, corn and tomato paste and simmer for 20 minutes, stirring often. Serve with corn chips and sour cream.

NUTRITION PER SERVE
Protein 7 g; Fat 10 g; Carbohydrate 18 g; Dietary Fibre 7 g; Cholesterol 8 mg; 780 kJ (185 cal)

STORAGE TIME: Chilli will keep for up to 3 days in the refrigerator (and can be frozen for up to 1 month).

Stir the garlic and spices into the pan with the onion and cook for a minute.

Add the crushed tomatoes, stock and burghul to the pan.

Stir in the beans, chickpeas, corn kernels and tomato paste.

POLENTA PIE

Preparation time: 20 minutes +
   15 minutes standing + refrigeration
Total cooking time: 50 minutes
Serves 6
Fat per serve: 8.5 g

2 eggplants, thickly sliced
1¹/₃ cups (350 ml/11 fl oz) vegetable
   stock
1 cup (150 g/5 oz) fine polenta
¹/₂ cup (60 g/2 oz) finely grated
   Parmesan
1 tablespoon olive oil
1 large onion, chopped
2 cloves garlic, crushed
1 large red capsicum, diced
2 zucchini, thickly sliced
150 g (5 oz) button mushrooms, cut
   into quarters
400 g (13 oz) can chopped tomatoes
3 teaspoons balsamic vinegar
olive oil, for brushing

1 Spread the eggplant in a single layer on a board and sprinkle with salt. Leave for 15 minutes, then rinse, pat dry and cut into cubes.
2 Line a 22 cm (9 inch) round cake tin with foil. Pour the stock and 1¹/₃ cups (350 ml/11 fl oz) water into a saucepan and bring to the boil. Add the polenta in a thin stream and stir over low heat for 5 minutes, or until the liquid is absorbed and the mixture comes away from the side of the pan.
3 Remove from the heat and stir in the cheese until it melts through the polenta. Spread into the prepared tin, smoothing the surface as much as possible. Refrigerate until set.
4 Preheat the oven to moderately hot 200°C (400°F/Gas 6). Heat the oil in a large saucepan with a lid and add the

onion. Cook over medium heat, stirring occasionally, for 3 minutes, or until soft. Add the garlic and cook for a further 1 minute. Add the eggplant, capsicum, zucchini, mushrooms and tomato. Bring to the boil, then reduce the heat and simmer, covered, for 20 minutes, or until the vegetables are tender. Stir occasionally to prevent catching on the bottom of the pan. Stir in the vinegar and season.
5 Transfer the vegetable mixture to a 22 cm (9 inch) ovenproof pie dish,

piling it up slightly in the centre.
6 Turn out the polenta, peel off the foil and cut into 12 wedges. Arrange smooth-side-down in a single layer, over the vegetables—don't worry about any gaps. Brush lightly with a little olive oil and bake for 20 minutes, or until lightly brown and crisp.

NUTRITION PER SERVE
Protein 8 g; Fat 8.5 g; Carbohydrate 23 g;
Dietary Fibre 4.5 g; Cholesterol 8 mg;
855 kJ (205 cal)

Cook the polenta, stirring, until all the liquid is absorbed and it is very thick.

Reduce the heat and simmer until the vegetables are tender.

Arrange the polenta wedges, smooth-side-down, over the vegetable mixture.

ROAST VEGETABLE QUICHE

Preparation time: 45 minutes
  + 25 minutes refrigeration
Total cooking time: 2 hours 30 minutes
Serves 6
Fat per serve: 10 g

cooking oil spray
1 large potato
400 g (13 oz) pumpkin
200 g (6¹/₂ oz) orange sweet potato
2 large parsnips
1 red capsicum
2 onions, cut into wedges
6 cloves garlic, halved
2 teaspoons olive oil
1¹/₄ cups (150 g/5 oz) plain flour
40 g (1¹/₄ oz) butter
45 g (1¹/₂ oz) ricotta
1 cup (250 ml/8 fl oz) skim milk
3 eggs, lightly beaten
¹/₄ cup (30 g/1 oz) grated reduced-fat
  Cheddar
2 tablespoons chopped fresh basil

1 Preheat the oven to moderate 180°C (350°F/Gas 4). Lightly spray a 3.5 cm (1¹/₄ inch) deep, 23 cm (9 inch) diameter loose-based flan tin with oil. Cut the potato, pumpkin, sweet potato, parsnips and capsicum into bite-sized chunks, place in a baking dish with the onion and garlic and drizzle with the oil. Season and bake for 1 hour, or until the vegetables are tender. Leave to cool.
2 Mix the flour, butter and ricotta in a food processor, then gradually add up to 3 tablespoons of the milk, enough to form a soft dough. Turn out onto a lightly floured surface and gather together into a smooth ball. Cover and refrigerate for 15 minutes.

3 Roll the pastry out on a lightly floured surface, then ease into the tin, bringing it gently up the side. Trim the edge and refrigerate for another 10 minutes. Increase the oven to moderately hot 200°C (400°F/Gas 6). Cover the pastry with crumpled baking paper and fill with baking beads or uncooked rice. Bake for 10 minutes, remove the beads or rice and paper, then bake for another 10 minutes, or until golden brown.
4 Place the vegetables in the pastry

base and pour in the combined remaining milk, eggs, cheese and basil. Reduce the oven temperature to moderate 180°C (350°F/Gas 4) and bake for 1 hour 10 minutes, or until set in the centre. Leave for 5 minutes before removing from the tin to serve.

NUTRITION PER SERVE
Protein 15 g; Fat 10 g; Carbohydrate 45 g;
Dietary Fibre 5.5 g; Cholesterol 115 mg;
1440 kJ (345 cal)

Put the vegetables in a baking dish and drizzle with the olive oil.

Ease the pastry into the flan tin, bring it up the side, then trim the edge.

Mix the milk, eggs, cheese and basil and pour over the vegetables.

VEGETABLE STRUDEL PARCELS

Preparation time: 1 hour
Total cooking time: 30 minutes
Serves 4
Fat per serve: 8 g

300 g (10 oz) pumpkin
2 carrots
1 parsnip
2 celery sticks
2 teaspoons sesame oil
1 onion, finely sliced
3 teaspoons finely chopped or
    grated fresh ginger
1 tablespoon dry sherry
1 teaspoon finely grated lemon rind
1 cup (185 g/6 oz) cooked long-grain
    rice
2 tablespoons plum sauce
1 tablespoon sweet chilli sauce
2 teaspoons soy sauce
16 sheets filo pastry
1/3 cup (35 g/1 1/4 oz) dry
    breadcrumbs
1 teaspoon butter, melted
1 tablespoon sesame seeds
sweet chilli sauce, for serving

1 Cut the pumpkin, carrots, parsnip and celery into thick matchsticks about 2.5 mm (1/8 inch) wide and 5 cm (2 inches) long.
2 Heat the sesame oil in a heavy-based pan or wok, add the onion and ginger and stir-fry, tossing well until brown, over medium heat. Add the pumpkin, carrot and parsnip, toss well and cook for 1 minute. Sprinkle 2 teaspoons of water all over the vegetables, cover and steam for another minute. Add the celery, sherry and lemon rind, toss and cook for 1 minute. Cover again and let steam for about 1 minute, or until the vegetables are just tender. Stir in the cooked rice and the plum, chilli and soy sauces. Set aside for about 20 minutes to cool.
3 Preheat the oven to moderately hot 190°C (375°F/Gas 5). Remove two sheets of filo pastry, keeping the remaining pastry covered with a damp tea towel. Place one sheet on top of the other, carefully brush the edges lightly with a little water, then scatter some breadcrumbs over the pastry. Top with another 2 sheets of pastry, fold over the edges to make a 2 cm (3/4 inch) border and brush lightly with a little water. Press the edges down gently with your fingertips to make the parcel easier to fold.
4 Place one-quarter of the filling about 5 cm (2 inches) from the short end, then firmly roll into a parcel to encase the filling, ensuring that the seam is underneath. Repeat with the remaining ingredients.
5 Brush the tops very lightly with butter, cut 3 slashes across the top of each and scatter any remaining breadcrumbs and the sesame seeds over the top. Arrange on a lightly greased baking tray and bake for 20–25 minutes, or until crisp and golden. Serve immediately, drizzled with sweet chilli sauce.

NUTRITION PER SERVE
Protein 15 g; Fat 8 g; Carbohydrate 95 g; Dietary Fibre 7 g; Cholesterol 3 mg; 2210 kJ (530 cal)

HINT: Cover the filo pastry that is waiting to be used with a damp tea towel to prevent it drying out.

Cut the pumpkin, carrot, parsnip and celery into similar-sized short matchsticks.

Stir the rice and plum, chilli and soy sauces into the vegetables.

Moisten the pastry before scattering the breadcrumbs over it.

Fold the pastry edges over, brush with water, then press down lightly.

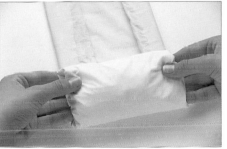

Put the filling on the pastry, then firmly roll it up into a parcel.

Cut 3 slashes on the top of each parcel to allow steam to escape.

213

SPICY BEANS ON BAKED SWEET POTATO

Preparation time: 20 minutes
Total cooking time: 1 hour 30 minutes
Serves 6
Fat per serve: 5 g

3 orange sweet potatoes
    (500 g/1 lb each)
1 tablespoon olive oil
1 large onion, chopped
3 cloves garlic, crushed
2 teaspoons ground cumin
1 teaspoon ground coriander
1/2 teaspoon chilli powder
400 g (13 oz) can chopped tomatoes
1 cup (250 ml/8 fl oz) vegetable stock
1 large zucchini, cubed
1 green capsicum, cubed
310 g (10 oz) can corn kernels,
    drained
2 x 400 g (13 oz) cans red kidney
    beans, rinsed and drained
3 tablespoons chopped fresh
    coriander leaves
light sour cream and grated reduced-
    fat Cheddar, to serve

1 Preheat the oven to hot 210°C (415°F/Gas 6–7). Rinse the sweet potatoes, then pierce with a small sharp knife. Place them on a baking tray and bake for 1–1½ hours, or until soft when tested with a skewer or sharp knife.
2 Meanwhile, heat the oil in a large saucepan and cook the onion over medium heat for about 5 minutes, stirring occasionally, until very soft and golden. Add the garlic and spices, and cook, stirring, for 1 minute.
3 Add the tomato and stock, stir well, then add the vegetables and beans. Bring to the boil, then reduce the heat and simmer, partially covered, for

20 minutes. Uncover, increase the heat slightly, and cook for a further 10–15 minutes, or until the liquid has reduced and thickened. Stir in the coriander leaves just before serving.
4 To serve, cut the sweet potatoes in half lengthways. Spoon the vegetable mixture over the top. Add a dollop of light sour cream and sprinkle with grated Cheddar cheese.

NUTRITION PER SERVE
Protein 15 g; Fat 5 g; Carbohydrate 72 g;
Dietary Fibre 17 g; Cholesterol 0 mg;
1665 kJ (397 cal)

Cook the spicy vegetable mixture until the liquid has reduced.

Cut the baked sweet potatoes in half lengthways and top with the spicy beans.

SILVERBEET PARCELS

Preparation time: 40 minutes
Total cooking time: 1 hour
Serves 6
Fat per serve: 6 g

2 cups (500 ml/16 fl oz) vegetable
    stock
1 tablespoon olive oil
1 onion, chopped
2 cloves garlic, crushed
1 red capsicum, chopped
250 g (8 oz) mushrooms, chopped
1/2 cup (110 g/31/2 oz) arborio rice
60 g (2 oz) reduced-fat Cheddar,
    grated
1/4 cup (15 g/1/2 oz) shredded
    fresh basil
6 large silverbeet leaves
2 x 400 g (13 oz) cans chopped
    tomatoes
1 tablespoon balsamic vinegar
1 teaspoon soft brown sugar

1 Heat the vegetable stock in a pan and maintain at simmering point. Heat the oil in a large pan, add the onion and garlic and cook until the onion has softened. Add the capsicum, mushrooms and rice and stir until well combined. Gradually add 1/2 cup (125 ml/4 fl oz) hot stock, stirring until the liquid has been absorbed. Continue to add the stock, a little at a time, until it has all been absorbed and the rice is tender (this will take about 20 minutes). Remove from the heat, add the cheese and basil and season to taste.
2 Trim the stalks from the silverbeet and cook the leaves, a few at a time, in a large pan of boiling water for 30 seconds, or until wilted. Drain on a tea towel. Using a sharp knife, cut away any tough white veins from the centre of the leaves without cutting them in half. If necessary, overlap the 2 sides to make a flat surface. Place a portion of mushroom filling in the centre of each leaf, fold in the sides and roll up carefully. Tie with string.
3 Put the tomato, balsamic vinegar and sugar in a large, deep non-stick frying pan and stir to combine. Add the silverbeet parcels, cover and simmer for 10 minutes. Remove the string and serve with tomato sauce.

NUTRITION PER SERVE
Protein 7.5 g; Fat 6 g; Carbohydrate 20 g;
Dietary Fibre 4 g; Cholesterol 7 mg;
725 kJ (175 cal)

Add the stock, a little at a time, until the rice is tender and has absorbed the liquid.

Using a sharp knife, cut away white veins from the centre of the leaves.

Place filling in the centre of each leaf, fold in the sides and roll up into parcels.

PASTA PRIMAVERA

Preparation time: 35 minutes
Total cooking time: 15 minutes
Serves 6
Fat per serve: 10 g

500 g (1 lb) pasta
155 g (5 oz) fresh asparagus spears
1 cup (155 g/5 oz) frozen (or fresh)
    broad beans
30 g (1 oz) butter
1 celery stick, sliced
1 cup (155 g/5 oz) peas
1 cup (250 ml/8 fl oz) light cream
1/2 cup (50 g/1 3/4 oz) grated
    Parmesan

1 Cook the pasta in a large pan of rapidly boiling salted water until *al dente*. Drain and return to the pan.
2 Snap the woody ends from the asparagus and cut into small pieces. Bring a pan of water to the boil, add the asparagus and cook for 2 minutes. Using a slotted spoon, remove the asparagus from the pan and plunge the pieces into a bowl of ice cold water to stop the cooking process.
3 Add the broad beans to the pan of boiling water. Remove immediately and cool in cold water. Drain, then peel by squeezing the beans out of their skins. If fresh broad beans are used, cook them for 2–5 minutes or until tender. If the beans are young, the skin can be left on, but old beans should be peeled.
4 Heat the butter in a heavy-based frying pan. Add the celery and stir for 2 minutes. Add the peas and the cream and cook gently for 3 minutes. Add the asparagus, broad beans, Parmesan, and salt and pepper. Bring the sauce to the boil and cook for 1 minute. Add the sauce to the cooked pasta and toss well to combine.

NUTRITION PER SERVE
Protein 20 g; Fat 10 g; Carbohydrate 95 g;
Dietary Fibre 10 g; Cholesterol 5 mg;
2295 kJ (545 cal)

NOTE: Spring vegetables are generally used for primavera. Choose your favourite from leeks, zucchini, beans, sugar snap peas or snowpeas.

Bend the asparagus spear gently and the woody end will snap off.

After cooking, plunge the asparagus into cold water to halt the cooking.

After cooking, squeeze the broad beans from their skins. If they are stubborn, slit with a knife.

Add the asparagus, broad beans and Parmesan to the sauce.

SUMMER POTATO PIZZA

Preparation time: 30 minutes
Total cooking time: 40 minutes
Serves 6
Fat per serve: 10 g

7 g (1/4 oz) sachet dry yeast
2¹/2 cups (310 g/10 oz) plain flour
2 teaspoons polenta or semolina
2 tablespoons olive oil
2 cloves garlic, crushed
4–5 potatoes, unpeeled, thinly sliced
1 tablespoon fresh rosemary leaves

1 Preheat the oven to hot 210°C
(415°F/Gas 6–7). Combine the yeast,
1/2 teaspoon of salt and sugar and
1 cup (250 ml/8 fl oz) of warm water
in a bowl. Cover and leave in a warm
place for 10 minutes, or until foamy.
Sift the flour into a bowl, make a well
in the centre, add the yeast mixture
and mix to a dough.
2 Turn the dough out onto a lightly
floured surface and knead for
5 minutes, or until smooth and elastic.
Roll out to a 30 cm (12 inch) circle.
Lightly spray a pizza tray with oil and
sprinkle with polenta or semolina.

3 Place the pizza base on the tray. Mix
2 teaspoons of the oil with the garlic
and brush over the pizza base. Gently
toss the remaining olive oil, potato
slices, rosemary leaves, 1 teaspoon of
salt and some pepper in a bowl.
4 Arrange the potato slices in
overlapping circles over the pizza base
and bake for 40 minutes, or until the
base is crisp and golden.

NUTRITION PER SERVE
Protein 9 g; Fat 10 g; Carbohydrate 50 g;
Dietary Fibre 4 g; Cholesterol 0 mg;
1415 kJ (340 cal)

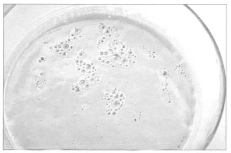

Leave the yeast mixture in a warm place until it
becomes foamy—this shows it is active.

Knead the dough until firm and elastic, then roll
out to fill a pizza tray.

Brush the dough base with garlic oil, then top
with a layer of potato slices.

POTATO GNOCCHI WITH TOMATO SAUCE

Preparation time: 1 hour
Total cooking time: 45 minutes
Serves 4
Fat per serve: 4 g

500 g (1 lb) floury potatoes, unpeeled
1 egg yolk
3 tablespoons grated Parmesan
1 cup (125 g/4 oz) plain flour

TOMATO SAUCE
425 g (14 oz) can tomatoes
1 small onion, chopped
1 celery stick, chopped
1 small carrot, chopped
1 tablespoon shredded fresh basil
1 teaspoon chopped fresh thyme
1 clove garlic, crushed
1 teaspoon caster sugar

1 Steam or boil the potatoes until just tender. Drain thoroughly and allow to cool for 10 minutes before peeling and mashing them.
2 Measure 2 cups of the mashed potato into a large bowl, mix in the egg yolk, Parmesan, 1/4 teaspoon of salt and some black pepper. Slowly add flour until you have a slightly sticky dough. Knead for 5 minutes, adding more flour if necessary, until a smooth dough is formed.
3 Divide the dough into four portions and roll each portion on a lightly floured surface to form a sausage shape, about 2 cm (3/4 inch) thick.
4 Cut the rolls into 2.5 cm (1 inch) slices and shape each piece into an oval. Press each oval into the palm of your hand against a floured fork, to flatten slightly and indent one side with a pattern. As you make the gnocchi place them in a single layer on a baking tray and cover until ready to use.
5 To make the tomato sauce, mix all the ingredients with salt and pepper in a pan. Bring to the boil, reduce the heat to medium-low and simmer for 30 minutes, stirring occasionally. Allow to cool, then process in a food processor or blender, until smooth. Reheat if necessary before serving.
6 Cook the gnocchi in batches in a large pan of boiling salted water for 2 minutes, or until the gnocchi float to the surface. Drain well. Serve the gnocchi tossed through the sauce.

NUTRITION PER SERVE
Protein 10 g; Fat 4 g; Carbohydrate 45 g;
Dietary Fibre 5 g; Cholesterol 50 mg;
1125 kJ (270 cal)

NOTES: The gnocchi can be prepared several hours in advance and arranged on a tray in a single layer to prevent them sticking together. Cover and keep refrigerated.

Gnocchi was traditionally made using potatoes baked in their skins. This results in a drier dough that is easy to work with, so if you have time you can use this method.

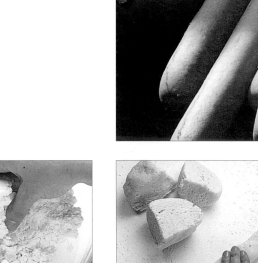

Slowly add flour to the potato mixture, until a slightly sticky dough is formed.

Knead the dough for about 5 minutes or until smooth, adding flour if necessary.

Roll each portion into a sausage shape, on a lightly floured surface.

Press each oval with a floured fork to flatten slightly and make an indentation.

Put all the ingredients for the sauce in a pan and season with salt and pepper.

Cook the gnocchi in a large pan of boiling water until they float to the surface.

LAYERED COUNTRY COB

Preparation time: 40 minutes +
   overnight refrigeration
Total cooking time: 25 minutes
Serves 8
Fat per serve: 9 g

2 red capsicums
1 eggplant, thinly sliced
1 large red onion, thinly sliced
450 g (14 oz) white cob loaf
1 tablespoon olive oil
2 cloves garlic, finely chopped
1 teaspoon chopped fresh lemon
   thyme
250 g (8 oz) English spinach
350 g (11 oz) ricotta

1 Preheat the grill to hot. Cut the
capsicums in half lengthways and
remove the seeds and membrane.
Arrange the capsicum, skin-side-up,
and the eggplant, sprayed lightly with
oil, on the grill. Grill for about
7 minutes, turning the eggplant over as
it browns, until the capsicum skin is
blackened and blistered; leave to cool.
Grill the onion for about 6 minutes,
turning once, until softened. Peel the
skin away from the capsicum.
2 Cut the top off the cob and pull out
the centre. Combine the oil, garlic and
thyme and brush lightly inside the
shell. Put the spinach leaves in a bowl
and pour boiling water over to cover.
Allow to soften for 1 minute, rinse
with cold water until cool, then drain
and pat dry with paper towels.
3 To fill the cob, arrange half the
eggplant in the base, followed by
capsicum and onion, then a layer of
ricotta, spinach and the remaining
eggplant. Season between layers. Press
down firmly. If the top of the cob is

empty, fill the space with a little of the
soft bread from the centre. Replace the
top of the loaf and wrap the whole
thing securely with foil. Top with a
brick wrapped in foil, or a heavy bowl
to weigh down. Refrigerate overnight.
Cut into wedges to serve.

NUTRITION PER SERVE
Protein 10 g; Fat 9 g; Carbohydrate 30 g;
Dietary Fibre 4 g; Cholesterol 20 mg;
1040 kJ (250 cal)

Cut the top off the cob loaf and pull the bread
from the centre.

Put half the eggplant in the cob, then capsicum
and onion.

Wrap the cob in foil and top with a brick
wrapped in foil, or a heavy bowl.

RED LENTIL AND RICOTTA LASAGNE

Preparation time: 30 minutes + soaking
Total cooking time: 2 hours 10 minutes
Serves 6
Fat per serve: 10 g

1/2 cup (125 g/4 oz) red lentils
2 teaspoons olive oil
2–3 cloves garlic, crushed
1 large onion, chopped
1 small red capsicum, chopped
2 zucchini, sliced
1 celery stick, sliced
2 x 425 g (14 oz) cans chopped
    tomatoes
2 tablespoons tomato paste
1 teaspoon dried oregano
350 g (12 oz) ricotta
12 dried or fresh lasagne sheets
60 g (2 oz) reduced-fat Cheddar,
    grated

WHITE SAUCE
1/3 cup (40 g/1 1/4 oz) cornflour
3 cups (750 ml/24 fl oz) skim milk
1/4 onion
1/2 teaspoon ground nutmeg

1 Soak the lentils in boiling water to cover for at least 30 minutes, then drain. Meanwhile, heat the oil in a large pan, add the garlic and onion and cook for 2 minutes. Add the capsicum, zucchini and celery and cook for 2–3 minutes.
2 Add the lentils, tomato, tomato paste, oregano and 1 1/2 cups (375 ml/ 12 fl oz) water. Bring slowly to the boil, reduce the heat and simmer for 30 minutes, or until the lentils are tender. Stir occasionally.
3 To make the white sauce, blend the cornflour with 2 tablespoons of the

milk in a pan until smooth. Pour the remaining milk into the pan, add the onion and stir over low heat until the mixture boils and thickens. Add the nutmeg and season with pepper, then cook over low heat for 5 minutes. Remove the onion.
4 Beat the ricotta with about 1/2 cup (125 ml/4 fl oz) of the white sauce. Preheat the oven to moderate 180°C (350°F/Gas 4). Spread one-third of the lentil mixture over the base of a 3-litre capacity ovenproof dish. Cover with a layer of lasagne sheets. Spread another third of the lentil mixture over the

pasta, then spread the ricotta evenly over the top. Follow with another layer of lasagne, then the remaining lentils. Pour the white sauce evenly over the top and sprinkle with the grated cheese. Bake for 1 hour, covering loosely with foil if the top starts to brown too much. Leave to stand for 5 minutes before cutting.

NUTRITION PER SERVE
Protein 25 g; Fat 10 g; Carbohydrate 65 g; Dietary Fibre 9 g; Cholesterol 40 mg; 1995 kJ (475 cal)

Chop the onion and capsicum into quite small pieces and slice the zucchini.

Build up layers of the lentil mixture, lasagne sheets and ricotta.

Pour the white sauce evenly over the top of the lasagne, then sprinkle with cheese.

FRITTATA

Preparation time: 25 minutes
Total cooking time: 25 minutes
Serves 6
Fat per serve: 5 g

200 g (6¹/₂ oz) zucchini, cubed
250 g (8 oz) pumpkin, cubed
300 g (10 oz) potato, cubed
100 g (3¹/₂ oz) broccoli florets
3 teaspoons oil
1 small onion, chopped
1 small red capsicum, chopped
2 tablespoons chopped fresh parsley
3 eggs
2 egg whites

1 Steam the zucchini, pumpkin, potato and broccoli until tender.
2 Heat 2 teaspoons of the oil in a non-stick frying pan, about 22 cm (9 inch) diameter. Add the onion and capsicum and cook for 3 minutes, or until tender. Mix with the steamed vegetables, along with the parsley.
3 Brush the pan with the remaining oil. Return all the vegetables to the pan and spread out with a spatula to an even thickness. Beat the eggs and whites together and pour into the pan.
4 Cook over medium heat until the eggs are almost set, but still runny on top. Wrap the handle of the pan in foil to protect it and place under a hot grill to brown the frittata top (pierce gently with a fork to make sure it is cooked through). Cut into wedges to serve.

NUTRITION PER SERVE
Protein 8 g; Fat 5 g; Carbohydrate 10 g;
Dietary Fibre 3 g; Cholesterol 90 mg;
515 kJ (125 cal)

Cook the finely chopped onion and capsicum until tender.

Beat the combined eggs and whites and pour into the pan over the vegetables.

The eggs should be almost set, but still runny on top, before you put them under the grill.

PUMPKIN AND BROAD BEAN RISOTTO

Preparation time: 35 minutes
Total cooking time. 50 minutes
Serves 4
Fat per serve: 12 g

350 g (11 oz) pumpkin
cooking oil spray
1 tablespoon olive oil
1 large onion, finely chopped
2 cloves garlic, finely chopped
3 cups (750 ml/24 fl oz) vegetable
   stock
1 cup (220 g/7 oz) arborio rice
200 g (6½ oz) Swiss brown
   mushrooms, halved
2 cups (310 g/10 oz) frozen broad
   beans, defrosted, peeled
4 tablespoons grated Parmesan

1 Preheat the oven to moderately hot 200°C (400°F/Gas 6). Cut the pumpkin into small chunks, place on a baking tray and spray lightly with oil. Bake, turning occasionally, for 20 minutes, or until tender. Set aside, covered.
2 Meanwhile, heat the oil in a large heavy-based pan, add the onion and garlic, cover and cook for 10 minutes over low heat. Put the stock in a different pan and keep at simmering point on the stove top.
3 Add the rice to the onion and stir for 2 minutes. Gradually stir in ½ cup (125 ml/4 fl oz) of the hot stock, until absorbed. Stir in another ½ cup (125 ml/4 fl oz) of hot stock until absorbed. Add the mushrooms and continue adding the remaining stock, a little at a time, until it is all absorbed and the rice is just tender (this will take about 25 minutes).
4 Stir in the cooked pumpkin and the broad beans. Sprinkle with the grated Parmesan.

NUTRITION PER SERVE
Protein 20 g; Fat 12 g; Carbohydrate 60 g;
Dietary Fibre 10 g; Cholesterol 20 mg;
1775 kJ (425 cal)

Put the chunks of pumpkin on a baking tray and spray with oil.

Add the stock to the rice, a little at a time, and stir until absorbed

Add the mushrooms, then continue stirring in the stock until absorbed.

Desserts & Baking

LEMON BERRY CHEESECAKE

Preparation time: 25 minutes +
  overnight refrigeration
Total cooking time: Nil
Serves 12
Fat per serve: 6 g

60 g (2 oz) plain biscuits, finely
  crushed
30 g (1 oz) butter, melted
300 g (10 oz) ricotta
2 tablespoons caster sugar
2 x 130 g (4¼ oz) tubs low-fat
  fromage frais or light vanilla Fruche
2 x 130 g (4½ oz) tubs low-fat lemon
  fromage frais or light lemon Fruche
2 teaspoons finely grated lemon rind
2 tablespoons fresh lemon juice
1 tablespoon gelatine
2 egg whites
250 g (8 oz) strawberries, halved

1 Lightly oil and line the base and
sides of a 20 cm (8 inch) diameter
springform tin with plastic wrap.
Combine the biscuit crumbs and butter
in a small bowl and press evenly over
the base of the tin. Refrigerate while
making the filling.

2 Combine the ricotta and sugar in a
food processor until smooth. Add all
the fromage frais, the lemon rind and
juice and mix well. Put ¼ cup (60 ml/
2 fl oz) water in a small bowl, sprinkle
the gelatine in an even layer onto the
surface and leave to go spongy. Bring
a small pan of water to the boil,
remove from the heat and put the
gelatine bowl in the pan. The water
should come halfway up the side of
the bowl. Stir the gelatine until clear
and dissolved, then cool slightly.
Stir the gelatine mixture into the ricotta
mixture, then transfer to a large bowl.
Beat the egg whites until soft peaks
form, then fold into the ricotta mixture.
3 Pour the mixture into the prepared
tin and refrigerate for several hours or
overnight, until set. Carefully remove
from the tin by removing the side and
gently easing the plastic from
underneath. Decorate with the
halved strawberries.

NUTRITION PER SERVE
Protein 5 g; Fat 6 g; Carbohydrate 8 g;
Dietary Fibre 1 g; Cholesterol 15 mg;
425 kJ (100 cal)

Combine the biscuit crumbs and butter, then
press evenly over the base of the tin.

Gently fold the beaten egg white into the ricotta
mixture with a large metal spoon.

FUDGE BROWNIES

Preparation time: 15 minutes
Total cooking time: 30 minutes
Makes 18 pieces
Fat per piece: 3.5 g

cooking oil spray
1/2 cup (60 g/2 oz) plain flour
1/2 cup (60 g/2 oz) self-raising flour
1 teaspoon bicarbonate of soda
3/4 cup (90 g/3 oz) cocoa powder
2 eggs
1 1/4 cups (310 g/10 oz) caster sugar
2 teaspoons vanilla essence

2 tablespoons vegetable oil
200 g (6 1/2 oz) low-fat fromage frais
140 ml (4 1/2 fl oz) apple purée
icing sugar, for dusting

1 Preheat the oven to moderate 180°C (350°F/Gas 4). Spray a 30 x 20 cm (12 x 8 inch) shallow baking tin with oil and line the base of the tin with baking paper.
2 Sift the flours, bicarbonate of soda and cocoa powder into a large bowl. Mix the eggs, sugar, vanilla essence, oil, fromage frais and purée in a large bowl, stirring until well combined. Add to the flour and stir until combined. Spread into the prepared tin and bake for about 30 minutes, or until a skewer inserted in the centre comes out clean.
3 The brownie will sink slightly in the centre as it cools. Leave in the pan for 5 minutes before turning onto a wire rack to cool. Dust with icing sugar before cutting into pieces to serve.

NUTRITION PER PIECE
Protein 2.5 g; Fat 3.5 g; Carbohydrate 2.5 g;
Dietary Fibre 5 g; Cholesterol 20 mg;
595 kJ (140 cal)

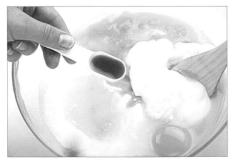

Stir together the eggs, sugar, vanilla essence, oil, fromage frais and apple purée.

Add the egg mixture to the flour and stir thoroughly until combined.

Test with a skewer. When the brownie is cooked, the skewer will come out clean.

RHUBARB AND PEAR CRUMBLE

Preparation time: 20 minutes
Total cooking time: 35 minutes
Serves 6
Fat per serve: 8 g

600 g (1¼ lb) rhubarb
2 strips lemon rind
1 tablespoon honey, or to taste
2 firm, ripe pears
½ cup (50 g/1¾ oz) rolled oats
¼ cup (35 g/1¼ oz) wholemeal plain flour
⅓ cup (60 g/2 oz) soft brown sugar
50 g (1¾ oz) butter

1 Trim the rhubarb, wash and cut into 3 cm (1¼ inch) pieces. Place in a medium pan with the lemon rind and 1 tablespoon water. Cook, covered, over low heat for 10 minutes, or until tender. Cool a little. Stir in the honey and remove the lemon rind.

2 Preheat the oven to moderate 180°C (350°F/Gas 4). Peel, core and cut the pears into 2 cm (¾ inch) cubes and combine with the rhubarb. Pour into a 1.25 litre dish and smooth the surface.

3 To make the topping, combine the oats, flour and brown sugar in a bowl. Rub in the butter with your fingertips until the mixture is crumbly. Spread over the fruit. Bake for 15 minutes, or until cooked and golden.

NUTRITION PER SERVE
Protein 3.5 g; Fat 8 g; Carbohydrate 30 g; Dietary Fibre 6 g; Cholesterol 0 mg; 885 kJ (210 cal)

Trim the rhubarb, wash thoroughly, then cut into short pieces.

Add the cubed pears to the cooked rhubarb and gently stir to combine.

Use your fingertips to rub the butter into the dry ingredients to make a crumble topping.

PEARS POACHED IN DARK GRAPE JUICE

Preparation time: 15 minutes +
  overnight refrigeration
Total cooking time: 1 hour 20 minutes
Serves 6
Fat per serve: 0 g

6 beurre bosc (or any firm) pears
2 tablespoons lemon juice
2 cups (500 ml/8 fl oz) dark grape
  juice
2 cups (500 ml/8 fl oz) blackcurrant
  juice
2 tablespoons sweet sherry
4 cloves
350 g (11 oz) black grapes
1 cup (250 g/8 oz) low-fat natural
  yoghurt
1/2 teaspoon ground cinnamon
1 tablespoon honey

1 Core and peel the pears, leaving the stalks on. Place the pears, as you peel, in a bowl filled with cold water and the lemon juice, to prevent browning.
2 Put the grape and blackcurrant juices, sherry and cloves in a saucepan large enough to hold the pears. (The size of the saucepan will depend on the size of the pears.) Add the pears.
3 Bring the liquid to the boil, then reduce to a simmer. Cover and cook for 35–40 minutes, or until tender. Remove from the heat and leave the pears to cool in the syrup. Transfer the pears and syrup to a bowl and cover with plastic wrap. Refrigerate overnight.
4 To serve, strain the syrup into a pan, bring to the boil, then reduce to a simmer and cook for 40 minutes, or until reduced by about two-thirds. Cool slightly, place a pear on each

plate and pour syrup over the pears. Arrange the grapes next to the pears. Just before serving, mix the yoghurt, cinnamon and honey and spoon over the pears or serve on the side.

NUTRITION PER SERVE
Protein 4 g; Fat 0 g; Carbohydrate 95 g; Dietary Fibre 4 g; Cholesterol 2 mg; 1630 kJ (390 cal)

Remove the core from the pears, then peel, leaving the stalks on.

Bring the liquid to the boil, then reduce the heat and simmer until tender.

Mix together the yoghurt, cinnamon and honey just before serving the pears.

FRUIT TARTS

Preparation time: 25 minutes +
   30 minutes refrigeration
Total cooking time: 20 minutes
Makes 8
Fat per tart: 8 g

1 cup (125 g/4 oz) plain flour
1/4 cup (30 g/1 oz) custard powder
1/4 cup (30 g/1 oz) icing sugar
40 g (11/4 oz) butter
2 tablespoons low-fat milk
2 x 130 g (41/2 oz) tubs low-fat
   strawberry fromage frais or light
   strawberry Fruche
100 g (31/2 oz) ricotta
strawberries, blueberries, kiwi fruit
2 tablespoons apricot jam

1 Grease eight 7 cm (23/4 inch) loose-based flan tins. Mix the flour, custard powder, icing sugar and butter in a food processor until fine crumbs form, then add enough of the milk to form a soft dough. Gather into a ball, wrap in plastic and chill for 30 minutes.
2 Preheat the oven to 200°C (400°F/ Gas 6). Divide the dough into eight portions and roll out to line the tins. Cover with paper and rice or dried beans. Bake for 10 minutes, remove the paper and rice and bake for another 10 minutes, or until golden. Cool and remove from the tins.
3 Mix the fromage frais and ricotta until smooth. Spread over the pastry bases and top with assorted fruit. Heat the jam until liquid, then brush over the fruit to glaze.

NUTRITION PER TART
Protein 3.5 g; Fat 8 g; Carbohydrate 20 g;
Dietary Fibre 1 g; Cholesterol 20 mg;
690 kJ (165 cal)

Add enough milk to the crumbly mixture to form a soft dough.

To blind bake, cover the pastry with baking paper and fill with uncooked rice or beans.

Remove the rice or beans and paper and return the pastry to the oven until golden.

MERINGUE BASKETS WITH FRUIT

Preparation time: 40 minutes + cooling
Total cooking time: 1 hour 30 minutes
Serves 6
Fat per serve: 0.5 g

2 egg whites
small pinch of cream of tartar
1/2 cup (125 g/4 oz) caster sugar
2 tablespoons custard powder
2 cups (500 ml/16 fl oz) skim milk
1 teaspoon vanilla essence
1 peach, cut into thin wedges
1 kiwi fruit, cut into thin wedges
2 strawberries, cut in half
2 tablespoons apricot jam

1 Preheat the oven to slow 150°C (300°F/Gas 2) and line a baking tray with baking paper. Beat the egg whites and cream of tartar with electric beaters until soft peaks form. Gradually add the sugar and beat until it is dissolved and the mixture is stiff and glossy.

2 Fit a piping bag with a medium star nozzle and pipe coiled spirals of the meringue (about 8 cm/3 inches) onto the tray. Pipe an extra ring around the top edge to make baskets. Bake for 30 minutes, then reduce the heat to very slow 120°C (250°F/Gas 1/2). Bake for 45 minutes, turn the oven off and cool with the oven door ajar.

3 Mix the custard powder with a little of the milk to form a smooth paste. Transfer to a pan with the remaining milk and the vanilla essence. Stir over medium heat until the mixture boils and thickens. Remove from the heat and place plastic wrap over the surface to stop a skin forming. Set aside and, when cool, stir until smooth. Spoon some of the cold custard into each basket. Top with fruit. Heat the jam until liquid, then brush over the fruit to glaze.

NUTRITION PER SERVE
Protein 5 g; Fat 0.5 g; Carbohydrate 30 g; Dietary Fibre 1 g; Cholesterol 3 mg; 590 kJ (140 cal)

Beat the egg whites and cream of tartar until soft peaks form.

Pipe an extra ring around the top edge of the coils to make baskets.

Lay a piece of plastic wrap directly onto the surface of the custard.

RASPBERRY MOUSSE

Preparation time: 30 minutes
   + refrigeration
Total cooking time: Nil
Serves 4
Fat per serve: 2 g

3 teaspoons gelatine
1 cup (250 g/8 oz) low-fat vanilla
   yoghurt
2 x 200 g (6$^{1/2}$ oz) tubs low-fat
   fromage frais or light vanilla Fruche
4 egg whites
150 g (5 oz) raspberries, mashed
fresh raspberries and mint leaves, for
   serving

1 Sprinkle the gelatine in an even layer onto 1 tablespoon water in a small bowl and leave to go spongy. Bring a small pan of water to the boil, remove from the heat and place the bowl in the pan. Stir until clear.
2 In a large bowl, stir the vanilla yoghurt and fromage frais together, then add the gelatine and mix well.
3 Using electric beaters, beat the egg whites until stiff peaks form, then fold through the yoghurt mixture. Transfer half to a separate bowl and fold the mashed raspberries through.
4 Divide the raspberry mixture into the bases of 4 long glasses or serving bowls. Top with the vanilla mixture. Refrigerate for several hours, or until set. Decorate with fresh raspberries and mint leaves.

NUTRITION PER SERVE
Protein 9.5 g; Fat 2 g; Carbohydrate 10 g;
Dietary Fibre 2 g; Cholesterol 4 mg;
355 kJ (85 cal)

You can use fresh raspberries or frozen. Thaw frozen raspberries completely before mashing.

Stir the vanilla yoghurt and fromage frais together until combined.

Gently fold the mashed raspberries through half the yoghurt mixture.

231

STRAWBERRY AND BANANA ICE

Preparation time: 10 minutes +
 freezing
Total cooking time: Nil
Serves 4
Fat per serve: 3 g

300 g (10 oz) silken tofu, chopped
250 g (8 oz) strawberries, chopped
2 ripe bananas, chopped
1/4 cup (60 g/2 oz) caster sugar

1 Blend the silken tofu, strawberries, banana and caster sugar in a blender or food processor, until smooth.
2 Pour the mixture into a shallow cake tin and freeze until almost frozen. Remove from the freezer and break up roughly with a fork or a spoon, then transfer to a large bowl and beat until it has a smooth texture. Pour the mixture evenly into a 15 x 25 cm (6 x 10 inch) loaf tin, cover and freeze again, until quite firm.
3 Alternatively, freeze the blended mixture in an ice cream machine until thick and creamy, then store in a covered container in the freezer.
4 Transfer to the refrigerator for about 30 minutes before serving to allow the ice to soften slightly.

NUTRITION PER SERVE
Protein 7 g; Fat 3 g; Carbohydrate 30 g;
Dietary Fibre 3 g; Cholesterol 0 mg;
710 kJ (170 cal)

Blend the tofu, strawberries, banana and caster sugar until smooth.

When partially frozen, use a fork or spoon to break up the mixture.

Transfer the chopped mixture to a bowl and beat until smooth.

PASSIONFRUIT BAVAROIS

Preparation time: 10 minutes
 + overnight refrigeration
Total cooking time: Nil
Serves 8
Fat per serve: 2.5 g

2 x 170 g (5 1/2 oz) cans passionfruit in
 syrup
300 g (10 oz) silken tofu, chopped
600 ml (20 fl oz) buttermilk
2 tablespoons caster sugar
1 teaspoon vanilla essence
6 teaspoons gelatine
3/4 cup (185 ml/6 fl oz) passionfruit
 pulp

1 Push the passionfruit in syrup through a sieve. Discard the seeds. Combine the strained syrup with the tofu, buttermilk, caster sugar and vanilla in a blender. Blend for 90 seconds on high, to mix thoroughly. Leave in the blender.
2 Put 1/3 cup (80 ml/2 3/4 fl oz) water in a small bowl and put the bowl in a slightly larger bowl of boiling water. Sprinkle the gelatine onto the water in the small bowl and stir until dissolved. Leave to cool.
3 Place eight 200 ml (6 1/2 fl oz) dariole moulds in a baking dish. Add the gelatine to the blender and mix on high for 1 minute. Pour into the moulds, cover the dish with plastic wrap and refrigerate overnight.
4 When ready to serve, carefully run a spatula around the edge of each mould and dip the bases into hot water for 2 seconds to make removal easier. Place each on a plate and spoon the passionfruit pulp around the bases. Serve, topped with a few halved strawberries.

NUTRITION PER SERVE
Protein 8 g; Fat 2.5 g; Carbohydrate 10 g;
Dietary Fibre 10 g; Cholesterol 3 mg;
455 kJ (110 cal)

Blend the strained passionfruit syrup, tofu, buttermilk, sugar and vanilla.

Sprinkle the gelatine over the surface of the water in the small bowl.

To remove, run a spatula around the edge and dip the base in hot water.

CARROT CAKE

Preparation time: 20 minutes
Total cooking time: 1 hour 15 minutes
Makes 14 slices
Fat per slice: 5 g

2¹/₂ cups (310 g/10 oz) self-raising
    flour
1 teaspoon bicarbonate of soda
2 teaspoons ground cinnamon
1 teaspoon mixed spice
¹/₂ cup (95 g/3 oz) soft brown sugar
¹/₂ cup (60 g/2 oz) sultanas
2 eggs, lightly beaten
2 tablespoons vegetable oil
¹/₃ cup (80 ml/2³/₄ fl oz) low-fat milk
140 g (4¹/₂ oz) apple purée
300 g (10 oz) carrot, coarsely grated

RICOTTA TOPPING
125 g (4 oz) ricotta
¹/₄ cup (30 g/1 oz) icing sugar
¹/₂ teaspoon grated lime rind

1 Grease a 10 x 18 cm (4 x 7 inch)
loaf tin and line the base with baking
paper. Preheat the oven to 180°C
(350°F/Gas 4). Sift the flour, soda and
spices into a large bowl. Stir in the
sugar and sultanas.
2 Mix the eggs, oil, milk and apple
purée and stir into the dry ingredients.
Stir in the carrot. Spread into the tin
and bake for 1¹/₄ hours, or until a
skewer comes out clean. Cool in the
tin for 5 minutes, then on a wire rack.
3 To make the topping, beat the
ingredients together until smooth.
Spread over the cake.

NUTRITION PER SLICE
Protein 4.5 g; Fat 5 g; Carbohydrate 30 g;
Dietary Fibre 2 g; Cholesterol 30 mg;
755 kJ (180 cal)

Stir the egg and apple mixture into the dry
ingredients, then stir in the carrot.

A skewer inserted into the centre of the cake
should come out clean when it is cooked.

Beat the topping ingredients together until
smooth and spread over the cake.

BRAZIL NUT AND COFFEE BISCOTTI

Preparation time: 20 minutes
Total cooking time: 45 minutes
Makes 40 pieces
Fat per piece: 1.5 g

3 teaspoons instant coffee powder
1 tablespoon dark rum, warmed
2 eggs
1/2 cup (125 g/4 oz) caster sugar
1 1/4 cups (155 g/5 oz) plain flour
1/2 cup (60 g/2 oz) self-raising flour
1 teaspoon ground cinnamon
3/4 cup (105 g/3 1/2 oz) brazil nuts,
    roughly chopped
1 tablespoon caster sugar, extra

1 Preheat the oven to 180°C (350°F/ Gas 4). Dissolve the coffee in the rum. Beat the eggs and sugar until thick and creamy, then beat in the coffee. Sift the flours and cinnamon into a bowl, then stir in the nuts. Mix in the egg mixture.
2 Divide the mixture into two rolls, each about 28 cm (11 inches) long. Line a baking tray with baking paper, put the rolls on it and press lightly to flatten to about 6 cm (2 1/2 inches) across. Brush lightly with water and sprinkle with the extra sugar. Bake for 25 minutes, or until firm and light brown. Cool until warm on the tray. Reduce the oven temperature to warm 160°C (315°F/Gas 2–3).
3 Cut into 1 cm (1/2 inch) thick diagonal slices. Bake in a single layer on the lined tray for 20 minutes, or until dry, turning once. Cool on a rack. When cold, store in an airtight container for 2–3 weeks.

NUTRITION PER BISCOTTI
Protein 1 g; Fat 1.5 g; Carbohydrate 7.5 g;
Dietary Fibre 0 g; Cholesterol 9 mg;
210 kJ (50 cal)

Beat the coffee and rum mixture into the beaten eggs and sugar

Put the rolls of dough on the lined baking tray and press lightly into shape.

Cut the cooked rolls into diagonal slices and bake until dry.

TIRAMISU

Preparation time: 15 minutes +
  overnight refrigeration
Total cooking time: 5 minutes
Serves 6
Fat per serve: 5.5 g

3 tablespoons custard powder
1 cup (250 ml/8 fl oz) skim milk
2 tablespoons caster sugar
2 teaspoons vanilla essence
2 x 130 g (4¹/₂ oz) tubs low-fat
  fromage frais or light vanilla Fruche
2 egg whites
1²/₃ cups (410 ml/13 fl oz) prepared
  strong coffee, cooled
2 tablespoons amaretto
250 g (8 oz) Savoyardi (sponge finger)
  biscuits
2 tablespoons unsweetened dark
  cocoa powder

1 Stir the custard powder in a small pan with 2 tablespoons of the milk until dissolved. Add the remaining milk, sugar and vanilla and stir over medium heat until the mixture boils and thickens. Remove from the heat. This custard will be thicker than the usual custard. Transfer to a bowl, cover the surface with plastic wrap and cool at room temperature.

2 Using electric beaters, mix the custard and the fromage frais in a bowl. Beat for 2 minutes. In a small bowl, whip the egg whites until soft peaks form, then fold into the custard mixture.

3 Pour the coffee into a dish and add the amaretto. Quickly dip the biscuits, one at a time, in the coffee mixture, just enough to cover (dip quickly, or they'll be soggy) and arrange in a single layer over the base of a 2.75 litre dish.

4 Using half the cream mixture, smooth it evenly over the biscuits. Dust half the dark cocoa over the cream and then repeat the layers with the remaining biscuits and cream. Cover with plastic wrap. Refrigerate overnight, or for at least 6 hours. Dust with dark cocoa powder to serve.

NUTRITION PER SERVE
Protein 5 g; Fat 5.5 g; Carbohydrate 26 g;
Dietary Fibre 1 g; Cholesterol 7.5 mg;
754 kJ (180 cal)

Stir the custard powder in a small amount of milk until dissolved.

Fold the whipped egg whites into the custard mixture with a large metal spoon.

Dip the biscuits quickly into the coffee mixture to cover evenly.

Use a strainer to dust half the cocoa over the cream. Dust with the rest before serving.

CREAMY RICE POTS

Preparation time: 15 minutes
Total cooking time: 1 hour
Serves 4
Fat per serve: 3.5 g

1/2 cup (110 g/3 1/2 oz) short-grain rice
1 litre skim milk
1/4 cup (60 g/2 oz) caster sugar
1 teaspoon grated orange rind
1 teaspoon grated lemon rind
1 teaspoon vanilla essence
20 g (3/4 oz) hazelnuts
1 tablespoon soft brown sugar

1 Wash the rice in a sieve, then drain thoroughly. Combine the skim milk and caster sugar in a non-stick pan and stir over low heat until dissolved. Add the rice and rind and stir briefly. Bring to the boil and reduce the heat to as low as possible. Cook for 1 hour, stirring occasionally, until the rice is tender and the mixture thick and creamy. Stir in the vanilla essence.
2 While the rice is cooking, spread the hazelnuts on a baking tray and toast in a moderate 180°C (350°F/Gas 4) oven for about 5 minutes. Rub the hot nuts in a tea towel to remove as much of the skin as possible. Cool and then grind in a food processor until coarsely chopped.
3 Spoon the rice into 4 heatproof 3/4 cup (185 ml/6 fl oz) capacity ramekins. Combine the brown sugar and ground hazelnuts and sprinkle over the surface of the rice. Cook briefly under a very hot grill until the sugar melts and the nuts are lightly browned. Serve immediately.

NUTRITION PER SERVE
Protein 12 g; Fat 3.5 g; Carbohydrate 55 g; Dietary Fibre 1 g; Cholesterol 7 mg; 1235 kJ (295 cal)

Cook the rice mixture over very low heat until thick and creamy.

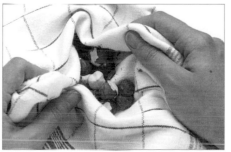

Transfer the hot nuts to a tea towel and rub to remove as much skin as possible.

Sprinkle the combined sugar and ground hazelnuts over the top of the rice.

PASSIONFRUIT TART

Preparation time: 25 minutes +
    30 minutes refrigeration
Total cooking time: 1 hour
Serves 8
Fat per serve: 6.5 g

3/4 cup (90 g/3 oz) plain flour
2 tablespoons icing sugar
2 tablespoons custard powder
30 g (1 oz) butter
3 tablespoons light evaporated milk

FILLING
1/2 cup (125 g/4 oz) ricotta
1 teaspoon vanilla essence
1/4 cup (30 g/1 oz) icing sugar
2 eggs, lightly beaten
4 tablespoons passionfruit pulp
    (about 8 passionfruit)
3/4 cup (185 ml/6 fl oz) light
    evaporated milk

1 Preheat the oven to 200°C (400°F/
Gas 6). Lightly spray a 22 cm (9 inch)
loose-based flan tin with oil. Sift the
flour, icing sugar and custard powder
into a bowl and rub in the butter until
crumbs form. Add enough evaporated
milk to form a soft dough. Bring
together on a floured surface until just
smooth. Gather into a ball, wrap in
plastic and chill for 15 minutes.
2 Roll the pastry out on a floured
surface to fit the tin, then refrigerate
for 15 minutes. Cover with baking
paper and fill with rice or dried beans.
Bake for 10 minutes, remove the rice
or beans and paper and bake for
another 5–8 minutes, or until golden.
Allow to cool. Reduce the oven to
warm 160°C (315°F/Gas 2–3).
3 Beat the ricotta with the vanilla
essence and icing sugar until smooth.

Add the eggs, passionfruit pulp
and milk, then beat well. Put the tin
with the pastry case on a baking tray
and pour in the filling. Bake for
40 minutes, or until set. Cool in the tin.
Dust with icing sugar to serve.

NUTRITION PER SERVE
Protein 8 g; Fat 6.5 g; Carbohydrate 25 g;
Dietary Fibre 3 g; Cholesterol 65 mg;
750 kJ (180 cal)

Remove the baking paper and rice or beans and
blind bake the pastry case again.

When the ricotta mixture is smooth, add the
eggs, passionfruit pulp and milk.

Put the tin on a baking tray to catch any drips
and gently pour in the filling.

FIGS WITH ORANGE CREAM AND RAISINS

Preparation time: 20 minutes +
  1 hour soaking
Total cooking time: 12 minutes
Serves 4
Fat per serve: 3.5 g

1 cup (150 g/5 oz) raisins
75 ml (2¹/₂ fl oz) tawny port
1 tablespoon custard powder
1 cup (250 ml/8 fl oz) skim milk
1 tablespoon sugar
100 g (3¹/₂ oz) ricotta
200 g (6¹/₂ oz) low-fat fromage frais or
  light vanilla Fruche

rind strips and juice of 1 orange
1 teaspoon ground cinnamon
8 fresh figs

1 Soak the raisins in the tawny port for 1 hour, or until plumped up.
2 In a small saucepan, blend the custard powder with the skim milk, add the sugar and stir over low heat until dissolved. Increase the heat and stir until the custard boils and thickens. Remove from the heat immediately, pour into a small bowl and cover with plastic wrap. Cool completely. Transfer to an electric mixer, add the ricotta and fromage frais and beat until smooth.
3 Warm the raisin mixture with the orange rind, juice and cinnamon in a small pan. Cover and keep warm.
4 Starting from the top, cut the figs into quarters, slicing only two-thirds of the way down so they hold together. Transfer to ramekins or a serving dish or platter. Place 2 heaped tablespoons of the custard cream mixture into the centre of each fig, top with a spoonful of the warm raisin and orange mixture and serve at once.

NUTRITION PER SERVE
Protein 7 g; Fat 3.5 g; Carbohydrate 45 g;
Dietary Fibre 4.5 g; Cholesterol 15 mg;
1510 kJ (360 cal)

Stir the custard continuously until it boils and thickens, then remove from the heat.

When the custard has cooled, mix it with the ricotta and fromage frais.

Cut the figs into quarters, slicing only two-thirds of the way down.

239

ALMOND AND PEAR POUCHES

Preparation time: 45 minutes +
  10 minutes standing
Total cooking time: 40 minutes
Makes 4
Fat per serve: 7 g

4 beurre bosc (or any firm) pears
1/4 cup (60 ml/2 fl oz) white wine
1/4 cup (60 g/2 oz) caster sugar
1 cinnamon stick
2 cloves
1 vanilla bean
4 dates, roughly chopped
2 tablespoons sultanas
2/3 cup (85 g/3 oz) plain flour
1 egg, lightly beaten
1 cup (250 ml/8 fl oz) skim milk
2 tablespoons ground almonds
1 tablespoon soft brown sugar
1/2 teaspoon ground cinnamon
2 teaspoons flaked almonds
icing sugar, for dusting

STRAWBERRY SAUCE
125 g (4 oz) strawberries, chopped
1 teaspoon caster sugar
2 tablespoons orange juice

1 Remove the cores of the pears through the base using a melon baller, then peel. Combine 2 cups (500 ml/ 16 fl oz) water with the wine, sugar, cinnamon stick and cloves in a pan that is just large enough to fit the pears. Split the vanilla bean in half lengthways and scrape the seeds out. Add to the pan with the vanilla pod and stir over medium heat until the sugar has dissolved.
2 Add the pears to the pan and simmer, covered, for 20 minutes, or until just soft when tested with a skewer. Remove from the heat and allow to cool in the syrup. Drain and stand the pears on paper towels. Fill the base of each with the combined dates and sultanas.
3 To make the crepes, sift the flour into a bowl, gradually beat in the combined egg and milk, beating until smooth. Strain into a jug and set aside for 10 minutes.
4 Preheat the oven to moderately hot 200°C (400°F/Gas 6). Lightly oil a 24 cm (9½ inch) non-stick pan with oil spray, heat the pan and pour in a quarter of the batter, swirling to cover the base of the pan. Cook until lightly browned, turn and brown the other side. Remove and repeat with the remaining mixture.
5 Place the crepes on a work bench, place a quarter of the combined ground almonds, brown sugar and cinnamon in the centre of each and top with a pear. Gather the crepes around the pears and tie with string. Sprinkle with the flaked almonds. Bake on a lightly oiled baking tray for 5 minutes, or until the almonds and the edges of the crepes are golden and the pears just warm. Discard the string.
6 To make the strawberry sauce, blend the strawberries, sugar and orange juice in a blender until smooth and then strain.
7 Dust the pear pouches with a little icing sugar and serve with strawberry sauce. For a special effect, you can tie a piece of raffia or ribbon around each pouch before serving.

NUTRITION PER SERVE
Protein 9.5 g; Fat 7 g; Carbohydrate 80 g; Dietary Fibre 7 g; Cholesterol 45 mg; 1740 kJ (415 cal)

Use a melon baller to remove the cores from the pears through the bases.

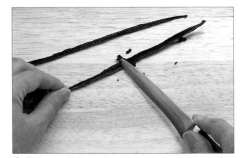

Split the vanilla bean lengthways, then scrape the seeds out with a knife.

Combine the dates and sultanas and fill the base of each pear.

Heat the pan and pour in a quarter of the batter, swirling to cover the base.

Put the ground almonds, sugar and cinnamon mix on the crepes.

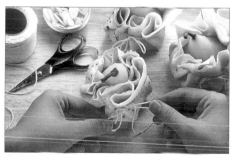

Gather the crepes around the pears and tie together with string.

BANANA PANCAKES

Preparation time: 20 minutes + 1 hour
Total cooking time: 25 minutes
Makes 10
Fat per serve: 0.5 g

2 very ripe bananas, mashed
1 cup (150 g/5 oz) wholemeal flour
2 teaspoons baking powder
1/2 teaspoon ground cinnamon
pinch of ground nutmeg
1 cup (250 ml/8 fl oz) skim milk
1 tablespoon maple syrup
maple syrup and banana, for serving

1 Put the mashed banana in a large bowl. Sift the flour, baking powder, cinnamon and nutmeg onto the banana and return the husks to the bowl. Stir until the flour is moistened but not totally combined with the mashed banana.
2 Make a well in the centre, add the milk and syrup and stir constantly until smooth. Set aside for 1 hour.
3 Heat a large non-stick pan over medium heat and coat with cooking oil spray. Cook the pancakes in batches, using 1/4 cup (60 ml/2 fl oz) of batter for each pancake. Cook for 3–4 minutes, or until small bubbles

appear on the surface. Using a spatula, gently turn the pancakes over, loosening the edges first so they don't stick to the pan. Cook for another 3 minutes. Remove from the pan and keep warm. Spray the pan with a little oil after each batch and continue with the remaining mixture. Serve drizzled with maple syrup and a few slices of banana.

NUTRITION PER PANCAKE
Protein 3 g; Fat 0.5 g; Carbohydrate 17 g; Dietary Fibre 2 g; Cholesterol 1 mg; 350 kJ (85 cal)

When you have sifted the wholemeal flour, return the husks to the bowl.

Stir the pancake mixture until smooth, then set aside for 1 hour.

Cook the pancakes over medium heat until small bubbles appear on the surface.

CHESTNUT HEARTS

Preparation time: 40 minutes
Total cooking time: 40 minutes
Makes 30 hearts
Fat per heart: 1 g

2/3 cup (160 g/5 1/2 oz) caster sugar
2 eggs
2 1/2 teaspoons coconut essence
6 egg whites
1 teaspoon cream of tartar
1 1/4 cups (155 g/5 oz) self-raising
    flour, sifted
1 cup (250 g/8 oz) canned sweetened
    chestnut purée
1/3 cup (90 g/3 oz) ricotta
2 teaspoons cocoa powder
icing sugar, to dust

1 Preheat the oven to 180°C (350°F/
Gas 4). Lightly spray two 20 x 30 cm
(8 x 12 inch) shallow baking tins with
oil and line with baking paper.
2 Beat the sugar and eggs in a bowl
with electric beaters for 3–4 minutes,
until light and fluffy. Transfer to a large
bowl. Add the coconut essence.
3 Beat the egg whites until foamy.
Add the cream of tartar and beat until
firm peaks form. Stir a third of the egg
white into the creamed mixture.
Slowly fold in the flour in small
batches, alternating with small
amounts of egg white. Fold in both
until just combined. Divide the
mixture between the trays. Bake for
20–25 minutes, until golden. Test with
a skewer. Turn out onto cooling racks
lined with greaseproof paper. Leave
until completely cold (if possible,
make a day in advance).
4 In a blender, mix the chestnut purée
with the ricotta and cocoa until very
smooth. Slice the cakes in half
horizontally and join with the chestnut
mixture. Cut out heart shapes using a
5 cm (2 inch) heart-shaped cookie
cutter. Clean the cutter between cuts or
dust it in icing sugar if the cake sticks.
Dust with icing sugar before serving.

NUTRITION PER HEART
Protein 1 g; Fat 1 g; Carbohydrate 8 g;
Dietary Fibre 0.5 g; Cholesterol 8.5 mg;
175 kJ (40 cal)

Beat the sugar and eggs together until the mixture
is light and fluffy.

Slowly fold the flour, in small batches, into the
mixture, using a large metal spoon.

Once the cakes are completely cooled, slice in
half horizontally.

When the cakes are joined with the chestnut
mixture, cut out heart shapes.

MANGO AND PASSIONFRUIT SORBET

Preparation time: 20 minutes + 8 hours
  freezing
Total cooking time: 5 minutes
Serves 6
Fat per serve: 0 g

1 cup (250 g/8 oz) caster sugar
1/3 cup (90 g/3 oz) passionfruit pulp
1/2 large mango (200 g/61/2 oz),
  chopped
1 large (250 g/8 oz) peach, chopped
2 tablespoons lemon juice
1 egg white

1 Stir the sugar in a pan with 1 cup
(250 ml/8 fl oz) water over low heat
until dissolved. Increase the heat,
bring to the boil and boil for 1 minute.
Transfer to a glass bowl, cool, then
refrigerate. Strain the passionfruit pulp,
reserving 1 tablespoon of the seeds.
2 Blend the fruit, passionfruit juice
and lemon juice in a blender until
smooth. With the motor running, add
the cold sugar syrup and 150 ml
(5 fl oz) water. Stir in the passionfruit
seeds. Freeze in a shallow container,
stirring occasionally, for about
5 hours, or until almost set.
3 Break up the icy mixture roughly
with a fork or spoon, transfer to a
bowl and beat with electric beaters
until smooth and fluffy. Beat the egg
white in a small bowl until firm peaks
form, then fold into the mixture until
just combined. Spread into a loaf tin
and return to the freezer until firm.
Transfer to the refrigerator, to soften,
15 minutes before serving.

NUTRITION PER SERVE
Protein 2 g; Fat 0 g; Carbohydrate 50 g;
Dietary Fibre 3 g; Cholesterol 0 mg;
850 kJ (200 cal)

VARIATION: To make a berry sorbet,
use 200 g (61/2 oz) blackberries or
blueberries, 200 g (61/2 oz) hulled
strawberries and 50 g (13/4 oz) peach
flesh. Prepare as above.

Leave the motor running and pour in the cold
sugar syrup and water.

Gently fold the egg white into the smooth fruit
purée with a metal spoon.

BANANA AND BLUEBERRY TART

Preparation time: 30 minutes
Total cooking time: 25 minutes
Serves 6
Fat per serve: 6 g

1 cup (125 g/4 oz) plain flour
1/2 cup (60 g/2 oz) self-raising flour
1 teaspoon cinnamon
1 teaspoon ground ginger
40 g (1 1/4 oz) butter, chopped
1/2 cup (95 g/3 oz) soft brown sugar

1/2 cup (125 ml/4 oz) buttermilk
200 g (6 1/2 oz) blueberries
2 bananas
2 teaspoons lemon juice
1 tablespoon demerara sugar

1 Preheat the oven to moderately hot 200°C (400°F/Gas 6). Lightly spray a baking tray or pizza tray with oil. Sift the flours and spices into a bowl. Add the butter and sugar and rub in until the mixture resembles breadcrumbs. Make a well and then add enough buttermilk to mix to a soft dough.
2 Roll the dough out on a lightly

floured surface to a 23 cm (9 inch) diameter round. Place on the tray and roll the edge to form a rim.
3 Spread the blueberries over the dough, keeping within the rim. Slice the bananas, toss them in the lemon juice, then arrange over the top. Sprinkle with the sugar and bake for 25 minutes, until the base is browned. Serve immediately.

NUTRITION PER SERVE
Protein 5 g; Fat 6 g; Carbohydrate 55 g; Dietary Fibre 3 g; Cholesterol 20 mg; 1215 kJ (290 cal)

Rub the butter into the flour until the mixture resembles breadcrumbs.

Pour the buttermilk into the well, using enough to form a soft dough.

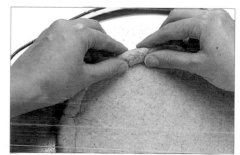
Put the circle of dough on the tray and roll the edge to form a rim.

POACHED PEARS IN SAFFRON CITRUS SYRUP

Preparation time: 10 minutes
Total cooking time: 30 minutes
Serves 4
Fat per serve: 0 g

1 vanilla bean, split lengthways
1/2 teaspoon firmly packed saffron threads
3/4 cup (185 g/6 oz) caster sugar
2 teaspoons grated lemon rind
4 pears, peeled
biscotti, to serve (see NOTE)

1 Place the vanilla bean, saffron threads, sugar, lemon rind and 2 cups (500 ml/16 fl oz) water in a large saucepan and mix together well. Heat, stirring, over low heat until the sugar has dissolved. Bring to the boil, then reduce to a gentle simmer.

2 Add the pears and cook, covered, for 12–15 minutes, or until tender when tested with a metal skewer. Turn the pears over with a slotted spoon halfway through cooking. Once cooked, remove from the syrup with a slotted spoon.

3 Remove the lid and allow the saffron citrus syrup to come to the boil. Cook for 8–10 minutes, or until the syrup has reduced by half and thickened slightly. Remove the vanilla bean and drizzle the syrup over the pears. Serve with biscotti.

NUTRITION PER SERVE
Protein 0.5 g; Fat 0 g; Carbohydrate 70 g; Dietary Fibre 4.5 g; Cholesterol 0 mg; 1155 kJ (276 cal)

NOTE: Biscotti are available in a wide variety of flavours. You can buy biscotti at gourmet food stores, delicatessens and supermarkets or use the recipe on page 235.

Stir the saffron citrus syrup until the sugar has completely dissolved.

Cook the pears until tender when tested with a metal skewer.

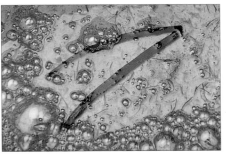
Bring the syrup to the boil and cook until it has slightly thickened.

WATERMELON AND VODKA GRANITA

Preparation time: 10 minutes +
 5 hours freezing
Total cooking time: Nil
Serves 6
Fat per serve: 0 g

1 kg (2 lb) piece of watermelon, rind
 removed (to leave 600 g/1¼ lb)
2 teaspoons lime juice
¼ cup (60 g/2 oz) caster sugar
¼ cup (60 ml/2 fl oz) citrus-flavoured
 vodka

1 Coarsely chop the watermelon, removing the seeds. Place the flesh in a food processor and add the lime juice and sugar. Process until smooth, then strain through a fine sieve. Stir in the vodka, then taste—if the watermelon is not very sweet, you may have to add a little more sugar.
2 Pour into a shallow 1.5 litre metal tin and freeze for about 1 hour, or until beginning to freeze around the edges. Scrape the frozen parts back into the mixture with a fork. Repeat every 30 minutes for about 4 hours, or until even ice crystals have formed.
3 Serve immediately or beat with a fork just before serving. To serve, scrape into dishes with a fork.

NUTRITION PER SERVE
Protein 0.5 g; Fat 0 g; Carbohydrate 18 g; Dietary Fibre 1 g; Cholesterol 0 mg; 410 kJ (98 cal)

SERVING SUGGESTION: A scoop of the granita in a shot glass with vodka is great for summer cocktail parties.

VARIATION: A tablespoon of finely chopped mint may be stirred through the mixture after straining the liquid.

Coarsely chop the watermelon flesh, removing the seeds.

Scrape the frozen parts around the edge back into the mixture.

Scrape the frozen parts back into the mixture until even ice crystals form.

FRUIT JELLIES

Preparation time: 20 minutes +
  refrigeration
Total cooking time: Nil
Serves 4
Fat per serve: 0 g

4 teaspoons gelatine
2 cups (500 ml/16 fl oz) cranberry and
  raspberry juice
330 g (11 oz) mixed berries, fresh or
  frozen

1 Sprinkle the gelatine in an even
layer onto 3 tablespoons of the juice,
in a small bowl, and leave to go
spongy. Bring a small pan of water to
the boil, remove from the heat and
place the bowl in the pan. The water
should come halfway up the side of
the bowl. Stir the gelatine until clear
and dissolved. Cool slightly and mix
with the rest of the juice.

2 Rinse four ³/4 cup (185 ml/6 fl oz)
moulds with water (wet moulds make
it easier when unmoulding) and pour
2 cm (³/4 inch) of the juice into each.
Refrigerate until set. Meanwhile, if the
fruit is frozen, defrost it and add any
liquid to the remaining juice. When
the bottom layer of jelly has set, divide
the fruit among the moulds (reserving
a few berries to garnish) and divide
the rest of the juice among the moulds,
pouring it over the fruit. Refrigerate
until set.

3 To turn out the jellies, hold each
mould in a hot, damp tea towel and
turn out onto a plate. Ease away
the edge of the jelly with your finger to
break the seal. (If you turn the jellies
onto a damp plate you will be able to
move them around, otherwise they
will stick.) Garnish with berries.

NUTRITION PER SERVE
Protein 3 g; Fat 0 g; Carbohydrate 25 g;
Dietary Fibre 1.5 g; Cholesterol 0 mg;
420 kJ (100 cal)

Lower the gelatine bowl into the water and stir the
gelatine until dissolved.

Divide the fruit among the moulds and pour in the
rest of the juice.

Use your finger to ease away the edge of the
jelly to break the seal.

BERRIES IN CHAMPAGNE JELLY

Preparation time: 10 minutes +
 refrigeration
Total cooking time: 5 minutes
Serves 8
Fat per serve: 0 g

1 litre champagne or sparkling wine
1¹/₂ tablespoons gelatine
1 cup (250 g/8 oz) sugar
4 strips lemon rind
4 strips orange rind
1²/₃ cups (250 g/8 oz) small
 strawberries, hulled
1²/₃ cups (250 g/8 oz) blueberries

1 Pour 2 cups (500 ml/16 fl oz)
champagne or sparkling white wine
into a bowl and let the bubbles
subside. Sprinkle the gelatine over the
top in an even layer. Leave until the
gelatine is spongy—do not stir. Place
the remaining champagne in a large
pan with the sugar, lemon and orange
rind and heat gently, stirring, until all
the sugar has dissolved.
2 Remove the pan from the heat, add
the gelatine mixture and stir until
thoroughly dissolved. Leave the jelly
to cool completely, then remove the
lemon and orange rind.

3 Divide the strawberries and
blueberries among eight ¹/₂ cup
(125 ml/4 fl oz) glasses or bowls and
pour the jelly over them. Chill until the
jelly has fully set. Remove from the
fridge 15 minutes before serving.

NUTRITION PER SERVE
Protein 3 g; Fat 0 g; Carbohydrate 37 g;
Dietary Fibre 1.5 g; Cholesterol 0 mg;
965 kJ (230 cal)

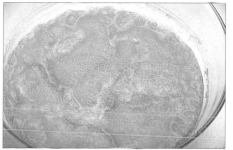

Sprinkle the gelatine over the champagne in an
even layer and leave until spongy.

Pour the jelly into the wine glasses or bowls,
covering the berries.

Muffins

It is always good to have a low-fat snack ready for between meals or breakfast on the run and these low-fat muffins all store and freeze well. All the following recipes are cooked in a 200°C (400°F/Gas 6) oven. Use a 12-hole muffin tin that has been lightly sprayed with oil—the holes should have a 1/2 cup (125 ml/4 fl oz) capacity.

OAT AND DATE

Sift 1 cup (125 g/4 oz) self-raising flour and 1 cup (150 g/5 oz) wholemeal self-raising flour with 1/2 teaspoon bicarbonate of soda into a large bowl. Return the husks to the bowl. Stir in 1 cup (100 g/3½ oz) quick rolled oats, 1/4 cup (55 g/2 oz) soft brown sugar and 1 cup (185 g/6 oz) chopped dates. Make a well in the centre. Beat together 1 egg, 2 tablespoons vegetable oil, 1/4 cup (90 g/3 oz) golden syrup and 1¼ (310 ml/ 10 fl oz) skim milk in a jug. Pour into the dry ingredients and stir with a large metal spoon until just combined. The mixture will look lumpy. Do not overmix. Spoon into the tin. Bake for

18 minutes, or until well risen and golden. Leave in the tin for 5 minutes before turning onto a wire rack to cool. Makes 12.

NUTRITION PER MUFFIN
Protein 5 g; Fat 5 g; Carbohydrate 15 g;
Dietary Fibre 4 g; Cholesterol 15 mg;
910 kJ (220 cal)

CORNMEAL AND CHILLI

Mix 1 cup (150 g/5 oz) polenta and 1 tablespoon caster sugar in a large bowl. Sift together 1½ cups (185 g/ 6 oz) plain flour and 1 tablespoon baking powder and add to the bowl. Mix and make a well. Stir 2 table-spoons vegetable oil and 1 lightly

beaten egg with 1¼ cups (315 ml/ 10 fl oz) skim milk in a jug, then pour onto the dry ingredients. Drain a 310 g (10 oz) can corn kernels and add to the mixture with 4 finely chopped spring onions and 1 finely chopped fresh small red chilli. Stir together with a large metal spoon to just combine. Do not overmix. Spoon into the tin. Sprinkle the tops with a little extra polenta. Bake for 20 minutes, or until well risen and golden. Leave in the tin for 5 minutes before turning onto a wire rack to cool. Makes 12.

NUTRITION PER MUFFIN
Protein 5 g; Fat 4 g; Carbohydrate 30 g;
Dietary Fibre 2 g; Cholesterol 15 mg;
735 kJ (175 cal)

RAISIN, BANANA AND APPLE

Place 1 cup (200 g/6½ oz) chopped raisins in a bowl, cover with boiling water, set aside for 30 minutes, then drain. Sift 1 cup (150 g/5 oz) wholemeal self-raising flour, 1 cup (125 g/4 oz) self-raising flour, 1 teaspoon ground cinnamon and ½ cup (95 g/3 oz) soft brown sugar into a large bowl. Mix ½ cup (135 g/4½ oz) apple sauce, 1 egg and 1 cup (250 ml/8 fl oz) skim milk in a bowl. Stir in 2 tablespoons vegetable oil and a mashed banana. Stir the apple mixture and raisins into the flour with a large metal spoon until just combined. The mixture will look lumpy. Do not overmix. Spoon into the tin and sprinkle with 2 tablespoons rolled oats combined with 1 tablespoon soft brown sugar. Bake for 20 minutes, or until cooked through. Leave in the tin for 5 minutes before turning onto a wire rack to cool. Makes 12.

NUTRITION PER MUFFIN
Protein 4.5 g; Fat 4 g; Carbohydrate 40 g; Dietary Fibre 3 g; Cholesterol 15 mg; 880 kJ (210 cal)

BLUEBERRY AND ALMOND

Sift 2 cups (250 g/8 oz) self-raising flour into a large bowl. Stir in ¼ cup (60 g/2 oz) caster sugar and make a well in the centre. In a jug, combine 1 cup (250 ml/8 fl oz) skim milk, 1 lightly beaten egg, 1 teaspoon vanilla essence and 2 tablespoons melted polyunsaturated margarine. Pour into the dry ingredients and stir with a large metal spoon until just combined. The mixture will look lumpy. Do not overmix. Quickly stir through 200 g (6½ oz) fresh blueberries. (Frozen blueberries can be used— add at the last minute while still frozen.) Spoon into the tin and sprinkle with 1 tablespoon demerara sugar combined with 30 g (1 oz) chopped almonds. Bake for 18 minutes, or until golden. Leave in the tin for 5 minutes before turning onto a wire rack to cool. Makes 12.

NUTRITION PER MUFFIN
Protein 3.5 g; Fat 3 g; Carbohydrate 25 g; Dietary Fibre 1 g; Cholesterol 15 mg; 595 kJ (145 cal)

PUMPKIN AND CHIVE

Combine 1 cup (250 g/8 oz) steamed and mashed pumpkin (375 g/12 oz uncooked, peeled), ¾ cup (185 ml/ 6 fl oz) skim milk, 2 tablespoons vegetable oil, 1 egg, 1 tablespoon soft brown sugar and ¼ teaspoon salt. Beat until smooth. Sift 1¼ cups (155 g/5 oz) self-raising flour and 1 cup (150 g/5 oz) wholemeal self-raising flour with ½ teaspoon bicarbonate of soda into a large bowl. Return the husks to the bowl. Stir in 2 finely chopped spring onions, ¼ cup (15 g/½ oz) chopped fresh chives and 2 tablespoons finely chopped fresh parsley. Make a well and pour in the liquid ingredients. Stir with a large metal spoon until just combined. The mixture will look lumpy. Do not overmix. Spoon into the tin. Sprinkle with fennel or dill seeds. Bake for 18 minutes, or until golden. Leave in the tin for 5 minutes before turning onto a wire rack to cool. Makes 12.

NUTRITION PER MUFFIN
Protein 4.5 g; Fat 4 g; Carbohydrate 20 g; Dietary Fibre 2 g; Cholesterol 15 mg; 550 kJ (130 cal)

Left to right: Oat and date; Cornmeal and chilli; Raisin, banana and apple; Blueberry and almond; Pumpkin and chive.

Index

USEFUL INFORMATION

The recipes in this book were developed using a tablespoon measure of 20 ml. In some other countries the tablespoon is 15 ml. For most recipes this difference will not be noticeable but, for recipes using baking powder, gelatine, bicarbonate of soda, small amounts of flour and cornflour, we suggest that, if you are using the smaller tablespoon, you add an extra teaspoon for each tablespoon.

The recipes in this book are written using convenient cup measurements. You can buy special measuring cups in the supermarket or use an ordinary household cup: first you need to check it holds 250 ml (8 fl oz) by filling it with water and measuring the water (pour it into a measuring jug or even an empty yoghurt carton). This cup can then be used for both liquid and dry cup measurements.

Liquid cup measures

1/4 cup	60 ml	2 fluid oz
1/3 cup	80 ml	2 1/2 fluid oz
1/2 cup	125 ml	4 fluid oz
3/4 cup	180 ml	6 fluid oz
1 cup	250 ml	8 fluid oz

Spoon measures

1/4 teaspoon	1.25 ml
1/2 teaspoon	2.5 ml
1 teaspoon	5 ml
1 tablespoon	20 ml

Nutritional Information

The nutritional information given for each recipe does not include any garnishes or accompaniments, such as rice or pasta, unless they are included in specific quantities in the ingredients list. The nutritional values are approximations and can be affected by biological and seasonal variations in foods, the unknown composition of some manufactured foods and uncertainty in the dietary database. Nutrient data given are derived primarily from the NUTTAB95 database produced by the Australian New Zealand Food Authority.

Oven Temperatures

You may find cooking times vary depending on the oven you are using. For fan-forced ovens, as a general rule, set oven temperature to 20°C lower than indicated in the recipe.

Note: Those who might be at risk from the effects of salmonella food poisoning (the elderly, pregnant women, young children and those suffering from immune deficiency diseases) should consult their GP with any concerns about eating raw eggs.

Alternative names

bicarbonate of soda	—	baking soda
besan flour	—	chickpea flour
capsicum	—	red or green (bell) pepper
chickpeas	—	garbanzo beans
cornflour	—	cornstarch
fresh coriander	—	cilantro
cream	—	single cream
eggplant	—	aubergine
flat-leaf parsley	—	Italian parsley
hazelnut	—	filbert
minced beef	—	ground beef
plain flour	—	all-purpose flour
polenta	—	cornmeal
prawn	—	shrimp
Roma tomato		plum tomato
sambal oelek	—	chilli paste
snow pea	—	mange tout
spring onion	—	scallion/shallot/green onion
thick cream	—	double/heavy cream
tomato paste (US)	—	tomato purée (UK)
zucchini	—	courgette

Weight

10 g	1/4 oz	220 g	7 oz	425 g	14 oz
30 g	1 oz	250 g	8 oz	475 g	15 oz
60 g	2 oz	275 g	9 oz	500 g	1 lb
90 g	3 oz	300 g	10 oz	600 g	1 1/4 lb
125 g	4 oz	330 g	11 oz	650 g	1 lb 5 oz
150 g	5 oz	375 g	12 oz	750 g	1 1/2 lb
185 g	6 oz	400 g	13 oz	1 kg	2 lb

Published by Murdoch Books® , GPO BOX 1203, Sydney, NSW 1045, AUSTRALIA
Ferry House, 51–57 Lacy Road, London SW15 1PR, UK

Editor: Jane Price **Designer:** Annette Fitzgerald **Chief Executive:** Juliet Rogers **Publisher:** Kay Scarlett
National Library of Australia Cataloguing-in-Publication Data. The complete low-fat cookbook. Includes index. ISBN 1 74045 074 4
1 74045 084 1 (pbk) I Cookery 2. Low-fat diet 641.5638 Printed by Toppan Printing Hong Kong Co. Ltd. PRINTED IN CHINA.
Reprinted 2002.